THE
VISITOR'S GUIDE TO
FINLAND

MPC

HUNTER
PUBLISHING INC

British Library Cataloguing in
Publication Data:
Lange, Hannes
   The visitor's guide to Finland.
   — (MPC visitor's guides).
   1. Finland— Description and
   travel — 1981- — Guide-books
   I. Title II. Finnland. *English*
   914.897'034   DL1010

Author: Hannes Lange
Translator: Andrew Shackleton

© Goldstadtverlag Karl A. Schäfer,
   Pforzheim
© Moorland Publishing Co Ltd
   1987 (English edition)

Published by:
Moorland Publishing Co Ltd,
Moor Farm Road,
Airfield Estate,
Ashbourne,
Derbyshire DE6 1HD
England

ISBN 0 86190 180 0 (paperback)
ISBN 0 86190 181 9 (hardback)

Published in the USA by:
Hunter Publishing Inc.,
300 Raritan Centre Parkway,
CN94, Edison, NJ 08818

ISBN 1 55650 007 6

Printed in the UK by Butler and
Tanner Ltd, Frome, Somerset.

Cover photograph:Traditional
Karelian house and farm, Nurmes
by D.G. Alcock

Colour photographs of Kerimäki
Church, Taivalkoski, sea plane
at Inari, Muonio and Lapp at
Enontekiö were supplied by M.
Upperton. The other colour
photographs were supplied by
H.W.A. Alcock. Black and white
photographs were kindly supplied
by the Finnish Tourist Board.

CONTENTS

Introduction

Tours and Excursions

The Tours and Excursions

Finland is a bilingual country. Swedish-speakers are a sizeable minority, and even form the majority in certain coastal areas to the west and the south. Many towns therefore have two names. The Finns are punctilious in this area, and are careful to avoid any possible linguistic or cultural conflict. For this reason the names of towns are given in the order determined by the majority language that is spoken. Where there is a Swedish-speaking majority, the Swedish name comes first — Nykarleby/Uusikaarlepyy, for example. The converse is true of towns with a Finnish-speaking majority, such as Turku/Åbo.

On major routes, the names of the important places have been entered in the margin, together with the distances between them. Recommended excursions and detours are also included.

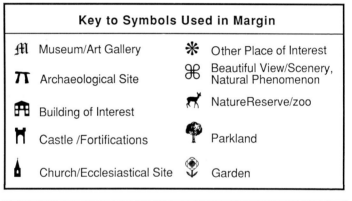

Key to Symbols Used in Margin

ᛗ	Museum/Art Gallery	✳	Other Place of Interest
𝝅	Archaeological Site	⌘	Beautiful View/Scenery, Natural Phenomenon
🏛	Building of Interest	🦌	NatureReserve/zoo
🏰	Castle /Fortifications	🌳	Parkland
⚱	Church/Ecclesiastical Site	❀	Garden

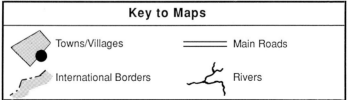

Key to Maps

◈	Towns/Villages	══	Main Roads
⌇	International Borders	⌇	Rivers

INTRODUCTION

The Country and its People

Geographical Situation

Finland, or Suomi as the Finns call it, has a total area of 338,127sq km. This makes Finland the second-largest country in Scandinavia (after Sweden), though it is only slightly larger than Norway. Its population of 4.9 million ranks third, being less than that of Sweden and Denmark. The population density is just over 16 per sq km, which is less than that of Sweden (18.5 per sq km) and slightly more than that of Norway (13 per sq km). The population density is greatest in the south-west of the country, where the major towns are; it becomes less towards the east and drops dramatically as one travels northwards.

Finland is geographically, ethnically and linguistically somewhat separate from the rest of Scandinavia, but its history is closely bound with that of Sweden and, because of its geographical proximity, with that of Russia. Modern Finland is so closely bonded with the rest of Scandinavia, whether economically, politically or from the tourist's point of view, that it can rightly be considered part of it.

The republic of Finland measures 1,160km from north to south, 540km from east to west, and fits almost exactly between the 60th and 70th parallels. The country is on average about 400km wide, its westernmost and easternmost points being at 19° 7' and 31° 35' respectively. The country is thus shaped rather like an elongated rectangle stretching from south to north. Almost 10 per cent of the land area is occupied by lakes. There are between 60,000 and 65,000 of them in all, though no one has yet counted them exactly. In parts of the south-east the lakes occupy as much as 50 per cent of the land area. About 70 per cent of the land area is covered by thick forests, and only 10 per cent is used for agricultural purposes. The

7

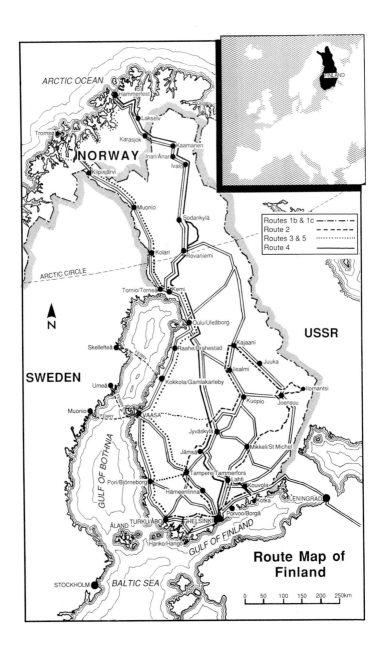

Route Map of Finland

The highly cultivated countryside of Häme

areas that remain consist mostly of barren land and swamp.

The country's position between East and West is clearly shown on the political map. For Finland shares a 1,200km-long border with Russia. At the end of World War II Russia took over large areas that had formerly belonged to Finland: the area around Vyborg/Viipuri in the south-east and most of Karelia further to the north, including the ice-free harbour of Petsamo on the Arctic Sea coast. Finland also shares its northern borders with Sweden (about 400km) and Norway (about 700km).

Finland now has only one length of coastline, bordering on the Gulf of Bothnia to the west and the Gulf of Finland to the south, both of them extensions of the Baltic Sea. The overall length of the sea coast measures some 1,100km, though it is many times longer if one counts the many irregularities such as inlets, islands and skerries. The lack of influence from the Gulf Stream means that the harbours are blocked by ice for much of the winter, especially along the fragmented western coast.

A quarter of the land area lies to the north of the Arctic Circle (66° 33'N). Finland can basically be described as a vast peneplain rising to an average of 100m (328ft), and sloping gently up towards the east. Its only mountains are mostly concentrated in the finger of territory that extends to the north-west between the Swedish and Norwegian borders. The highest point is Haltiatunturi (1,328m (4356ft)) on the border with Norway. During the last Ice Age the glaciers eroded the rocks right down to the ancient continental shield. The result is a vast peneplain criss-crossed with glacial trenches, most of which run from north-west to south-east. This undulating landscape is especially characteristic of the southern part of Finland, where the trenches have been dammed and flooded to form many thousands of irregular-shaped lakes.

These lakes (in Finnish *järvi*) occupy about 10 per cent of the land surface of Finland, but most lie in the south. By far the largest is Saimaa in the south-east; with an area of 4,400sq km, it is not much smaller than Lake Vänern in Sweden, the largest lake in Scandinavia. Finland's second-largest lake is Päijänne (1,065sq km), which stretches for 150km between Lahti and Jyväskylä. This is followed by Lake Inari (1,000sq km) in Finnish Lapland, well north of the Arctic Circle. The thousands of other lakes, especially those in the south-east, form long chains linked by rivers and canals, and are thus extremely important for transporting timber. The same is true of the country's many rivers, which form highways through the trackless forests of the interior. Most of them drain into the Gulf of Bothnia.

The undulating nature of the landscape is particularly noticeable when travelling along the roads that run perpendicular to the glacial drift, which often go up and down like a switchback. Only recently, with the advent of modern blasting techniques, have the road builders begun to smooth these bumps out. The basalt rock is at most covered by only a thin layer of soil, and is often completely exposed.

The undulations are also reflected in the irregular coastline. There are numerous offshore islands and skerries, especially in the south-western corner near the islands of Åland/Ahvenanmaa. Åland forms a link with Sweden, and not only in the geographical sense. Although the inhabitants are Swedish-speaking, the islands have belonged to Finland for many years and enjoy a certain degree of autonomy.

Geology

Finland is a very unified country from a geological point of view. The rocks consist mostly of ancient granites and gneisses, including some of the oldest and hardest rocks in the world. About a million years ago the country was covered by a thick layer of ice. This melted between 12,000 and 8,000 years ago, about 10,000 years later than in regions further south. Nowhere are the effects of glaciation more dramatic than in Finland.

The advancing ice scraped away the surface of even the hardest of rocks, pushing up enormous piles of debris in front of it. As the ice retreated these were left behind in the form of long barriers called terminal moraines, which mark the different stages in the melting of the ice. They are made up of a chaotic mixture of different rocks and boulders that the ice had carried along with it. A dramatic example of a terminal moraine is the Salpausselkä, which forms the southern boundary of the south-eastern lake region. It runs in two parallel arcs from Riihimäki past Lahti and Kouvola to Lappeenranta.

The soil layer is thin, and provides very little rooting area for trees. Only the hardier trees such as pines, spruces and birches can grow here. Their roots spread out among the boulders, penetrating into the finest of cracks in the rocks and forming the basis for the development of humus.

Also typically glacial are the eskers (in Finnish *harju*): long causeways formed by gravel deposits from rivers that trickled beneath the ice. These again were left behind as the ice retreated. They can be as much as 100km long, and some of them form dams and causeways across the lakes, often providing vital east–west land routes through the complex pattern of lakes that cover the south-east of the country. The Punkaharju near Savonlinna is perhaps the best known example of this phenomenon.

As the ice melted the sea level rose, flooding many of the glacial valleys to form inlets. But as the land was relieved of the enormous weight of the ice, it too rose dramatically, re-exposing many of the areas that had been flooded. The islands of Åland/Ahvenanmaa and the hills along the south coast are typical examples of this. They are covered with glacial deposits that have since been eroded by the action of the sea.

Another typical postglacial feature is the kettlehole: a funnel-shaped depression that occurred where the ice was covered by a layer of drift. This insulated the ice from the sun so that it melted more slowly than elsewhere. It broke down the land surface beneath it, forming a thicker layer of humus than is usual in Finland. The result is some of the country's best agricultural land. Otherwise the soil layer is extremely thin; it is often said of Finnish soil that it must be dug with dynamite instead of with a spade.

The unusual hardness and evenness of the underlying rock has meant that the glaciers have not carved out the deep valleys that characterise the more mountainous parts of Scandinavia. Also, river valleys are virtually never found in Finland. The few glacial valleys that have formed in the north are broad and swampy. They occupy about 10 per cent of the land surface (as much as the lakes) in that part of the country.

Fauna and Flora

Nearly three-quarters of the land surface of Finland is covered with forest. Apart from that, the landscape is dominated by lakes in the south and by swamps in the north. One should bear in mind that Finland was covered by ice until only 10,000 years ago, which is relatively recent from a geological point of view. Only since then has the vegetation had a chance to develop.

The agricultural areas in the south are little different from those in Central and Western Europe, and the crops are much the same too. The big difference lies in the predominance of forest even in these areas. Much deforestation occurred indirectly as a result of Finland having had to fulfil certain obligations (war reparations) to Russia. The war caused a decrease in Finland's wood reserves, a loss of large areas of first-class forest land in Karelia and Finland had to clear much forest for agricultural land within its own borders. Forest growth is now good due to effective farming.

The Finns pay great attention to the state of their forests. The forests belong to the boreal vegetation zone and consist mostly of hardy conifers. The only deciduous tree to be found outside the parks in the south is the birch, which grows where other trees cannot. The commonest tree in the south is the spruce, which accounts for about 38 per cent of the total tree population. Further north, however, it is the pine that predominates, occupying as much as 43 per cent of the

Small mammals like the squirrel are a common sight in Finland

total forest area. The birch occupies about 19 per cent; all over Finland it creates light patches among the dark-coloured conifers, while in the north it forms the forest fringe where the trees gradually dwindle into swamp and tundra.

Tundra accounts for surprisingly little of the land surface of Finland, considering how much of the country lies north of the Arctic Circle. However, the northern climate, with its cold, dark winters and warm, bright summers, has an effect on tree growth in these northern regions. The trees grow more slowly and have shorter branches. The weight of snow breaks the weaker branches, so that the remaining branches become sparse and knotted. The predominant tree in the far north is a dwarf birch that is of minimal use for forestry.

Coniferous forests allow for very little undergrowth. But the clearings and river banks, and the sparser northern birchwoods, support a rich variety of fruiting bushes and shrubs. There are not only the familiar bilberries and cranberries, but exclusively northern species such as the *lakkoja* or '*mossberry*' (a hardy species of cranberry) and the *mesimarjoja*, which is similar to the blackberry. There are also many forms of edible fungi, which are mostly collected in areas of commercial forestry.

The fauna consists mostly of forest species, but not of those commonly associated with forests elsewhere such as red deer and roe deer, which prefer a mixture of forest and fields. The largest animal is the elk, which occurs predominantly in swampy areas. There is an estimated population of 122,700 elks in Finland although there are fewer than in Sweden.

The reindeer of the north are semi-domesticated, and make seasonal migrations in search of food. They are not suited to thick forests, since their diet consists of ground vegetation, including the mosses and lichens that grow on the tundra. Reindeer herding in Finnish Lapland is less exclusively confined to the Lapps than in Norway and Sweden. The herds are followed by lone herdsmen. Once a year they are rounded up at specific northerly locations and divided among their owners so that the young deer can be marked. The marking is done by means of small incisions in the ears, the form of which is laid down by a long-held tradition. The division of the reindeer herds is also an occasion for an annual market and folk festival. In the far north the reindeer are never hunted.

Brown bears and wolves are occasionally to be seen, especially in the large nature reserves. In hard winters wolves wander over the Russian border from Karelia and other areas to the north of Lake Ladoga. The lynx is among the rarest of the carnivores, while the fox is the most common — so much so that it often has a price on its head. The same applies to the glutton, the European equivalent of the North American wolverine, which is closely related to the marten; the Finnish name for it is *ahma*.

The Finnish climate is well suited to the breeding of fur animals, and the fur trade is an important part of the Finnish economy. The most common fur animals to be bred are the muskrat or musquash, the Siberian squirrel and Arctic fox and the mink. Fur animal farming is especially concentrated on the coast between Vaasa and Kokkola. The Finnish Fur Centre holds one of the biggest fur auctions in the world.

Small game include hares and various species of grouse. Many of the northern species turn white during the winter, including the Lapland ptarmigan, the snowy owl and the Arctic hare. The lakes in the south are full of waterfowl which feed on the plentiful fish.

Industry and the consequent pollution is mostly confined to the coastal areas. The lakes remain clean, and are the ideal breeding ground for trout and perch. The pike are often particularly impressive, while the salmon rivers are a veritable paradise for anglers.

The sea fish off the coast are typical of the Baltic, and include herring, cod, salmon and trout. The lovely sea trout is becoming increasingly rare. Coastal habitats have been occasionally damaged by industrial pollution, in particular by the poisonous wastes from cellulose factories, which at present are the subject of a world-wide clean-up campaign. The once-common crayfish is becoming scarce because of the so-called 'crayfish plague', and may only be caught in certain specified areas. A favourite delicacy, it still forms an essential part of Finnish cuisine, although nowadays large quantities have to be imported.

Without doubt the most bloodthirsty creature in Finland is the midge, which is a source of great discomfort on warm summer days in the north. It often reaches plague proportions around midsummer, only to disappear as suddenly as it came when the weather turns cooler. Nowadays there are plenty of skin preparations to protect against midge bites — a rather pleasanter solution than the birch tar that hunters used to rub into their skin. People who live in the north, the Lapps in particular, have long since become immune to midge bites.

Domestic animals are much the same as elsewhere in Europe, though sheep are noticeable by their relative absence, as are the goats that are so common on the richer pastures of Norway.

The Population

Finland has a total land area (including lakes) of 338,127sq km, and a population of 4.9 million. If one discounts the lakes and swamps, the overall population density is 16 per sq km. This, however, ignores the fact that the majority of the population live in the south-western triangle of the country. The three most populous of the twelve provinces are Uusimaa (including Helsinki itself), Turku Pori and Häme (including the second-largest city, Tampere). The population dwindles rapidly as one travels northwards, so that the northernmost province of Lappi (Finnish Lapland) has a population density of only 2 per sq km. About half the population live in towns, of which there are only ninety altogether, most of them not far from the coast. The other half live in scattered villages and farmsteads in the country. The loss of the provinces of Karelia and Vyborg deprived 10 per cent of

Finnish girl in national costume

the Finns of their homeland. They were forced to resettle, some of them in the towns, where most of the industry grew up.

The Finns

The Finns are outwardly very similar to the Swedes, especially in coastal regions. They are typically tall and strong with fair hair and blue eyes. These mostly Nordic features are often tempered by the broad cheekbones and short nose of the Baltic peoples. Further north there is a greater predominance of dark hair, brown eyes and slighter build.

The origin of the Finns has puzzled anthropologists for many years. But it is now generally accepted that around the time of Christ the Finns lived a long way further east, just beyond the Urals. The Finnish language and the closely related Estonian language are not Indo-European, but belong to the so-called Finno-Ugric family of languages. This family also includes Lapp and probably Hungarian, suggesting that these people also originated from beyond the Urals.

The original Finnish settlers must have looked much more like the Lapps than the present-day Finns, although the Lapps settled in Scandinavia at a very much earlier date. It would therefore appear that the original Finns were swamped by the Swedes and the people of northern Russia. But in spite of this the language remained intact — a common phenomenon among the races of the world.

Finland was ruled by Sweden for several centuries and subsequently by Russia; it did not become independent until 1917. Swedish was the official language for so long that it became part of the Finnish culture. Because of its high status, many Finns adopted it as their own language, especially in the south and west of the country. Since independence the large Swedish-speaking minority has been constantly decreasing, but Finland can still be considered a bilingual state. Nearly 94 per cent of the population are Finnish-speaking, and about 6 per cent are Swedish-speaking; an increasingly tiny minority of 1,500 speak Lapp (see below).

Bilingualism causes practical problems, but it does not detract from the Finnish sense of identity. Whatever their language, the people are Finns first and foremost. They have no universal characteristics, but their strongest trait is a fierce sense of family loyalty, which is probably a reaction to the harshness of the climate and the environment. The same applies to their other two strongest traits: their almost overwhelming hospitality and their selfless devotion to the welfare of their neighbours. Otherwise the Finns are rather reserved in character, though they can at times be fierce and passionate. Their most treasured virtues are reliability, fortitude and a strong sense of honour and duty — traits that have been continually reflected in the history of their people.

The Finns are a hard-working race. This is especially true of the women, who show great independence in the pursuance of their careers, often entering professions that remain exclusively male in other countries. Moreover, certain areas such as teaching and hairdressing are almost totally female professions.

Countryfolk and townsfolk are very similar in character, and tend to be very formal and conservative. It is still normal to uncover one's head immediately on entering a hotel or restaurant. Only a few years ago, a casually-dressed man or a woman in a trouser-suit could be turned away from a restaurant that was in no way exclusive. This is no longer the case, but a visitor who is too informal, either in manner or dress, is still likely to be looked on with a certain amount of suspicion.

The Lapps

There are between 30,000 and 40,000 Lapps in northern Europe. Their language, like Finnish, is Finno-Ugric in origin, but unlike the Finns they have retained their physical racial characteristics. They are slightly built with black hair, brown eyes and distinctly mongoloid features. The majority of Lapps live in Norway and Sweden, and there are only about 2,000 or 3,000 in Finland. Of these only about half still speak Lapp, which is divided into a number of different dialects.

In Finland the Lapps have been assimilated much more than in Norway and Sweden, where they have retained a much stronger individual identity. There are several reasons for this, one being the undoubted resemblance between the Lapp and Finnish languages. When the Finns arrived in the region, they found the northern areas already settled by Lapps. A certain amount of assimilation was inevitable, although the Finns did not settle much in the empty regions of the north. On the other hand, the mountains and fjords of Norway and Sweden hindered the Germanic peoples from spreading northwards, so that the Lapps could preserve their culture intact.

The Lapps are traditionally nomadic, following their reindeer herds around the northern tundra and paying scant attention to national boundaries. But now all Lapps in Finland have become permanently settled, and reindeer herding is practised by the Finns

Lapp, Saariselkä, selling souvenirs

as much as by the Lapps. There is no specific area of Lapp settlement. Most of them live in scattered villages inhabited by a single family and consisting of no more than a few houses.

Wherever one comes across Lapps in their brightly-coloured costumes, one can be sure that they are there mainly for the benefit of tourists. One can also see the traditional Lapp tents made of reindeer hide with a hole through which smoke can escape. However, these tents are virtually never used except by summer herdsmen, and most people live in settled (albeit seasonal) accommodation.

Even in warm weather the Lapps often pose for photographers in their traditional winter clothing. It is much too hot to wear in summer, but the beautifully embroidered costumes, tasselled headgear and reindeer-skin boots are attractive to tourists, and one cannot really blame them for cashing in on the tourist trade. The Lapps sell some lovely examples of traditional handiwork, most of which have been skilfully crafted from reindeer hide and antlers. If one glances inside a tent surrounded by barking huskies and grazing reindeer, one need not be surprised to see a television set.

The Lapps are good-natured but crafty, and consider cunning to be more important than strength. They were not converted to Christianity until the nineteenth century, and are in many ways still bound up in the beliefs of their forebears. The Lapps who still live in scattered settlements send their children to special boarding schools in centres such as Inari, where they are educated in their own Lapp culture.

Unlike the Lapps of Norway and Sweden, who are totally dependent on reindeer, some groups of Finnish Lapps have lived traditionally from fishing or agriculture. At one time their occupation was an indication of which group they belonged to, though nowadays such distinctions have become blurred. However, Lapps cannot be persuaded to work in industry. They also avoid the towns, which to them are like anthills, full of panic and confusion. They prefer the privations of the open tundra, where they can be freer and more self-reliant.

One exceptional group is that of the Skolt Lapps, who originally lived in northern Karelia. They were uprooted by the Russians, and resettled in the far north-east of Finland. Their present homeland is an area of about 40sq km lying between Lake Inari and the eastern end of the Finnish–Norwegian border. It is centred on the village of Sevettijärvi, which consists of no more than a few houses with a hospital, a church and a Lapp boarding school. They are Eastern Orthodox by faith, and their patriarch is the archbishop of Constantinople. A priest comes to take services at the church only a few times a year. Because of their isolated position a long way from the tourist routes, the Skolt Lapps have retained many of their traditional customs.

The Lapps of Finland have the same rights and duties as other Finnish citizens, apart from certain special hunting privileges in Lapland. This means that they are also obliged to do military service.

The Social Structure

Finland's gross national product is the lowest in Scandinavia, but this does not mean that the country is poor. On the contrary, Finland enjoys increasing affluence and prosperity thanks to its healthy industrial growth. Incomes are high and differentials are low, while the social structure is much the same in the country as in the town.

After independence in 1917, the Finns had to build up their

economy from nothing. 1945 saw great changes towards urbanisation when the country suddenly had to accommodate refugees from the east. They had lost all their land and possessions, and were in great need of rehabilitation. Finland made the best it could of this, and the result was a thriving industrial economy.

Like other countries in Europe, Finland has its generation problems, but they are not nearly as bad as those of its neighbour Sweden. Alcoholism is a big problem, as in other Scandinavian countries. Drastic measures have been introduced to combat this. They include a state monopoly of alcohol sales, a ban on alcohol advertising, strict control of sales by means of rationing cards, and the imposition of exorbitant taxes. Offences due to drunkenness are always punished severely; one can be arrested simply for being drunk, while those caught drinking and driving are usually given prison sentences.

The period of reconstruction and industrialisation also saw the development of a comprehensive welfare state. It compares well with those of Denmark and Sweden, which are probably the most advanced of all. Finland spends more on its social and welfare services than on any other area of public expenditure.

The pension system is particularly well funded. Every Finnish citizen, indeed anyone who has lived in the country long enough, has a right to a state pension that ensures at least a minimum level of comfort. Retirement age varies between 60 and 65 depending on the person's profession. The state pension is further supplemented by a vocational pension, which varies according to the person's earned income. These pensions are financed by the taxpayers, the employers and the local authorities.

The Finnish health service is equally advanced. The number of hospital beds has multiplied in the last few years, and the facilities provided both by the state and by the local communities are correspondingly good. The patient pays a maximum of 11 per cent of the cost of care, while the rest is paid under the state insurance scheme. The Finnish government introduced comprehensive health insurance in 1963. The local authorities also make a vital contribution to the public health system as the employers of doctors, midwives and nurses.

The Constitution

Finland is an independent parliamentary republic. The constitution was laid down in 1919 and revised in 1928. Legislative power rests with parliament with the consent of the state president. Executive power lies in the hands of the state president, who makes decisions with the assistance of the relevant cabinet minister. Judicial power is exercised independently by the courts.

A new law (2 June 1987) has been passed with regard to the election of the state president. The citizens elect both the president and 300 'electors'. If one of the presidential candidates gets more than 50 per cent of the votes he is elected. If none of the candidates get over 50 per cent, the 'electors' elect the president. The state president is elected for a period of 6 years. His powers are fairly wide, and he is also the commander-in-chief of the armed forces. The parliament consists of one chamber with 200 members elected by free secret ballot according to a system of proportional representation. All citizens are eligible to vote from the age of 18.

The country is administered by a cabinet led by the prime minister and including between eleven and eighteen departmental ministers plus two non-political experts who are in charge of the judiciary. The cabinet is appointed by the president but must enjoy the confidence of the parliament.

Seven political parties are represented in parliament. Of these, the Social Democrats have had the largest number of seats for more than 40 years. Since no party has ever achieved an absolute majority, most governments have consisted of a stable coalition of parties. Elections take place every 4 years, but voting patterns have so far changed very little.

The country is divided into twelve provinces for administrative purposes. These in turn are divided into a number of independent local authorities. The province of Åland/Ahvenanmaa is exceptional in having a much greater degree of autonomy than the others.

All Finnish citizens are required to do a period of military service. It usually lasts 240 days, though 330 days is required in certain specialised areas. The treaty of 1947 imposed limitations on the strength of the armed forces. They are divided into two sections, one responsible for internal security and the other for border defences.

Finland enjoys complete religious freedom —an Eastern Orthodox Church Festival

Education

The last few years have seen sweeping educational reforms, which have brought Finland more in line with most other European countries. Children previously spent only 8 years at one school. But nowadays they spend 10 years of basic education at a primary/secondary school up to the equivalent of 'O' levels (to be replaced by GCSE)in England. This is followed by 3 years at the equivalent of an English sixth-form college. Their final school qualification is similar to 'A' levels in England.

All children have the same curriculum for their first 6 years of schooling, and are then streamed according to ability. They must then achieve a certain standard in order to qualify for 'sixth-form college'. About 20,000 children a year leave school with an 'A' level equivalent qualification. Most of these 'sixth-form colleges' are private schools, although 90 per cent of their costs are financed by the state. Examinations are now gradually being replaced by forms of continuous assessment.

Those who do not go on to 'sixth-form college' may instead go to a vocational school, which in certain circumstances can also qualify them for higher education at a specialist college or university. Finland has seven universities, including the Swedish university at Turku/Åbo, and a large number of other colleges of higher education. The number of students registered at present totals about 100,000.

About 5 per cent of pupils attend schools that teach through the medium of Swedish. All children must learn two foreign languages, beginning in their third year at school with the other native language of their country, be it Swedish or Finnish. They begin their second foreign language in their seventh year of schooling, and have a choice of English, German, French or Russian. In special circumstances they may study a second one of these in place of Finnish or Swedish.

Education is free for the 10 years of basic education. Travel to school and accommodation at school are also free — a vital provision in far-flung regions of the country. The costs of basic and subsequent education are met by the local authorities, who may receive a considerable amount of state support, depending on their financial situation.

Agriculture, Fisheries and Forestry

Until the middle of the nineteenth century the overwhelming majority of the Finnish population lived from agriculture, fishing and hunting. But these occupations have long since dwindled in importance. In 1948 they still accounted for 21.4 per cent of the gross national product, whereas the figure has now dropped to only 7.5 per cent.

The poor soils and the unfavourable climate mean that agriculture is not very productive, and this has resulted in the continuous depopulation of the countryside. Arable farming is practically limited to the southern parts of the country. Farms are usually small, and frequently combine agriculture with forestry. The chief crops are grain crops, potatoes and root beets like sugar beet. Livestock farming is less affected by the climate, and the dairy industry often proves highly profitable.

Commercial fisheries are not confined to the south coast, but often the harbours along the west coast are blocked by ice during the winter. The southern harbours are sometimes blocked too. Fishing is often carried out by small firms, who work in forestry during the

The wood-processing industry is vital to Finland's economy

winter months. Fishing and agricultural products are used for home consumption only.

The fact that 70 per cent of Finland is covered by forest is sufficient indication alone of the importance of forestry in the Finnish economy. Yet forestry itself creates only 7 per cent of the country's gross national product. The associated wood-processing industries, on the other hand, are much more important to the economy. Finland has the largest area of forest of any European country apart from the Soviet Union: 21 million hectares of woodland, or some 5 hectares of woodland per inhabitant. Large areas of forest were cut down after the war to satisfy demands for reparations, but these have long since been replanted.

By far the majority of the trees are conifers, most of them pine and spruce, which account for about 80 per cent of the total. Birch is the next most important, making up about 17 per cent, and is followed by other foliage trees, especially alder and aspen. In earlier times the wood was mostly exported in its natural state, but nowadays an increasing proportion of it is processed at home.

Wood-processing has become one of Finland's most important industries. The long-fibred conifers are of high quality because they grow slowly in the harsh Finnish climate; they are mostly turned into paper, cellulose and chipboard. Strong birch trunks provide the raw material for the plywood industry. The Finnish birch is prized throughout the world as a wood for furniture. Branches and shorter trunks are broken down and made into chipboard.

The extent of the Finnish forests creates an interesting natural phenomenon. On sunny days the white clouds over the countryside take on a greenish shimmer, produced by the light that is reflected up from the forest.

Industry

Up until World War II Finland had a purely agrarian economy. But the years since then have seen the rapid development of a comprehensive industrial base, which now creates more than a third of the gross national product. This growth is a positive consequence of the enormous efforts which Finland was forced to make in order to fulfil the reparations demanded by the Soviet Union. The industry had literally to be built up from nothing, because the income from agriculture and forestry would simply not have been enough.

The first industries to develop were centred around the country's chief natural resource, which is timber. The chief products of wood-processing are cellulose, plywood, paper and chipboard.

In the 1950s, metal industries were introduced, which have since far surpassed the wood-processing industries in terms of output. The high manpower requirements also make them the country's chief employers. Their 165,000 employees account for a good third of the country's industrial workforce. Both these areas of industry are still expanding.

The mining industry now employs about 6,000 workers, or 1.2 per cent of the industrial workforce. Its growth has meant that more raw materials are now available, including mainly copper and nickel, but also zinc, chromium and cobalt. Mining products account for a large portion of Finland's exports.

The main exports as always are of timber and its associated products, which make up 55 per cent of the total. The chief export in

An old industry — lace-making at Rauma

the area of finished metal products is machinery for the paper industry. The shipbuilding industry specialises in car ferries and icebreakers.

The textile and clothing industries employ 14 per cent of the workforce, and the export of these products is double that of imports. The food and drink industries account for 12 per cent of the workforce. In recent years, high-quality glass and ceramics have formed an important part of the Finnish export market.

Germany is the chief buyer of Finnish furniture. Finland's chief export partners are the fellow-members of EFTA, which buy about 44 per cent of its exports. About 24 per cent of exports go to EEC countries and about 20 per cent to countries in the Eastern Bloc. About 50 per cent of Finland's imports consists of raw materials and industrial consumer goods. Finland has a consistent slight balance-of-payments deficit.

Co-operatives play an important part in the Finnish economy. Indeed, almost the whole of its agriculture is structured around co-operatives.

As far as transport is concerned, Finland is effectively an island. The one rail link with the West is insignificant economically; the line gauge is different from that in the West, so that all goods must be reloaded at the Swedish border. The rail link with Leningrad in the Soviet Union is somewhat more important. There is a railway–ferry traffic link between Hanko in Finland and Travemünde in Germany.

More than 90 per cent of Finland's freight and passenger traffic is carried by sea. Great efforts are required to keep the harbours free of ice in the winter, and this has resulted in the development of special icebreaker ships that are renowned throughout the world. The Finnish merchant navy has a gross tonnage of 1.3 million, and most of its ships are modern in design.

Finland has had an exceptionally small rise in the retail prices index over the past 10 years or so, while income levels have noticeably improved.

The Arts and Sciences

In order to understand Finnish culture one must go right back to its origins. The Finnish peasants were the custodians of its culture. They were free in Finland, where landlords and serfs were unknown. The farmers in their isolated farmsteads spent the long winters creatively in the development of numerous handicrafts. The beautifully carved furniture and fine wood carvings that remain show how skilful they have always been with wood. Other fine examples of Finnish folk art are their handwoven Ryijy carpets and tapestries.

The great distances between farmsteads meant that the peasants felt a great need to get together. At these gatherings they told stories, and with time developed a vast legacy of folk legends, sagas and poetry. It was not until the beginning of the nineteenth century that Elias Lönnrot first wrote these works down. He made a vast collection of them, which he published under the name *Kalevala*. This formed the basis for modern Finnish literature, and established Finnish as a language of culture and learning.

The country's many museums contain some marvellous examples of Finnish peasant culture, especially the National Museum in Helsinki. Finland also has its share of open-air museums like those found elsewhere in Scandinavia. One of the best examples is the Seurasaari Museum on an island just outside Helsinki. It is a reconstructed village made up of old farmsteads of various kinds. Near Turku there is its urban counterpart: a fortified monastery which has been reconstructed in the form of a medieval town, made up of buildings from all over the country.

Finnish scientists have naturally been primarily concerned with the everyday problems of Finland. They have achieved much, for example, in the areas of geology and of forestry, which was pioneered by A. K. Cajander. But the country's universities contain scholars in all the modern scientific disciplines, some of whom have produced work of world-wide significance. In the natural sciences, for example, the biochemist A. I. Vitanen won the Nobel Prize for chemistry in 1945.

As far as music is concerned, the name Jean Sibelius has almost become synonymous with Finland. But this does not mean that Sibelius is the last word in Finnish music. Finland has a rich musical heritage, and the Sibelius Academy in Helsinki is as prestigious as many conservatoires in other European countries. Helsinki's two symphony orchestras are internationally famous. Famous singers from all over Europe appear at the National Opera House in Helsinki, while its own resident artists make many guest appearances abroad.

Finnish literature began in 1548 with a translation of the New Testament by a pupil and friend of Luther called Mikael Agricola, who at the same time produced a Finnish primer. Another milestone was Lönnrot's publication of the *Kalevala* at the beginning of the nineteenth century (see above). The years which followed saw the publication of much folk literature, most of which remained unknown outside Finland. This was no doubt because the Finnish language was

Nineteenth-century icon

so difficult and was spoken by so few people. There were, however, some notable exceptions. These included Johann Ludvig Runeberg, honoured as Finland's 'national poet', Aleksis Kivi, author of *The Seven Brothers*, and Nobel Prize winner F. E. Sillanpää, who wrote *Silja the Maid*. More recent works include Väinö Linna's war diary, known as *Crosses in Karelia*, and the historical novels of Mika Waltari.

The only historical examples of Finnish architecture are medieval stone churches. All other buildings were made of wood, and have long since fallen victim to fire or decay. Finnish architects first made their mark in modern times with the building of factories and blocks of flats. Beauty was sacrificed for the sake of function and the best use of materials. Finnish architects and builders are well known internationally for their skills in such matters, and often get contracts abroad. The Finns themselves revel in the contrast to their former way of life, and lay more store by these 'concrete castles' than the buildings would appear to merit.

Finnish painting and sculpture has in the past been little known outside Finland, partly as a result of the country's isolated position in

Birthplace of author Aleksis Kivi, Nurmijärvi

Europe. Only recently have exhibitions at last been mounted to bring the work of modern Finnish artists to people abroad.

It is a different story with Finnish applied art, which attempts to combine traditional folk art with modern forms and styles. Finland has gained a world reputation in this field, especially with glass and ceramics. The distinctively Finnish designs mean that these products make ideal tourist souvenirs. Finnish design skills are responsible for some outstandingly beautiful manufactured goods, including lamps, textiles and wood carvings. The Finnish Design Centre in Helsinki contains a permanent exhibition of such items.

In the area of dramatic art, the Finnish theatre and film industries have been almost exclusively limited to Finland itself, simply because no one else speaks Finnish. There is a large number of professional theatre companies, four of which perform in Swedish. These are further supplemented by numerous small amateur companies. Amateur drama is a popular activity in rural areas, and the standard is remarkably high.

Some Finnish radio stations are controlled by a single organisation in which the state has a 90 per cent share. It is financed by a system of listeners' licences. There are also private local radio stations in most main cities. Finland has had its own television channel since 1958. Satellite television programmes like Sky-channel and Super-channel are transmitted by cable TV to most main centres. The number of television sets is fast increasing; there are now well over a million, or one for nearly every household in the country.

The Finnish press is free and independent. There are about ninety separate titles, producing a total print-run of over two million, and including fourteen daily papers in Swedish. The most popular papers are the more politically orientated dailies, which are produced in the cities, but are widely read in the country. Local papers have smaller print-runs and are less likely to be published daily. Weekly and monthly journals are also very popular, and are published widely.

Religion

Finland enjoys complete religious freedom. About 93 per cent of the population belongs to the Protestant Lutheran Church, which is theoretically administered by the government and the state president. In practice, however, it is allowed complete administrative independence.

About 1.4 per cent of the population is Eastern Orthodox, and is subject to the patriarch of Constantinople. Their church is also theoretically administered by the state. About 5 per cent of the population have no church allegiances, while the rest belong to other faiths.

Some Facts about Finland

Constitution: independent republic
Area: 338,127sq km, of which about 300,000sq km are land
Population: 4.9 million
Population density: 16 per sq km
Longest river: Kemijoki 512km
Largest lake: Saimaa 1,400sq km
Highest point: Haltiatunturi 1,328m (4,356ft)
Largest cities: Helsinki 500,000; Tampere 175,000;
  Turku 165,000

Modern sculpture

Land Use
Forest: about 70 per cent of the land surface
Barren land and swamp: about 20 per cent
Agricultural land: about 10 per cent
Lakes: 10 per cent of the total area

Landscape
In the south: cultivated land with large towns and extensive forests
to the north, and with lakes occupying 50 per cent of the south-east
In the north: forests, becoming increasingly sparse further north, and
eventually turning to scrub, swamp and tundra, with most towns near
the coast

Trade
Strongly orientated towards EFTA, the EEC, the Eastern Bloc and Western Europe, with a slight balance-of-payments deficit
Imports
Primarily raw materials for industry, but also finished consumer items such as cars and fuel and investment goods
Exports
Timber, paper, other wood products, specialist machinery, ships and valuable metal ores such as copper, zinc and cobalt
Industrial Workforce
Metal industry: 33 per cent

Wood and paper: 17 per cent

Shoes and clothing: 13.4 per cent

Food and drink: 11.6 per cent

Co-operatives: 5.6 per cent

Others: about 19.5 per cent
National Flag
A light-blue cross on a white background
National Coat of Arms
A gold lion rampant facing left (heraldic right) on a red background, holding a sword in the raised right paw and accompanied by nine silver roses

A Short History

Finnish history can be said to have begun at about the time of Christ, when the Finns arrived in the area of present-day Finland. They were originally a nomadic Finno-Ugrian tribe that came over from beyond the Urals. They were preceded by the Lapps, who though closely related had arrived much earlier via a more northerly route. Presumably some interbreeding occurred. However, the Finns mostly arrived from the east, and some of them across the sea from the south; they probably drove the original inhabitants further north.

During the first millennium AD the Finns settled along the coast, and gradually moved inland along the river banks into the dense forests of the interior. They lived mostly from hunting and fishing, and from agriculture in the south, where a landowner class soon devel-

Saimaa, Finland's largest lake

oped. The people divided into three main groups: the Finns proper settled in permanent farmsteads in the south-west; the Häme or Tavaste occupied the lake country of the interior; and the Karelians remained in the east. The Lapps meanwhile became somewhat isolated in the north, where they lived from reindeer herding, fishing and a little agriculture; they had little influence on the subsequent history of Finland.

The Finns had not formed themselves into a nation, so it was not difficult for the Swedes to invade the country. Their ostensible reason for doing so was to convert the Finns to Christianity. The first signs of Christianity on the south coast of Finland date back to about AD1000. By this time the Finns had begun a flourishing fur trade with Sweden and other Baltic states. In 1154 Eric IX of Sweden (St Eric) led his army in a 'crusade', in which south-western Finland was annexed to the Swedish Crown. In further 'crusades' in 1249 and 1293, the Swedes advanced into Finland, and pushed back the Eastern Orthodox influence that was being exercised by the Russians in central Finland. In 1323, at the Treaty of Schlüsselburg, Karelia was divided between Sweden and Russia, so that the boundary of Swedish Finland became fixed.

Finland was soon given full rights as a Swedish province. In 1362 it gained the right to vote in the election of the Swedish king, and to be represented in the Swedish parliament (the Riksdag). Swedish became the language of administration, and many Swedes came to settle in Finland. The Finnish culture was never suppressed, but neither was it fostered or encouraged. Swedish became the language of the gentry, and was adopted by Finnish families who wanted to advance themselves socially or professionally.

The Swedish settlers interbred with the Finns to the extent that their racial type became general in the south and west of the country. Today the people in these areas are tall, fair and blue-eyed, and look much more like the Nordic Swedes than the Lapps to whom the Finns were originally much more closely related. It is significant that the Finns elsewhere tend to be more like the Lapps — shorter with dark hair and brown eyes.

But such physical characteristics make no difference to the Finnish consciousness, as is amply demonstrated by the fact that the Finnish language and culture have been preserved intact. The people have always thought of themselves as Finns, and the Swedish minority have retained a separate cultural identity in their coastal communities. There were never any serious conflicts between the two linguistic communities.

In the fifteenth and sixteenth centuries there were repeated Russian incursions, and the Finns learned to appreciate the protection afforded by their Swedish rulers. By now they had developed profitable trade links, especially in furs, with the merchants of the Hanseatic League but the areas exposed to invasion were devastated and trade in maritime towns suffered.

In 1523 Finland followed Sweden into the Reformation. In 1548 Martin Luther's pupil Mikael Agricola translated the New Testament into Finnish. He thus established Finnish as a written language, just as his mentor had done with German. So began education for all children. In 1581 the king of Sweden made Finland into a Grand Duchy. There followed a series of peasant uprisings against the nobility — the so-called 'Cudgel War'; but they were ruthlessly suppressed.

From 1611–17 King Gustav II Adolf of Sweden went to war with Russia, and expanded his territory around the shores of Lake

Ladoga. During the Thirty Years' War the Finns were involved in Sweden's religious campaigns in Germany. Finland flourished in the mid-seventeenth century under its Swedish governor Count Per Brahe. Several cities were founded, and Finland's first university was established at Turku/Åbo in 1640, which was then the capital of the Grand Duchy of Finland.

The end of that century saw a sudden downturn in the country's fortunes. Famine and disease killed more than 100,000 people — a quarter of the population at the time. The Finnish people soon became discontented, and could no longer trust Sweden to satisfy their interests.

Finland continued to suffer throughout the eighteenth century as it was devastated by repeated Russian invasions. In 1721 Sweden was forced to cede Karelia to Russia, and in 1743 lost yet more territory in the area around Vyborg. At the end of the eighteenth-century, a growing tendency towards separatism led to an abortive rebellion by Finnish Military Officers against the Swedish Crown (see page 71). But Finland was not yet ready for independence from Sweden, although many attempts were made to obtain this.

In 1808 Russian troops conquered the whole of Finland. They drove back the Swedes, and absorbed the Grand Duchy into the Russian empire. Under the Treaty of Fredrikshamn in September 1809, Sweden ceded the whole of Finland and the Åland Islands to Russia. Tsar Alexander I established himself as the Grand Duke of Finland, but at the same time gave full recognition to the constitutional rights granted to Finland under Swedish rule. He made a formal acknowledgement to this effect at the provincial assembly in Porvoo/Borgå. This meant that Finland had its own government, judiciary, currency, postal system, and even its own army. The areas that had been lost (Karelia and Vyborg) were reunited with the Grand Duchy, and Helsinki became the capital.

The end of the nineteenth century saw increasing Russian domination, which found expression in the gradual suppression of Finnish autonomy. The Finns could do no more than offer passive resistance as their rights were whittled away. One by one the post, currency and other autonomous institutions were taken over by the Russians. A Russian Orthodox diocese was set up at Vyborg, and Russian became the official language. The final step was the dissolution of the

Turku Castle. Turku was once the capital of the 'Grand Duchy' of Finland.

Finnish army in 1903. In 1912 Finnish citizenship was granted to Russians.

These changes made the Finns all the more determined to fight for total independence, and their opportunity came with the Russian Revolution in 1917. On 6 December 1917, Finland finally declared itself independent, and the provincial assembly elected P. E. Svinhufvud as its first head of government. But the civil war in Russia spilled over into Finland, and the Finns were forced to take up arms against Red Revolutionaries assisted by the Russian troops. The Finnish military leader was General Mannerheim (1867–1951).

In 1919 K. J. Ståhlberg became Finland's first president. He strove valiantly to unite the country and to put an end to war and political instability. At the Treaty of Dorpat (Tartu) in 1920, Finland at last made peace with Russia and was recognised internationally as an independent state. It also gained territory around the ice-free port of Petsamo on the Arctic Ocean. In 1919–21, the Åland Islands sought reunion with Sweden but the League of Nations assigned them to Finland. They were however, granted their own constitution and demilitarised.

There followed a long period of economic struggle, with the continued threat of Russia in the east, with whom relations were still somewhat strained. Finland at this stage followed an international policy of strict neutrality.

In 1939 the Russians demanded territory from Finland as a bulwark to Leningrad. The breakdown of negotiations led in November to the outbreak of the so-called Winter War, which lasted for 3 months. The Finns fought valiantly under the military leadership of Mannerheim, but the war ended with the loss of nearly a tenth of their territory. Finland again lost the Vyborg region, eastern Karelia and the Petsamo area bordering on the Arctic Ocean. Moreover, Hanko had to be leased to the Russians for use as a naval base.

In 1941 war broke out between Russia and Germany. The Finns resumed the struggle against Russia, and with the help of German troops they regained most of the territory they had lost. But with the collapse of the Eastern Front, these areas fell once and for all into Russian hands, while Porkkala had to be leased to the Russians in exchange for Hanko. Marshal Mannerheim became state president, and nearly half a million people (a tenth of the population) had to be resettled in the areas that still belonged to Finland.

In 1946 Marshal Mannerheim was replaced by Dr J. K. Paasikivi, who set up a new civilian government. Peace was finally declared in the Treaty of Paris in 1947, and the Finns set out with determination to rebuild their shattered nation. Other countries were amazed at the success of their efforts to put Finland on a sound financial footing.

Hauho, the oldest parish in the province of Häme, first mentioned in 1329

The result was an increasing affluence based on a strong industrial economy.

In 1956 Russia gave back the port of Porkkala, which they had used as a military base. Also in that year, Urho Kekkonen became president, a prominent figure in Finland's post-war history. Finland had returned to its pre-war policy of strict neutrality — so much so that until 1972 there was no Finnish embassy in either East or West Germany. Since September 1982 Dr Mauno Koivista has been the president of Finland. Today, Finland is secure, independent, neutral, and, more recently, prosperous.

Relations with East and West
The state of Finland is only about 70 years old, but the Finns have existed as a people for many centuries. During this time they have been shunted back and forth between their eastern and western neighbours, and have suffered atrocities from both sides. Relations have never been easy either way, so it is understandable that Finland should pursue a policy of strict neutrality.

Finland is a member of the United Nations. But the country still remains sandwiched between often opposing nations to the east and the west. The situation is best summed up by a government declaration made on the occasion of Finland's entry into the United Nations: 'Finland is a small neutral country that has neither sought nor found security by trusting in military alliances or in the protection of one power group against others. Its foreign policy is therefore geared towards staying out of international conflicts and controversies. It is in Finland's ultimate interests to promote a world order in which peace and reason prevail. Such a situation depends on the kind of system of world security that is foreseen in the United Nations charter. Finland can contribute most towards achieving that end by adhering strictly and consistently to a policy of neutrality.'

For many years Finland remained especially hostile towards its eastern neighbours, partly as a result of Russia's insistent demands for territory. But since World War II the Finns have tried to put such things behind them. They managed by superhuman efforts to fulfil all the reparations demanded by the Soviet Union, and wrote off the territories they had lost. Thus relations have improved between the two nations, and both sides have tried to overcome the understandable mistrust that has grown up between them in the past.

In 1948 Finland and the Soviet Union signed a treaty of mutual friendship, co-operation and support. It was renewed in 1970, and gives full recognition to Finland's policy of neutrality. The Soviet Union receives nearly 20 per cent of Finland's exports, the main items being ships and machinery for the paper and wood-processing industries. Conversely, Finland imports fuel and industrial raw materials from the Soviet Union, together with cars and machinery.

One indication that relations have improved is the treaty regarding the Saimaa Canal. This waterway forms a vital transport link between the Finnish lakes and the eastern end of the Gulf of Finland, and is a much-used route to the Baltic. The southern part of the canal fell to the Soviet Union when they occupied the region around Vyborg, and the canal fell into disuse. But the Russians have now leased the canal zone back to the Finns, who have thus been able to redevelop this canal link between the lakes and the Baltic.

For historical and cultural reasons, Finland has always had close links with the rest of Scandinavia. In 1955 Finland joined the so-called

Nordic Council, which had already been formed by the other three countries. Its chief purpose is to co-ordinate the job market and welfare legislation. This means, for example, that over 100,000 Finns work in Sweden alone. Another result is the Nordic Passport and Customs Union, whereby citizens of member countries are exempt from passport and customs control when travelling to other countries within the union. Finland, however, retains a certain amount of independence from the rest of the union, which is symbolised by its somewhat more isolated position to the east.

Finland has also enjoyed close relations with Germany, going back to its trading links with Lübeck and the other Hanseatic cities. Small German enclaves grew up in Finnish ports, and cultural links were further encouraged by the large number of Finns who went to study at German universities. One typical example of this is that great figure of the Finnish Reformation, Mikael Agricola, whose friendship with Luther was instrumental in his pioneering of Finnish as a written language.

Finnish-UK relations have been traditionally commercial with Finland exporting to the UK the products of its metal, textile and timber industries and importing machinery, vehicles, textiles, chemicals etc. Finnish companies have recently invested in the building of two paper mills in Wales and Scotland. Relations between Finland and the USA are also largely commercial, with about 5 per cent of Finland's exports going to the States. Import figures are about the same.

Finland's important role as host country for the Helsinki Human Rights Convention has formed a bridge between East and West. It is to be hoped that its policy of strict neutrality will enable it to maintain this role, and will prevent it from becoming a battlefield yet again at some future date.

Climate and Travel

Finland has a predominantly continental climate, characterised by cold winters and warm summers. But even Finland benefits a little from the effects of the Gulf Stream, so that the extremes are very slightly moderated. In northern Finland there is no spring or autumn

Helsinki, host for the Human Rights Convention

to speak of, and the summer seems almost to explode into life. Even in the south the autumn and spring are curtailed, though the weather then is usually fairly pleasant.

The country's northern situation means that the days are very long in the summer. There are at least 20 hours of daylight at the summer solstice, while the midnight sun shines in areas north of the Arctic Circle. North of the 70th parallel there is non-stop daylight for 70 days in the summer, although the same areas must suffer 50 days of continuous darkness in the winter.

In northern Finland the night frosts begin in late August or early September, and the ground is usually covered with snow from mid-November to mid-May. In the south the snow normally lies from mid-December to mid-April. The average annual precipitation (including both snow and rainfall) is about 700mm (27in) in the south and about half that in the north.

Travellers to the north should choose the midsummer period from late June until mid-August. Before then the weather can still some-times turn nasty, and after that the nights are often very cold. The

In northern Finland, snow covers the ground from mid-November to mid-May

lakes warm up rapidly in the summer, and reach their warmest by late July. But the water temperature rarely exceeds 20°C (68°F) except in certain specially favoured stretches of water. The weather in southern Finland is usually fairly pleasant from mid-May onwards. The landscape is particularly beautiful at this time as the deciduous trees become green, and similarly in September as the leaves turn brown again.

Southern Finland has a well-defined skiing season that is mainly concentrated in the period from mid-January to mid-April. Although winter temperatures are so low, the cold is usually a very dry cold, and is therefore less unpleasant than the low temperatures would suggest.

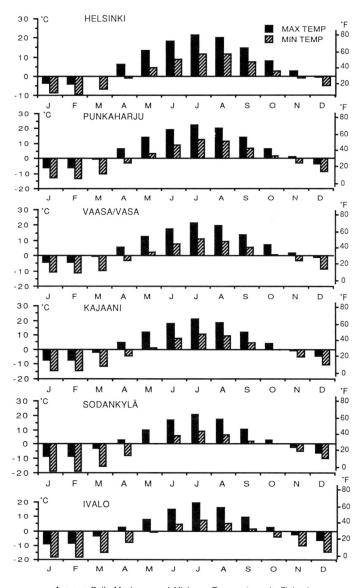

Average Daily Maximum and Minimum Temperatures in Finland

The Midnight Sun and the Northern Lights

The phenomenon of the midnight sun is basically due to the tilt in the earth's axis. The earth turns on its axis once every 24 hours, and one half is turned towards the sun. This results in the cycle of day and night, which if the earth's axis were vertical would each last 12 hours. But because the earth's axis is tilted, this is only the case at the equator — and elsewhere at the spring and autumn equinoxes in late March and late September.

From late March to late September the northern hemisphere is tilted towards the sun, and daylight there lasts for longer than 12 hours. The change in the duration and intensity of sunlight is also the reason for the seasonal changes in weather. The further one travels northwards, the longer the summer daylight becomes, until in a certain area around the North Pole the sun never sets for days on end. Conversely, the sun never rises for a similar period in the winter. (In the southern hemisphere the seasons are the opposite way round.)

There are 90° of latitude (the difference between the horizontal and vertical axes) between the equator and either pole. The latitude of all places on the globe is calculated accordingly, with the equator at 0° and the poles at 90°. The earth is tilted at an angle of 23° 27'. If subtracted from 90°, this gives 66° 33', which is the latitude at and above which the midnight sun shines at the summer solstice in late June.

In the northern hemisphere this line is called the Arctic Circle (in Finnish Napapiiri). As one travels north from here, the period of the midnight sun becomes gradually longer. Thus Sodankylä, for example, enjoys permanent daylight from 31 May to 16 July, and the North Cape from 12 May to 30 July. However, the height above sea level also increases the period of the midnight sun, which is experienced at Kuusamo even though it is south of the Arctic Circle (see below).

Even in southern Finland the sun rises for almost 20 hours at midsummer. At Helsinki, for example, the dawn begins to show as early as one o'clock in the morning, and it turns dark as late as ten or eleven o'clock in the evening.

The midnight sun has an understandable effect on plants, animals and even people. At midsummer the whole of Scandinavia is full of the joys of life. People sleep much less, and tend to be on an emotional 'high'. It is a time of endless feasting and celebration, especially in Finland. The plant life is affected too. In the north the summer explodes into life, so that the period from bud to fruit, which elsewhere lasts up to 6 months, can be concentrated into a period of 3 or 4 weeks.

The midnight sun can be seen. . .

at Kuusamo	(65° 58')	from 15 June to 27 June
at Rovaniemi	(66° 34')	from 6 June to 5 July
at Pello	(66° 48')	from 4 June to 7 July
at Sodankylä	(67° 22')	from 31 May to 12 July
at Ivalo	(68° 36')	from 24 May to 19 July
at Utsjoki	(69° 45')	from 18 May to 25 July
at the North Cape	(71° 10')	from 12 May to 30 July

The other occurrence that is common in the far north is a wierd phenomenon known as the northern lights. It is a truly remarkable sight that has puzzled scientists down the centuries. At first the sky is illuminated with red and yellow light, and gradually the whole sky is filled with multicoloured bands of bright light, which are constantly changing in colour, intensity and form. It is as if the whole sky has become the stage for a vast *son et lumière* performance.

One can quite understand why the ancients were so afraid of this ghostly phenomenon, in which the sky was filled with a shimmering veil of bright lights like the reflection of a great fire. It was for them as though the gods had drawn a great curtain across the sky, and it could only have a supernatural explanation. Indeed, they regarded it as an omen of great evil.

The causes of the northern lights or aurora borealis have yet to be fully explained. They are more accurately called polar lights, since they also occur in Antarctic regions (the southern lights or aurora australis).

The phenomenon is strongly associated with sunspot activity — gigantic explosions in the sun's atmosphere. These explosions emit vast numbers of protons and electrons (subatomic particles) into space, which hurtle towards the earth at nearly the speed of light. As they come into the earth's magnetic field, they are deflected towards the magnetic poles. This is why the aurora is commoner in polar regions, though it can very occasionally occur in other parts of the globe. As these particles collide with the outer edge of the earth's atmosphere, at heights of between 100km and 1,000km, they cause ionisation and emit vast amounts of light. (Neon lights work on a roughly similar principle, though on a vastly smaller scale.) The many different colours that make up the display are due to the variable wavelengths of the light that is emitted.

1 HELSINKI AND THE SURROUNDING AREA

There are not many European capitals in such beautiful settings as the Scandinavian capitals, and Helsinki (in Swedish Helsingfors) is no exception to this. For the city is built on a rugged granite peninsula between two fjord-like inlets, and is surrounded by a whole host of rocks and islands.

Known as the 'Daughter of the Baltic', Helsinki has a population of 500,000. It was founded in 1550 by King Gustav I Vasa of Sweden at the mouth of the River Vantaa and to the north of the present city centre. People from the surrounding area were compulsorily re-settled there. It was intended as a port and garrison town to rival the Russian Baltic ports, especially Reval (now Tallinn) in Estonia, and to profit from flourishing trade links with the Hanseatic League and the Dutch ports.

This development was not entirely successful. All that remains of the old town are the foundations of a church. In 1639 Queen Christina of Sweden resited the town on its present peninsular site, but this did not improve matters particularly. In 1808 this town of wooden buildings was destroyed in the last of several fires.

Paradoxically, the present city owes its existence to the Russians, who took over Finland in 1809. In 1812 this small settlement on the Vironiemi Peninsula was turned by the Russians into the capital of the Grand Duchy of Finland. Their decision was no doubt reinforced by the fact that the previous capital of Turku/Åbo had similarly been burned to the ground.

As a result of this, by far the majority of Helsinki's historical buildings go back to the early nineteenth century, when the Classical Revival was at its height. Most of them were designed by Carl Ludwig Engel from the Schinkel school of architecture in Berlin.

What Helsinki Has to Offer

Helsinki is an ideal place for starting or finishing a tour of Finland. Though not typical of Finland in general, it is an important part of Finland as a whole. Nowhere else can one find so much information on the country's history and culture. One can trace the history of the Finns, from their arrival in Finland, through the period of Swedish settlement and the Russian occupation, to their final emergence as an independent state.

Even without the rest of Finland, a visit to Helsinki is an experience in itself. Thanks to modern transport facilities, it is accessible throughout the year. It can also be combined with other Scandinavian capitals such as Stockholm and Copenhagen. Helsinki is a thriving modern city in a rapidly developing country, and has much to offer the visitor.

The best way to see the city centre is on foot. It is relatively compact, and the regular road layout makes it fairly easy to find one's way around. The tour suggested below includes all the most important sights. The oldest surviving buildings go back no further than the Classical Revival. But there is much else to see besides, including no less than twenty-five museums. There are theatres, opera houses and concert halls, although most of these are closed in the summer.

The Best Time to Visit

Helsinki itself can be visited throughout the year. Summer is the best time for those wishing to visit the many parks and islands in the area around Helsinki. But winter is more attractive for visitors who wish to sample the city's cultural life, and a voyage through the ice of the Gulf of Finland is an unforgettable experience.

Essential Information

The city tourist office is in the Northern Esplanade, and its address is as follows:

Helsingin kaupungin matkailutoimisto
(Helsinki Tourist Information Office)
Pohjoisesplanadi 19
00100 Helsinki 10
☎ (9)1-174 088/1-693 757

Helsinki Market Square

The tourist office provides much useful information in English, including up-to-date details of things to see, both in and around the city. A good city plan is essential for touring Helsinki. This can also be obtained from the tourist office.

1a In and Around the City

The City Centre

The tour begins at the city tourist office (see above). Just to the north of it is the Senaatintori (Senate Square), which forms the centre of the city. In the middle of it is a statue of Tsar Alexander I of Russia, who did much for Finland. To the north of the square a broad flight of steps leads up to **St Nicholas' Cathedral** (the Lutheran cathedral). This enormous white, domed structure was built by Carl Ludwig Engel in the Classical Revival style of the early nineteenth century. On the western side is **Helsinki University**, designed by Engel in 1830. The building to the north of it is the university library.

The route leaves the square in an easterly direction past the

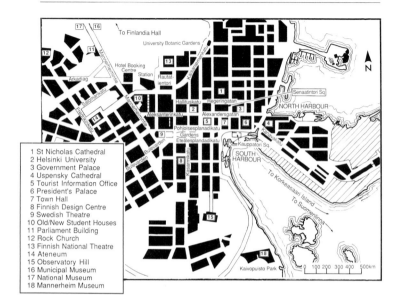

1 St Nicholas Cathedral
2 Helsinki University
3 Government Palace
4 Uspensky Cathedral
5 Tourist Information Office
6 President's Palace
7 Town Hall
8 Finnish Design Centre
9 Swedish Theatre
10 Old/New Student Houses
11 Parliament Building
12 Rock Church
13 Finnish National Theatre
14 Ateneum
15 Observatory Hill
16 Municipal Museum
17 National Museum
18 Mannerheim Museum

Government Palace, which is yet another Engel creation. One then continues past the **Knights' House**, where the nobility once held their formal assemblies, and eventually comes out by the North Harbour. Just across the water is the **Uspensky Cathedral** (the Eastern Orthodox cathedral). Built in 1868, it is a beautifully exotic structure, with gold-painted onion-shaped domes.

Turning south, one quickly comes to the **President's Palace**, which was originally built for the Russian Tsars. In front of it is the market square (Kauppatori), which is always full of activity. Further to the west is the **town hall** — another of Engel's Classical buildings, which looks out across the water.

Beyond here is the Esplanade, Helsinki's main central boulevard, which runs due west into the city. The well-kept gardens along the centre are flanked by two grand avenues: the Northern Esplanade (Pohjoisesplanadikatu) to the right, and the Southern Esplanade (Eteälesplanadikatu) to the left. The gardens contain a statue of Runeberg, Finland's national poet, and a beautifully decorative fountain created by Ville Vallgren in 1908. Known as the *Havis Amanda*, it is in the form of a young woman, and is supposed to symbolise the youthful Helsinki emerging from the sea.

Uspensky Cathedral

The first building on the left is the former Governor's Palace, which is now used for festivals and exhibitions. Visitors who are interested may care to look at the World Health and Safety at Work Exhibition. It is concerned with the prevention of accidents at work, and with safety and rehabilitation. Another interesting place to visit is the **Finnish Design Centre**, which is just south of the Esplanade along the Kasarmikatu. It contains a permanent exhibition of modern Finnish craft and design.

At the western end of the Esplanade is the **Swedish Theatre**, beyond which one may turn north-west along the city's busiest thoroughfare, the Mannerheimintie. It passes a statue called the *Three Smiths* on the right before arriving at the **Old Student House** (now a theatre) and the **New Student House.** There is a view of the central station to the right. Further along on the left is the **Parliament Building** (1927–30).

The **Municipal Museum** (Kaupunginmuseo) is in a park on the right. The large modern building beyond it is the **Finlandia Hall**, which is a true masterpiece of modern Finnish architecture. It includes a large conference centre where important international conventions are held, and two concert halls. The larger hall seats 1,700, and is well known for its outstanding acoustics; the smaller one is used for more intimate chamber concerts.

If one crosses the Mannerheimintie, one comes to the **Finnish National Museum** (Suomen Kansallismuseo), built in 1912. This imposing structure with a spire contains important cultural and historical collections from all periods of Finnish history. A prehistoric section is also included. Not far away to the left is the fascinating **Temppeliaukio** or **Rock Church**. This underground church is a remarkable feat of architecture, having been hewn out of bare granite.

If one returns to the Mannerheimintie and leaves it past the main post office building, one quickly arrives at the **central station**. This building was hailed in its time as one of the most remarkable structures in Scandinavia, and was to establish the reputation of Finnish architects throughout the world. Such functional buildings are less in fashion these days, but it nonetheless remains an impressive structure.

Beyond the station is the Station Square (Rautatientori), on the northern side of which is the **National Theatre**. The gardens to the north of here include the **University Botanic Gardens**, which are full of fascinating trees and other plants, together with exotic green-house collections. Immediately to the south of the Station Square is the **Ateneum** (Athenaeum), which houses the country's most impor-tant art collections. Of particular interest are paintings by modern Finnish artists, whose work is unjustly neglected outside Finland.

If one goes south past the Ateneum and turns left along the Aleksanterinkatu, one quickly comes back to the Senate Square, and to the starting point of the tour.

If the weather is decent, visitors are recommended to take a further stroll towards the city's south-eastern point. The route goes due south along the South Harbour, where the ships dock that come in from abroad (there is also a car park).

It is only a short distance to the **German Church**, which is on the northern edge of a park. A path through the park leads to the **Observatory Hill** (Tätitorninvuori), which is the site for the obser-vatory of the Ursa Astronomical Society. From the top of the hill there is a marvellous view of the city and the harbour. The statue close by is a monument to shipwrecked mariners, created by Richard Stigell in 1897.

Helsinki National Museum in winter

If one continues south along the harbour, one first passes the great customs sheds, which ship passengers pass through on arrival in Finland. The **Mannerheim Museum** is further along on a road that goes up to the right. It is housed in the former residence of Marshal Mannerheim, Finland's national hero at the time of both World Wars.

The coast road eventually comes out into a lovely park called the **Kaivopuisto** on the south-eastern corner of the peninsula. The islands adjoining it form ideal centres for yachting and bathing.

Things to See Outside the City Centre

Helsinki Zoo

Founded in 1888, this is the most northerly zoo in the world, and contains over 1,000 animals in pleasant parkland surroundings. It is situated on an island called **Korkeasaari** to the east of the city, and can be reached by boat from a pier on the North Harbour at the bottom end of the Aleksanterinkatu.

❋ **Hietaniemi Cemetery**

This extensive cemetery is spread out along the rocky western shore of the peninsula. It contains the graves of many Finnish and German soldiers who died in Finland during World War II. Among them are the tombs of Finnish national heroes such as Marshal Mannerheim.

❋ **Olympic Stadium and Linnanmäki Park**

The Olympic Stadium is due north of the city, not far from the Mannerheimintie, and can be reached by car or public transport. It was built in 1938 for the Olympic Games which were postponed until 1948 (London). They eventually took place in Helsinki in 1952. The tower provides a magnificent view of the city. In front of the stadium is a statue of another Finnish hero, the great runner Paavo Nurmi.

The park to the east of the Olympic site is an extensive amusement park called Linnanmäki (in Swedish Borgbacken) that is typical of Scandinavian cities. There is plenty going on, including the famous Peacock Varieties, where world-famous artists perform, and an open-air theatre, which is open during the summer.

ℍ **Seurasaari Open-air Museum**

This is situated due west of the Olympic Stadium on an island of the same name that is linked to the mainland by a bridge. The route to it goes past the Mannerheim Children's Hospital, next to which is an institute called Lastenlinna (Children's Castle), a home and training centre for the care of handicapped children.

Seurasaari Museum consists of a collection of reconstructed houses and farmsteads from all over Finland. They are beautifully restored, and give a vivid impression of the cultural development of Finland, especially in country communities.

❋ **Helsinki Harbour and Suomenlinna**

Visitors should not leave Helsinki without taking a boat trip around the harbour, which cannot be seen properly from the land.

Not to be missed either is a boat trip through the skerries in the harbour to the island of Suomenlinna (in Swedish Sveaborg), commonly known as the 'Gibraltar of the North'. The boat goes from a pier on the South Harbour adjoining the market square. The island is dominated by an eighteenth-century castle, with a wonderful view across the harbour to the city. There is also an open-air theatre and a military museum.

Helsinki Olympic Stadium and statue of Paavo Nurmi

Theatres

Helsinki is the artistic and cultural centre of Finland. There are four important theatres and several smaller ones, all of which unfortunately are closed for the 3 months of the summer holidays.

The **National Theatre** (Kansallisteatteri), near the central station, stages perfomances in Finnish, mostly of classical plays. The **Swedish Theatre** (Ruotsalainenteatteri) presents plays and musical productions in Swedish. The **Municipal Theatre** (Kaupunginteatteri) is the largest and most modern theatre in Finland. The **National Opera House** (Suomen Kansallisoopera) is the home of Finnish opera.

There are open-air theatres at Linnanmäki and on the island of Suomenlinna (see above), both of which are open only during the summer holiday period.

Museums

Helsinki has no fewer than twenty-five major museums, plus numerous smaller museums of a more specialised nature. The most important museums are given below, of which those with an asterisk are mentioned in the main text above:

Seurasaari Open-air Museum

Agricultural Museum Viikki Estate
The history of agriculture in Finland, from its beginnings to the
development of modern technology.

Ateneum (Athenaeum) Museum of Art* Kaivokatu 2-4
(Temporary address while under repair: Kansakoulukatu 3)
Collections of paintings and drawings by modern Finnish artists, plus
classical works from overseas. Expected to be under repair for 3–4
years.

Gallén Kallela Museum Gallén-Kallelantie 27, Leppävaara
The artist's studio for 20 years, containing 120 of his paintings.

Mannerheim Museum* Kalliolinnantie 22
Home of Finland's national hero, preserved exactly as he left it,
including numerous personal mementos.

Sibelius Monument,
Sibelius Park

Military Museum* Suomenlinna.

Municipal Museum* Karamzininkatu 2
Cultural and historical collections from Helsinki's past.

National Museum* Mannerheimintie 34
Prehistoric, historical and ethnographical collections, with specific reference to Finland.

Seurasaari Open-air Museum* Seurasaari
Historical collection of houses and farmsteads from all over Finland.

1b To the West of Helsinki

This section covers the area between Helsinki and the south-western port of Turku/Åbo. Both are significant ports on the Baltic shipping network. The two routes described are those from Helsinki to Turku and from Helsinki to Hanko/Hangö.

Helsinki to Hanko/Hangö (145km)

Helsinki   One should leave Helsinki along the E3, or Finnish Road 1, which is signposted for Salo and Turku/Åbo. It is a motorway for the first 42km.

· 14km   The exit for Espoo is about 14km out of Helsinki.

Espoo   **Espoo/Esbo** (population 157,000) is typical of modern industrialised towns in southern Finland. Although one of the oldest settlements in the country, it was so small that until recently it did not even appear on maps, and was not given town status until 1972. But its recent growth has been so explosive that it is now the fourth-largest town in Finland. The earliest parish records go back to 1450, which is the date when the old stone church was founded.

The new town has swallowed up a number of other towns that were previously separate entities. They include the famous garden city of **Tapiola/Hagalund**, which is popular with visitors, and the rather older town of **Kauniainen**. The district of **Otaniemi** is the site for the Helsinki College of Technology, the main building of which was designed by the famous architect Alvar Aalto. Its most impressive building is the Dipoli Hall — a student residence that doubles as a prestigious conference centre. It is a particularly outstanding example of modern Finnish architecture.

Some of these districts are linked to Helsinki by a separate motorway route across the Ruoholahti Peninsula. This is also the route to the beaches along the irregular coastline to the south-west of Helsinki.

The E3/Road 1 continues from Espoo. The motorway section

28km   ends somewhere between Veikkola and Lohjanharju. At **Lohjan-**
Lohjanharju   **harju** there is an important road junction. The E3 goes straight on for Salo and Turku/Åbo (see below), while the present route goes left along Road 53 for Hanko.

Road 53 runs through lush green countryside that is reminiscent

15km   of southern Sweden. After another 15km it arrives at the small

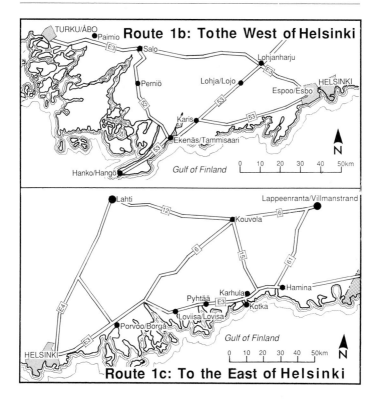

Route 1b: To the West of Helsinki

Route 1c: To the East of Helsinki

industrial town of **Lohja/Lojo** (population 14,500). Standing in the old part of the town is the lovely fourteenth-century stone church of St Laurence. It contains some beautiful frescos that date back to the time of its foundation.

Lohja

The road passes the shore of the Lohjajärvi, and continues via Virkkala/Virkby to the small industrial town of **Karis/Karjaa**, which is the railway junction for the line to Hanko. From here it is another 20km further to Ekenäs.

35km
Karis

Ekenäs/Tammisaari is a popular holiday resort surrounded by oak woodlands. It has been a town since the Middle Ages, and its park is famous for its many rare plants. The coast around here is much fragmented into inlets and islands, and there are many excellent beaches with chalet and bathing facilities.

20km
Ekenäs

There is a turning at Ekenäs along Road 52 to Salo, where one may rejoin the E3 Helsinki–Turku road (see below). It passes through **Perniö**, with its fourteenth-century church. From Perniö there is another road going down to the beautiful fragmented coastline of south-west Finland. The landscape is densely wooded, with gentle hills formed by glacial moraines.

Road 53 covers the final 35km from Ekenäs to Hanko. It passes through the seaside resort of Lappvik/Lappohja, which is beautifully situated among the woods along the coast.

35km
Hanko

Hanko/Hangö (population 12,000) is the most southerly town in Finland. There are records of a port here from as early as the thirteenth century. After the coming of the railway, Hanko soon developed into the biggest winter port in Finland, although even here considerable effort was required to keep the harbour free of ice. The big ships dock in the outer harbour to the west of the town. Hanko and the islands around it have become a popular holiday region. The whole area is still peppered with the ruins of old Swedish forts, destroyed by the Russians in 1854.

Helsinki to Turku/Åbo (164km)

Helsinki
42km
Lohjanharju

This route follows the same course as the previous one from Helsinki as far as Lohjanharju (see above) — at which point it carries straight on for Salo and Turku, while the previous route turns left towards Hanko.

The E3/Road 1 continues through a landscape of wooded hills, passing a number of small villages and lakes. It is an area where numerous Stone Age sites have been discovered, some of which are as much as 8,000 years old. The Finns call the area Varsinais Suomi, or 'Finland proper'.

70km
Salo

Salo (population 20,000) is picturesquely situated at the mouth of the Uskelanjoki next to the bay of Halikko. It was once purely a market town in an area full of large arable farms and estates. But the town now has a number of industries, including a large sugar factory and a television factory (Salora–TV).

The E3/Road 1 passes through the village of **Halikko**, with its fifteenth-century church, and crosses the Paimionjoki near Paimio.

52km
Turku

Near Piikkiö it runs along the shore of a long inlet, and soon after that enters the suburbs of Turku.

Perniö Church

Turku/Åbo (population 165,000)

Turku is the third-largest town in Finland, and also the oldest. It was once the capital of Finland and the centre of its Swedish-speaking community. Now only about 10 per cent of the population are Swedish-speaking. Turku is the capital of the province of Turku Pori. It has both a Swedish and a Finnish university, with 11,000 students altogether. Finland's first university was founded here by Per Brahe in 1640, but was moved to Helsinki following the great fire of 1827. The seat of government had already been moved to Helsinki in 1819, so that Turku was no longer the capital.

Very little of the old city remains. Like other cities in Norway, Sweden and Finland, it was built primarily of wood, and was repeatedly burned to the ground. All that remain are the old castle, the Gothic cathedral and some wooden houses that have been turned into an open-air museum.

The castle, **Turun Linna**, is the largest fortified structure in Finland. It stands at the entrance to the harbour overlooking the mouth of the Aurajoki. One can see the ferries docking here from

ports in Sweden and across the Baltic. It was originally founded by
the Swedes in the thirteenth century, destroyed by Duke Albert of
Mecklenburg in the fourteenth century and rebuilt in the fifteenth. It
changed hands several times during the fifteenth and sixteenth
centuries, as Denmark and Sweden fought one another for suprem-
acy. It was finally rebuilt in 1599.

It later fell into disrepair, and was further damaged by bombs in
1941. However, thanks to 14 years' restoration work, it has now been
turned into a fascinating and unusually comprehensive historical
museum. The collections cover all aspects of the city's culture, and
include furniture, tiled stoves, carpets, woven goods and other
handicrafts. Nowhere is there a fuller presentation of the interlocking
cultural development of the Finnish and Swedish communities.

Most of the other things to see are in the city centre, which can be
reached from the castle along the west bank of the river via the
Linnankatu/Slottsgatan. There are two old sailing ships moored near
St Martin's Bridge (Martinsilta). Of these, the frigate *Suomen Joutsen*
('Swan of Finland') is used as a naval training ship, while the wooden
barque *Sigyn* is still seaworthy but has now been turned into a
museum.

The sports park across the river contains a number of interesting
buildings. Directly by the river is the **Wäinö Aaltonen Museum**,
which is filled with sculptures. The **Natural History Museum** is
positioned further back, and provides a comprehensive display of
Finnish fauna. The **Municipal Theatre** is again next to the river,
and is particularly impressive when floodlit at night.

The town hall is further along on the western shore, just before the
Aura Bridge (Auransilta). Next to it are the Municipal Information
Office and the **Qwensel House**, which is the oldest surviving
wooden building in Turku. It has now been turned into a fascinating
museum of pharmacy. Close by is the pier for local boat tours and
excursions.

Returning to the eastern shore, there is another park area
adjoining the Kaskenkatu. It is sited on a hill called the Vartiovuori,
and contains both the former observatory and an open-air theatre.
Nearby is the so-called **Abbey Quarter**, a group of old wooden
houses that survived the fires. They have been turned into a
handicrafts museum.

The President's Palace, Helsinki

Helsinki's unusual Protestant Cathedral

Kerimäki Church, on the eastern bank of the Peruvesi. Built in 1847 it seats 5,000.

Finnish lakes coffee house

Turku Music Festival at Turun Linna

If one leaves the park at the opposite end and crosses the Uudenmannkatu, one quickly comes to the **Swedish University** (Åbo Akademi). Beyond it is the Old Academy, the home of the old university, which was moved to Helsinki in 1827.

Turku Cathedral stands on a hill behind, surrounded by trees. This massive thirteenth-century brick structure is the best example of early Gothic architecture in Scandinavia apart from Uppsala Cathedral. The tower is 98m (320ft) high.

The interior contains the remains of some remarkable Gothic frescos and the tombs of several important historical figures. These include members of the Horn family, who did much to shape the history of both Sweden and Finland, and also Queen Karin Månsdotter, a commoner's daughter who became consort to King Erik XIV. The king was overthrown by his brother Johan, and the couple were imprisoned at Turku.

Two glass cabinets contain special editions of the Bible. One is a decorative edition from the seventeenth century. The other is the famous Agricola Bible, the first book to have been printed in Finnish. In front of the cathedral is a statue of its translator Mikael Agricola, who was a pupil and friend of Martin Luther.

Just to the north of the cathedral is the **Sibelius Museum**. The building also includes the music faculty of the Swedish University and the Ett Hem ('Old House') Museum. Beyond here is the site of the **Finnish University** (Turun Yliopisto).

If one returns across the river, and continues via the Aninkais-tenkatu and left along the Eerikinkatu, one quickly comes to the old market square. The market is usually full of activity. On one side is the Orthodox church, built by Carl Ludwig Engel in the style of the Classical Revival. There is also a tourist information office, where visitors can find out about all there is to see and do.

If one turns left by the old market hall, it is only a short distance back to the Aura Bridge. This is the starting point for boat trips to the local holiday islands and to the nearby coastal resort of Naantali. It is also possible to travel from here to the island province of Åland (see page 162).

The beginning of August is the time of the famous Turku Music Festival and the Naantali Music Festival, also an important event, is held in June. Apart from classical performances, there is also a rock music festival known as the 'Ruisrock' on the nearby island of Ruissalo.

1c To the East of Helsinki

This section is primarily for visitors to Helsinki who do not have enough time to see much of Finland. The routes suggested below are short enough for a day excursion. They provide glimpses of the inlets and islands along the Gulf of Finland, and also of the lake country inland.

Visitors with a little more time may combine these routes with parts of the longer routes described later in the book, especially Route 2. One possible combination would be to go via Lappeenranta, Imatra, Savonlinna and Mikkeli, returning via Heinola and Lahti. This option would take about 3 days.

The three routes described below are: Helsinki to Kotka; Kotka to Lahti (linking with Routes 2 and 4); and Kotka to Lappeenranta (linking with Route 2).

Turku Cathedral

Helsinki · Porvoo · Kotka (127km)

The route leaves Helsinki along the E3/Road 7 for Porvoo/Borgå, Helsinki
which for the first 50km is a motorway. It runs east along the coast,
passing several side turnings to local seaside resorts. The town of 51km
Porvoo is just beyond the end of the motorway section. Porvoo

Porvoo/Borgå (population 20,000)

Finland's second-oldest town was founded in the fourteenth century, and is the main cultural centre of the Swedish-speaking community. Porvoo is situated at the mouth of the river of the same name (Porvoonjoki). The population almost doubled at the end of World War II, when Finnish-speaking refugees arrived from the territories lost to the Soviet Union. Thus only the old part of Porvoo has managed to preserve the town's exclusively Swedish character.

The town is important culturally because of the many famous artists who worked here. It was the home of Finland's national poet J. L. Runeberg (1804–77), who is buried in the cemetery across the river. It was also the birthplace of his son Walter Runeberg and of Valle Vallgren (1855–1940), both of whom made a name for themselves as sculptors.

According to tradition, the town was originally founded by Danish Vikings, who built a fortified camp here. Remnants of it have been found together with those of later fortifications on the Linnanmäki/ Borgbacken (Castle Hill) overlooking the town. The hill also provides a good view of the town and the bay.

The narrow streets of the old town cluster below the small Gothic cathedral. The main structure is from the early fifteenth century, but the interior was later refurbished in the Rococo style. Inside the cathedral is a bronze statue of Tsar Alexander I of Russia. It was cast by Walter Runeberg in 1909 to commemorate the centenary of the assembly in 1809, at which the Tsar formally upheld the Finnish constitution, and guaranteed the religious freedom of its citizens.

Adjoining the cathedral are the bell tower and a small wooden church where Finnish services are held. There has been a Lutheran bishopric at Porvoo since 1723. Nearby are the bishop's palace (1923) and the old Swedish grammar school, which now houses a collection of sculptures by Walter Runeberg. His father Johan Ludwig Runeberg taught at the school from 1837 to 1857. The poet's former residence has been turned into a museum. It is situated at the southern end of the old town, on the corner of the Runeberginkatu and the Aleksanterinkatu. There is a statue of the poet at the entrance to the Runeberginkatu.

The old town hall (1764) is on the opposite side of the cathedral; it is now the municipal museum. Next to it is an art gallery containing

Old Porvoo

works by the sculptor Valle Vallgren and the painter Albert Edelfelt (1854–1905), both of whom worked here for many years. The edge of the town is occupied by a number of wood-processing industries.

The route continues along the E3/Road 7. After 22km the road forks at Forsby/Koskenkylä: Road 6 goes north-east towards Kouvola (see below), while the E3/Road 7 continues eastwards along the coast, which at this point forms several long inlets.

Porvoo

40km

Loviisa

Another 18km further on is the small town of **Loviisa/Lovisa**. This picturesque little fishing port is situated at the northern end of an inlet called the Lovisavik. It was founded in 1745, and named after Queen Luise Ulrike of Sweden, sister of Frederick the Great. Loviisa was originally intended as a garrison post against the Russians, who in 1743 had pushed the border to within 15km of here. The garrison was later taken over by the Russians. The Russian fort on the nearby island of Svartholm was destroyed by the British and French fleets in 1855 during the course of the Crimean War. Nowadays Loviisa is a popular seaside resort, in spite of the proximity of two nuclear power stations.

Kotka

16km
Pyhtää
Sixteen kilometres further east is a small place called **Pyhtää/ Pyttis**. It has a fifteenth-century stone church with a free-standing bell tower. The road crosses the five channels that form the delta of the Kymenjoki/Kymmeneälv. This river forms the main outflow from the Finnish lakes. It comes out of Lake Routsalainen just north of Heinola. That in turn is linked to the Päijänne lake system that stretches far to the north of Jyväskylä. Between 1743 and 1809, this river formed the border with Russia.

20km
Kotka
Beyond the Kymenjoki delta is the port of **Kotka**, which together with the neighbouring town of **Karhula** has grown into an important industrial centre (population 62,000). The main industries include sugar, glass and wood-processing, especially cellulose. Kotka today has one of the largest export harbours in Finland, handling products from the Kouvola region.

Kotka itself is situated on an island, which is linked to the mainland by a bridge. It was founded as a Russian border garrison, together with several forts on the islands along the coast, in opposition to the Swedish garrison of Lovisa (now Loviisa). In 1855 all these defences

Tsar Alexander's fisherman's hut, Kotka

were destroyed by the British and French fleets during the Crimean War. All that remained of Kotka itself was the Russian Orthodox church, built in 1795 for the Russian garrison. It is now surrounded by the municipal park. The great town hall by the market square was built in 1934, and was designed by E. Huttunen.

Also worth seeing is an old fisherman's hut next to the nearby rapids of Langinkoski. It was a present to Tsar Alexander III, and has now been turned into a museum.

Kotka · Kouvola · Lahti (114km)

Road 15 goes due north from Kotka and its industrial neighbour Kotka Karhula. The road is very busy, but has been rebuilt on a generous scale so as to bypass all the towns and villages on the way to Kouvola.

One of the places to be bypassed is the village of **Anjala**, which is where the Anjala Association was formed in 1788. This was a conspiracy against Gustav III by Swedish-speaking officers in the Finnish army, with the ultimate purpose of freeing Finland from Swedish domination. Anjala is now a busy centre for the wood-processing industries, and especially paper manufacture.

The same is true of the next town, **Myllykoski**. Between here and Kouvola the road passes through a range of hills called the Salpausselkä, which was formed from glacial deposits left behind after the last Ice Age.

52km
Kouvola

Kouvola (population 31,600) is a thriving industrial centre, whose population has trebled in the last two decades. It is an important road and rail junction, and the capital of the south-eastern province of Kymi. The town is situated on the banks of the Kymijoki, after which the province was named. This important river provides hydroelectric power for the area's many wood-processing industries. Kouvola is a typical example of post-war industrialisation in Finland. Industry is especially concentrated in the towns immmediately to the north, such as Kuusankoski and Voikka, which can boast the largest paper mills in Europe.

62km
Lahti

From Kouvola one can return directly to Helsinki along Road 6 via Porvoo (see above). Alternatively, one can continue due west along Road 12, which leaves Road 6 near Koria in the direction of **Lahti** (see page 79). From Lahti one can either return southwards to Helsinki, or else join one of the longer routes described later in the book (see Routes 2 and 4).

Kotka · Hamina · Lappeenranta (140km)

Kotka

The E3/Road 7 continues eastwards from Kotka towards the Soviet border. About 8km beyond the turning for Kouvola (Road 15 — see above) there is another left turn along Road 61 for Lappeenranta.

18km
Hamina

Only a few kilometres east of this junction (along the E3) is the port of **Hamina/Fredrikshamn** (population 11,000). Hamina is located on a peninsula in an inlet of the Gulf of Finland. As a major export outlet, it handles much of Finland's trade with the Soviet Union.

Hamina was founded in the fourteenth century. The old church is all that remains from that period; it was restored in 1828. In the early eighteenth century the Swedes built a garrison here against the Russians, the outlines of which are still recognisable in the plan of the old town. The so-called Peace Tower is a remnant of these old fortifications; it is now a museum. In 1743 Hamina was taken by the Russians, who built the town hall in 1798. This was later restored by

Sailing on Lake Saimaa, near Lappeenranta

Carl Ludwig Engel (1840), who also designed the Orthodox (1837)
and Lutheran (1843) churches.

The route returns to Road 61, which continues north-eastwards
until it meets the hills of southern Finland (the Salpausselkä). Near
Taavetti it joins Road 6, which has come across from Kouvola (see
above). The road continues along the shores of the Kivijärvi and
meets the southernmost point of the Saimaa lake system.

Lappeenranta/Villmanstrand (see page 86) lies on the
southern shore of Lake Saimaa, 138km from Kotka. It is a popular
holiday centre and an ideal place from which to visit the Finnish lake
country. Travellers who wish to join Route 2 should continue north-
eastwards along the shore, crossing the Saimaa Canal at Lauritsala,
and eventually arriving at Imatra (see page 84).

122km
Lappeen-
ranta

2 THE FINNISH LAKE COUNTRY

The Land of a Thousand Lakes

Helsinki • Lahti • Heinola • Joutsa • Kangasniemi • Mikkeli • Puumala • Imatra (Lappeenranta) • Savonlinna • Joensuu (Ilomantsi) • Ahmovaara (Koli Hills) • Juuka • Vuokatti • Kajaani (Oulujärvi) • Iisalmi • Kuopio • Rautalampi • Jyväskylä • Jämsä • Mänttä • Ruovesi • Tampere • Hämeenlinna (Helsinki) • Turku

What the Route Has to Offer

There are said to be three faces of Finland: the fertile agricultural south, described in Routes 1b and 1c; the wild tundra of Lapland, covered in Routes 4 and 5; and perhaps most typical, the region of endless lakes and forests, which is primarily dealt with here.

The description 'a land of a thousand lakes' is very much an understatement, since Finland has somewhere between 60,000 and 65,000 lakes, the majority of which are concentrated in the south-east of the country. Flying over this region in an aeroplane, one can see nothing but water and forest, mixed together in a gloriously irregular pattern. It is almost as though the land has not yet been divided from the water.

This route passes quickly through the populous south of Finland, passing through interesting towns such as Helsinki and Lahti on the outward journey, Tampere and Turku on the return. Apart from that the towns are usually small, and most of the people live in small villages and lonely farmsteads.

The majority of the tour runs through vast systems of lakes interlinked by numerous waterways, some of them natural and some artificial. These are vital for the transport of timber, the region's chief natural resource. The trees are mostly felled during the winter, and the logs are piled up on the frozen lakes, so that when the ice melts

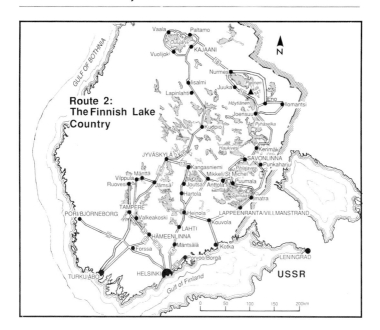

they can be easily carried away. The ice thaws gradually from south-west to north-east; this prevents any congestion as the logs are transported to destinations in the south and west, because those in the south-west will have been cleared by the time that the logs from the north-east arrive. Thus the climatic differences are turned to commercial advantage.

The lakes are often divided by narrow causeways, many of which have castles built on them. These were strategically important in that they enabled the Finns and Swedes to fend off numerous Russian attacks during the course of several centuries. One of these cause-ways, the Punkaharju, is possibly the most remarkable of its kind in the world. Although 6km long, it measures only 30m (98ft) wide, rising to a height of about 30m (98ft) along the centre. It divides the great Lake Saimaa from the lake systems to the north.

The tour ranges northwards into the endless forests of Karelia, which extend far beyond the Soviet border. There is for the most part no sign of human habitation here, except perhaps the telegraph wires that run alongside the road.

The northernmost point of the route is the Oulujärvi. This beautiful lake lies between the 64th and 65th parallels. Although this is well short of the Arctic Circle, the midsummer sun is never far below the horizon, and the short nights take the form of twilight rather than darkness.

The route returns southwards along the shores of yet more lakes, passing through pleasant lakeside towns such as Kuopio and Tampere, idyllically situated at the junction of two of the most beautiful lakes. The road reaches the coast again at Turku, or alternatively back at Helsinki.

Although this route passes through some deserted areas, it never goes too far from civilisation, and no special precautions need be taken on that account. Indeed, even in the vast forests of the interior, one is lucky to find the place totally to oneself.

Only the most important camping sites are mentioned in the description below, and there are many more smaller sites available. It is also possible to camp on open land, provided that certain courtesies are observed (see page 188). The lakes tend to be infested with midges, so it is essential to take an insect spray plus a supply of insect-repellent and antiseptic creams.

Another very useful item is a small boat — perhaps a rubber dinghy with an outboard motor. Keen anglers should not forget to take a rod, though they can admittedly buy them on the spot. Fishing permits are not difficult to obtain, though it should be noted that the trout and salmon season in the north is in July and August.

Access Routes

The fastest route is undoubtedly by air to Helsinki. There are no direct sea routes from the UK, although visitors with more time may care to combine the holiday with a cruise along the Baltic. There are regular ferry connections to Turku and Helsinki from ports in West Germany, Denmark and Sweden.

It is also possible to combine parts of the route with others described in this book. And given the regular ferry services across the Gulf of Bothnia, the route can also be combined with a holiday in Sweden (see *The Visitor's Guide to Sweden*). More details about possible travel options are given in the final section of this book.

Finnish lakeland scenery

Length and Timing

The tour on its own is about 1,800km long, though the exact length will vary depending on which optional routes are chosen. As a general guideline, the lakes tour takes about 10 days to complete without appreciable stops on the way. On the other hand, visitors who have travelled as far as Finland would be foolish not to stop off at points on the way. So a much longer time is recommended if possible, perhaps including a relaxing break by one of the lakes.

The exact timing of the holiday will, of course, depend on the type of transport used to get to Finland. Air travel obviously takes much less time than a sea voyage or an overland journey interspersed with ferries.

The Best Time to Travel

Visitors who like to bathe in the lakes should travel between mid-June and late August. Before then the lakes are not usually warm enough for bathing, and the cool nights of autumn normally begin with the month of September

The Route

Helsinki One should leave Helsinki by the E4/Road 4/5, which is signposted for Lahti. The road is of motorway standard as it passes through the sprawling suburbs of the city; the villas include some interesting examples of modern architecture. The motorway soon comes out into the countryside, which at this stage is heavily cultivated and distinctly 'un-Finnish' in character. The route bypasses Kerava, and

38km the motorway section ends just before **Järvenpää**. The E4 contin-
Järvenpää ues towards **Mäntsälä**, where there is a major crossroads with Road
22km 55.
Mäntsälä

Detour via Porvoo/Borgä

This delightful detour forms an alternative route from Helsinki to Lahti, rejoining the main route at Mäntsälä. It not only provides glimpses of the coast, but also includes a visit to the old town of Porvoo.

Helsinki   The route leaves Helsinki along the E3/Road 7 for Porvoo/Borgå (see Route 1c), which runs through dense mixed forest along the much-indented coastline of the Gulf of Finland. Perched on the granite domes that poke up through the trees are wooden chalets used by people from Helsinki as weekend retreats. The road is of

51km motorway standard, and quickly arrives at Porvoo.
Porvoo   **Porvoo/Borgå** (population 20,000) has a distinctly Scandinavian air, typical of older towns in southern Finland. Once a sleepy

little backwater, it now boasts a busy harbour and a lively industry based mostly on timber. Porvoo has a Gothic cathedral and a Baroque town hall. It was the location for the first Finnish assembly under Russian rule in 1809, at which Tsar Alexander I upheld the Finnish constitution and promised religious freedom. The town is famous culturally; it was the home of Runeberg, Finland's national poet, and the birthplace of his famous sculptor son, many of whose works can be seen in Helsinki; many other important artists also lived and worked here. According to tradition, the town was founded by

Danish Vikings; there are remains of both the original and subse- ✳
quent fortifications on a nearby hill. For a more detailed description
of Porvoo, please turn to page 68.

The detour route now turns north-west along Road 55, which
initially follows the banks of the Porvoonjoki/Borgå. The road runs
through an undulating landscape of moraines to rejoin the main route   37km
at **Mäntsälä**.   Mäntsälä

The main route continues northwards from Mäntsälä, passing a
number of small villages. The landscape becomes increasingly
wooded, but is still partially occupied by cornfields. The road passes
the first of many lakes — the Hunttijärvi — on the left. The road   66km
remains dual carriageway as far as Lahti.   Lahti

Lahti (population 100,000) lies on the southern shore of the
Vesijärvi. To the south are the fertile soils of Salpausselkä ridge,
which is glacial in origin; to the north is the Finnish lake country, with
its thousands of lakes and its endless forests. Lahti is a bustling town
full of ultra-modern apartment blocks that contrast strangely with the
landscape around. It received its municipal charter only 80 years
ago, when it was no more than a small market town. The decades
since then have seen an enormous expansion, thanks mostly to
modern industrial development. Furniture manufacture is the town's
chief industry. Lahti is best known as a winter skiing centre, with
annual ski races and ski-jumping competitions. The Historical Mu- ♨
seum in Kirkkokatu presents a good historical survey of the province
of Häme. Other places of interest include the Museum of Art in ♨
Vesijärvenkatu, and the Radio Museum at the radio station.

Boat Trip from Lahti to Heinola
The 'waterbus' from Lahti to Heinola provides a marvellous foretaste
of the delights to come. It runs past the lush green shores of the
Vesijärvi, and continues by canal past the lovely little town of Vääksy.
It enters the Päijänne, a vast lake flanked by innumerable isolated
beaches. Another canal leads off past Kalkkinen into the beautiful
Ruotsalainen, at the other end of which is Heinola (see below).

The land route runs north-west from Lahti along Road 5. At   Lahti
                                                                  24km
Vierumäki there is a right turn along a side road to the famous Vierumäki

✳ National Sports College (4km), which is largely responsible for Finland's great advances on the international sports scene. It can be reached on foot from Heinola (see below) via the so-called Lynx Path (12km), which makes a pleasant forest walk.

♨ Several kilometres to the left of the main road is the old country estate of Urajärvi, which has now been turned into a museum. The area contains yet more historical estates, including a famous library 12km belonging to the University of Helsinki.

Heinola It is only another 12km to **Heinola** (population 17,000). The road enters the town across the Kymijoki, which is the country's most important river. It drains a vast lake system comprising a large ♋ proportion of the lakes of southern Finland. The bridge into Heinola commands an impressive view of the town.

Heinola is prettily situated next to where the Kymijoki passes over a stretch of rapids called the Jyrängönvirta. The town's favourable position has enabled it to grow rapidly in recent years. There are several important industries on a development area to the east. The town is spread over several islands, all of them linked by bridges. Some of these bridges, especially the railway bridge, provide a wide panorama of the nearby lakes: the Ruotsalainen immediately to the west, with its many bays and inlets; and the Konnivesi to the east, linked by the waters of the Jyrängönvirta. An important timber transport route runs right through the middle of the town. A tug pulling a raft of logs is a frequent and familiar sight.

♋ The best view of Heinola is from the café in the water tower, which stands on a ridge (*harju*) overlooking the town. The Siltakatu and the Kauppakatu form the centre of the town. One of the old houses in the ✳ Siltakatu bears a memorial plaque to P. E. Svinhufvud, the country's first president, who was born here. Most of the old wooden buildings have been destroyed in the many fires that have ravaged the town. ▲ Notable exceptions to this include the octagonal church, built by Carl Ludwig Engel, and a few wooden houses from around 1800, when Heinola was important as the seat of local government. The most ⌂ impressive of the modern buildings is a clinic for the treatment of rheumatic complaints.

The tourist office in Kauppakatu provides ample information on things to see and do in the area, some of which have already been mentioned (see above). Heinola is an ideal centre for a boating or

Waterbus cruising the lakes

angling holiday. There is a wide selection of boat trips, and the rapids are famous for their trout and salmon. It is easy to obtain an angler's licence for waters in Heinola and the area around. Information on this is available from the local traffic and forestry offices. A permit is needed to fish along the shores of the lake.

Heinola is also an ideal centre for a camping holiday. The

Heinäsaari site is one of the best in the whole of Scandinavia. It provides all necessary facilities, including a sauna. It is well sign-posted, and is situated to the north-west of the town on a peninsula that sticks out into the lake.

Short Cut from Heinola to Mikkeli/St Michel (127km) The direct route to Mikkeli can only be recommended if time is extremely short, since it completely misses out some of the most beautiful parts of the route. The short cut simply follows Road 5, which goes north-west from Heinola to Mikkeli (see page 83).

Heinola The preferred route follows Road 5 from Heinola for only 12km before turning left onto Road 59 for Hartola. The landscape is now typically Finnish. The road winds and twists around the gently undulating terrain, passing through patches of forest interrupted by lakes. The people live in scattered communities of brightly painted wooden 45km houses.

Hartola   After **Hartola** the road runs along a narrow strip of land between two lakes: the Jääsjärvi to the right and the Rautavesi to the left. The 21km shoreline of both lakes is extremely irregular and indented. The Joutsa isthmus ends at **Joutsa**, where the route leaves Road 59 and turns right onto a small country road.

           Though unclassified, this road is a decent one, and is much more ⌘ scenic than the main road through Toivakka. The scenery is glorious, with dense forests, rocky lake shores and scattered wooden cot-tages. The road passes over a complex sequence of bridges, islands and causeways as it wends its way between the numerous lakes and 28km inlets.

Kangas-   At **Kangasniemi** the road comes into Road 13. At this point the niemi route turns right and continues in a south-easterly direction. It runs near to the shores of the great Puulavesi, although only the occa-sional inlet is visible.

           The road crosses an irregular range of hills called the Harjunmaa, ⌘ covered in forest and divided into irregular folds. The depressions are filled by lakes, while the ridges form obstacles which the road must either climb over or bypass. It is impossible to imagine a more typically Finnish landscape. The brightly painted wooden cottages and farmsteads peep through gaps in the forest.

The road finally arrives at **Mikkeli** (population 29,500). Marshal Mannerheim had his headquarters here during the Finnish campaigns of World War II. His office was simply a room at the local secondary school, which is typical of the attitude of Mannerheim and his army. The town is pleasantly situated among the lakes. It has been a provincial capital since the middle of the last century. At the northern end of the town is the sacristy (*kivisakasti*) of an early fourteenth-century church that has been resited here and turned into a museum. There is a cabinet full of waxworks of characters from Finnish history. There is also a Museum of Infantry in one of the old military barracks in the middle of the town. At the nearby village of **Visulahti** (to the east along Road 5) is Finland's first model village.

62km
Mikkeli

Short Cut from Mikkeli to Savonlinna (101km)

Like the previous short cut, the direct route from Mikkeli to Savonlinna misses out a lot of beautiful and interesting scenery. It is therefore only useful for visitors who are short of time. The route follows Road 5 as far as Juva, then continues along Road 14 to Savonlinna (see page 88).

The recommended route leaves Mikkeli to the south along Road 13. After only 6km there is a left turn along a more minor road (Road 62) to **Anttola**, which runs through some picturesque scenery. Anttola is delightfully situated on the gentle shores of Lake Luonteri. The pier and bathing area are shaded by a grove of ancient birch trees, with camping facilities nearby.

Mikkeli
29km
Anttola

The next part of the route is along a road that has only recently been built. A section through the forest is followed by a complex area of interlocking lakes and inlets. The road negotiates them by means of bridges and causeways, sometimes going from island to island. At one point the road plunges into a tunnel through a vast block of granite. The views along the way are some of the most delightful one could possibly imagine. The lakes are full of tiny islands covered by trees. It is a real holidaymaker's paradise. At one point there is a swing bridge. Shortly afterwards the road comes to a stretch of water that must be crossed by ferry (in Finnish *lossi*). A right turn at Luukkosenkylä brings one quickly to **Puumala**.

46km
Puumala

Direct Route from Puumala to Savonlinna (77km)

⌘ Travellers who choose this route should retrace their steps as far as Luukkosenkylä, then turn right along an unclassified road. The scenery which follows is just as delightful as that before Puumala. The road meanders through a landscape of forest interspersed by numerous lakes and inlets, crossing some surprisingly steep ridges on the way. After Sulkava the road comes into Road 14, where one must turn right for the final section to Savonlinna. For a description of Savonlinna and the subsequent route, please turn to page 88.

For travellers who wish to see the area along the Soviet border, there is a much longer alternative route via Imatra, Simpele and the Puumala Punkaharju. It begins with a ferry from the southern end of Puumala across an arm of Lake Saimaa.

⌘ Not only is **Lake Saimaa** the largest of the Finnish lakes, with an area of 1,400sq km, but the whole associated lake system comprises an area of nearly 7,000sq km. Not for nothing is Lake Saimaa known as 'the lake of a thousand islands'. The road runs through tracts of dense forest, and little of the lake is visible apart from a few bays and inlets.

At **Käyhkää** the road crosses a bridge over another arm of Lake Saimaa, and carries on through the deserted regions of the Karelian Forest. It crosses the Virmutjoki, and after Ruokolahti comes at last 65km into Road 6. If one turns right here, it is only a short distance to Imatra.

Imatra **Imatra** (population 36,000) is only 6km away from the Soviet border. It is an important centre for industry. The approach road from Ruokolahti passes an enormous cellulose factory, where hundreds of thousands of spruce logs are stockpiled.

⌘ To the north of the town are the famous Imatra Falls, where the waters of Lake Saimaa once emptied into the River Vuoksi. The lake is held back by a rocky barrier that is breached at this point, and the Vuoksi once came thundering down through a channel about 20m (66ft) wide. This mighty waterfall has been diverted to provide the power for a hydroelectric scheme. With an output of some 158MW, it produces enough electrical power to supply the needs of most of southern Finland. The dam and the power station are a spectacle in themselves, and are well worth a visit. The river bed is now sadly empty, though its dimensions are still impressive. On Sundays in the

Fourteenth-century museum-church, Mikkeli

summer the great sluice gates are opened to let the water through again, and for a short time the falls are returned to their former glory. The course of the Vuoksi is mostly through Soviet territory, and the river eventually comes out into Lake Ladoga.

Five kilometres south of Imatra is the village of **Pelkola**, which is directly next to the Soviet border. The area is covered with warning signs to the effect that car drivers must not stop or take photographs. The actual border is indicated by yellow circles and signs; a special permit is needed even to approach it.

Excursion to Lappeenranta/Villmanstrand (40km each way)
The holiday centre of Lappeenranta (population 54,000) is only a short distance south-west of Imatra along the southern shore of Lake Saimaa. There is everything here that a tourist could want, from hotels, camping sites and holiday villages to boat trips, tennis courts, spa facilities, riding and ramblers' centres. There is even the possibility of a trip to Leningrad, though this requires a visa. The airport is served by flights from all over the Finnish national network.

The industrial suburb of Lauritsala is the starting point for the Saimaa Canal that links Lake Saimaa with the Gulf of Finland. The canal runs from here to the former Finnish port of Vyborg/Viipuri, which is now inside the Soviet Union. It was first opened up to ships in 1856, but fell into disuse following the Russian occupation in World War II. But in the 1960s a treaty was signed in which the canal zone was leased back to Finland. The canal was refurbished, and the route to the sea was reopened.

The Eastern Orthodox church, built in 1785, is the oldest of its kind in Finland. The Municipal Museum presents the history of the town, which has been an important east–west trading point since the Middle Ages. In 1741 Lappeenranta was the scene of a bloody struggle between the Swedes and the Russians. This is commemorated by a monument in the Old Park on a promontory by the lake, where there are also the remains of the old town defences.

The old wooden town hall was built in 1829 according to the plans of Carl Ludwig Engel (it almost goes without saying!). The market square opens out onto the lake in typically Finnish style. Moored next to it is a boat called the *Prinsessa Armada*, which has now been turned into a museum. Lappeenranta has been a popular spa resort since the discovery of mineral springs in 1824.

The Central Park contains the old church of the rural parish of Lappee, from which the town later grew. It was built in the early eighteenth century, but the separate bell tower was added almost a century later. Adjoining the park is the largest war cemetery in Finland. It includes a memorial to the Karelians who fell between 1941 and 1948 — a permanent reminder of the most recent conflict between the peoples of Eastern and Western Europe.

Lappeenranta is a popular starting point for boat trips across Lake Saimaa. There are regular services to the lake's other main towns, including Mikkeli and Savonlinna, plus a wide choice of cruises and excursions, varying in length from a few hours to several days. Information on these is available from the following address: Saimaatouring, Valtakatu 23, 53100 Lappeenranta 10.

The main route continues north-east from Imatra along Road 6, Imatra passing again through the industrial suburb of Immola. The road runs parallel to the Soviet border through the forests of Karelia. It eventu- 48km ally arrives at **Simpele** on the shores of the Simpelejärvi. Between Simpele Simpele and Parikkala, the Soviet border comes to within 100m (about 300ft) of the road. This happens at a point where the road crosses a channel between two lakes. The route stays with Road 6 until **Särkisalmi**, where one bears left along Road 14 for Savonlinna.

M/S Väinämöinen, Lappeenranta

40km   It is only a short distance before the road arrives at the
Punkaharju **Punkaharju**. This remarkable natural causeway is 6km (about 3$^1/_2$
ℋ   miles long) and only 30m (98ft) wide, with a height of between 20m
(65ft) and 40m (131ft). It divides Lake Saimaa from the lake system
to the north. The road winds along the crest of the causeway between
Punkaharju and Punkasalmi, the villages at either end. The railway
ℋ   runs along parallel to the road. There is a lovely view of the lakes
either side, with their many islands covered in spruce and birch
爪   woodlands. In Punkaharju regular art exhibitions and concerts are
held at the Retretti building. The art is always of a high standard and
music lovers from all over the world flock here especially during the
Savonlinna Opera Festival (see below).

          The road crosses a channel called the Tuunaansalmi, and contin-
ues north-west through a typically undulating landscape. At the point
where Road 71 comes in from the right, it is only another 14km to
34km   Savonlinna.
Savonlinna **Savonlinna/Nyslott** (population 28,500) is beautifully situated
in the middle of the Saimaa lake system. It has been burned down so
many times in its long history that few of the original wooden buildings
remain. The only exceptions are a few houses in the old town, which
is on an island sandwiched between the Haapavesi and the
Pihlajavesi. There is a strong current running between the two lakes.
♘   The old castle stands on an island to the south-east of the old
town. It is called Olavinlinna (in Swedish Olofsborg) after King Olaf
the Holy of Norway. It was built in the fifteenth century by the then
Swedish governor, Count Erik Tott, as a bulwark against the Russians. From then until 1809, it was the site of frequent skirmishes
between the Finns and the invading Russians, which is indicative of
its strategic importance. It has so often been destroyed, rebuilt and
strengthened that little of the original structure remains. It has also
been used as a prison. It is, however, the best-preserved medieval
castle in the whole of Finland. A boat service is laid on for sightseers
who wish to visit the castle and there is also a bridge to Olavinlinna.
In July it is the site for an international opera festival. Information on
the festival can be obtained from the following address: Savonlinna
Opera Festival, Olavinkatu 37, 57130 Savonlinna 13.

          Savonlinna is situated at the junction of several timber transport
routes, and is consequently the site for a number of wood-processing

industries. The town received its municipal charter in 1639, but did not develop as a port until the opening of the Saimaa Canal in 1856. This opened up the Finnish lake region, Savonlinna included, to new trade links with ports on the Gulf of Finland and the Baltic. Trade was interrupted by the closure of the canal when the Russians occupied Vyborg, but since 1968 the canal has been open again. The boats dock at the quay by the market square (Kauppatori), which also has a daily fish and vegetable market.

Excursion to the Punkaharju (34km each way)
Visitors who have come via the direct route from Puumala to Savonlinna (see page 84) are recommended to make an extra trip to see this remarkable natural phenomenon. The Punkaharju is to the south-east of Savonlinna along Road 14 to Parikkala. It is a natural causeway formed by debris deposited beneath the glaciers during the last Ice Age. It runs for 6km between the villages of Punkasalmi and Punkaharju.

The route leaves Savonlinna in an easterly direction along Road 14, Savonlinna and for the first 14km retraces the route from Imatra and Punkaharju (for those travellers who have arrived by that route). Then after Anttola there is a left turn along Road 71 (signposted to Toroppala). 28km This road soon arrives at **Kerimäki** on the shores of the Puruvesi. Kerimäki Kerimäki is the site of the largest wooden church in the world, with a seating capacity of more than 3,300.

The road turns north-east along the wooded shores of the 37km Puruvesi, and leaves it again after **Väärämäki**. After another 22km Väärämäki it enters Road 6, which has come north from Imatra and Parikkala. The route turns north along Road 6, which follows a straight track through the vast, uninhabited forests. The trees become perceptibly sparser as one continues northwards, and deciduous woodland is totally replaced by conifers. After Onkamo the road approaches the shores of the great Pyhäselkä, which is part of a vast system of lakes. 92km

The town of **Joensuu** (population 46,300) is in stark contrast to Joensuu the wildness of the surrounding forest. It is situated at the outflow of the Pielisjoki into the Pyhäselkä. Few other towns in Finland have grown so fast since World War II. Large numbers of Karelian refugees settled here after the Russian occupation of the eastern territories. They were able to find a living from the new developing industries, especially wood-processing.

There are several bridges across the river, including several to the island of **Ilosaari**. The building on the island is called the Karelian House, and contains a museum. There are numerous canals linking the nearby rivers and lakes. It is fascinating to watch the timber being floated along them, especially at the rapids upstream, which are a favourite haunt for anglers.

There is a camping site by the lake just to the north of the river mouth. Joensuu is an ideal centre for visiting the lovely province of North Karelia, including the Ilomantsi region and the beautiful Koli Hills (see below).

Excursion to Ilomantsi and Eno (163km)

This excursion takes the form of a round trip through the uninhabited forests of North Karelia. Road 74 goes east from Joensuu through vast tracts of virgin forest, interrupted only by the occasional lake. The dark conifers are mixed with the lighter foliage of birch and aspen.

Joensuu

76km
Ilomantsi

There are virtually no villages for the whole of the first part of the route, until the road arrives at **Ilomantsi**. This small village is in an idyllic forest setting on the banks of the Ilomantsijoki and not far from the Soviet border.

55km
Eno

The route back is equally delightful. It follows unclassified roads via Sonkaja to **Eno**. This small village is situated between Lake Jouhtinen and the Pielisjoki, and is an important timber collection point.

32km
Joensuu

A road over a swing bridge leads to the Jakokoski road fork (near a farm), where one should bear right along Road 73. This road crosses the railway twice, and eventually comes into Road 18. A left turn brings one quickly back to Joensuu. Travellers who are continuing northwards should turn right towards Kontiolahti.

Joensuu

The main route leaves Joensuu in a northerly direction along Road 18. It passes through Kontiolahti, and follows the shore of Lake Höytiäinen through a mixture of forest and fields. Having left the lake shore, it eventually arrives at **Ahmovaara**.

60km
Ahmovaara

Olavinlinna Castle, Savonlinna

Excursion to the Koli Hills (12km each way)
The road to the Koli Hills turns right off Road 18 at Ahmovaara. It is
a good road through partly rocky and partly wooded scenery. After
about 9km (near Osuuskaupa) there is a right turn along a winding
road up the hillside, which comes to a dead end at a height of about
250m (820ft). From here it is about 5 or 10 minutes' walk to the Koli
Hotel. The path carries on up to the highest summit, the Ukko-Koli
(347m (1,138ft)). There is a wonderful view across Lake Pielinen and
beyond to the Soviet border. There is a camping site nearby, and also
plenty of other places to camp.

Road 18 carries on northwards from Ahmovaara, and soon arrives at
Juuka on the shores of Lake Pielinen. This vast lake empties into the
Pielisjoki near Eno (see above), and is thus linked to lakes Pyhäselkä
and Saimaa. The whole lake system is vital for the transport of timber

Ahmovaara
26km
Juuka

Joensuu on the Pielisjoki

from the forests of North Karelia. The road continues along the shore as far as the northern end of the lake. There is a right turn along Road 75 to **Nurmes**, which has a reconstructed Karelian village.

58km
Valtimo

Road 18 carries straight on via Vanhakylä and Valtimo. The landscape is undulating and covered with forest. Road and railway run side by side, and frequently cross over. The road passes a timber loading bay next to a railway station, and runs along the shore of the Kiantajärvi. At **Vuokatti** the road climbs over a steep ridge, affording a fine panorama of the forests and lakes to the east of Kajaani.

60km
Vuokatti
40km

Kajaani

The road bears left towards **Kajaani** (population 36,000). Kajaani was founded in 1651 under the Swedish governor Per Brahe. The ruined castle on the island of Linnasaari was originally built at the beginning of the seventeenth century, and was repeatedly captured and destroyed. The Swedish poet Johan Messenius was imprisoned here from 1620 to 1637, during which time he wrote an epic poem about the history of Finland.

Kajaani was also the home of the doctor and poet Elias Lönnrot, creator of the *Kalevala*. The old wooden town hall was built by Carl

The Koli Hills

Pielinen Open-air Museum, Lieksa

Ludwig Engel in 1831. The town has a number of important wood-processing industries. It is served by an airport, and is well supplied with hotel, restaurant and camping facilities.

About 10km to the north of Kajaani, by the shore of the great Oulujärvi, is the village of **Paltaniemi**. Its 250-year-old church has paintings by E. Grauberg inside. Nearby is the so-called Tsar's Stable, commemorating the visit of Tsar Alexander I in 1819.

✳ Tour of the Oulujärvi (196km)

Visitors are strongly recommended to take a trip around this lake, which has a total area of just over 1,000sq km. The Oulujärvi is practically divided in two by the large island of **Manamansalo**. It lies at an altitude of 125m (410ft), and empties into the Gulf of Bothnia via the fast-flowing Oulujoki. Vast amounts of timber pass through on their way from the forests down to the great timber port of Oulu at the mouth of the river. The area was once an important producer of wood tar, now long since replaced by the cheaper coal tars. But the area now has a variety of modern wood-based industries that bring in twice or three times the income once obtained from wood tar.

Kajaani
36km

Paltamo

The route leaves Kajaani along Road 5 in the direction of Ristijärvi. After only 20km there is a left turn along Road 22, which runs parallel to the railway along the shore of the lake. At **Paltamo** there is a bridge over the Paltamojoki, and soon after that a side turning to the island of Manamansalo.

Road 22 turns inland, and crosses a steep ridge of which the island is a continuation. The road drops down again through dense forest to the shores of the Kivesjärvi, a small lake that flows out into the Oulujärvi. This is a marvellous place for camping. The road goes inland again before returning to the Oulujärvi near Liminpuro. It continues close to the shore past Kankari.

It is fascinating to watch the timber floating down from the forests along the fast streams that flow into the lake. This cheap method of transport is what makes forestry viable in these isolated regions. Transporting a log overland for a distance of some 350km costs as much as the value of the log itself. But floating the same log down-river over the same distance costs no more than the value of an ordinary postage stamp.

These rivers are not only useful for timber transport, but also provide energy for hydroelectric power. Unfortunately, many of the most impressive falls and rapids have been channelled off to produce electricity. But those few that remain untouched are an angler's dream. Salmon fishing used to be very profitable in this area in the summer. But where rivers have been harnessed for power, the migrating salmon are diverted through artificial channels or over specially constructed salmon ladders.

60km
Vaala

The road soon arrives at **Vaala**, which is situated at the point where the Oulujoki flows out of the lake. This river once formed two impressive waterfalls: the nearby Niskakoski, and the Pyhäkoski further downstream, which dropped 60m (197ft) within a distance of 20m (66ft). Both alas have been sacrificed for hydroelectricity, and are no longer worth visiting.

17km
Säräisniemi

The route turns south along the shore towards the village of Säräisniemi, which is perched scenically at the base of a promontory. One can bypass the village; or alternatively one can go through the village and out onto the point, where there is an idyllic bathing beach with opportunities for camping.

The road carries on around the bay, and there is yet another left turn down to a beautiful bathing beach. As the road continues southwards, almost all the side roads down to the lake lead to beaches that are ideal for bathing, camping or fishing.

38km
Vuolijoki

The road continues through **Vuolijoki** to the southern end of the lake, which at this point forms an inlet called the Vuottilahti. Just past the end of the lake, there is a left turn along a small road which follows the lake shore back to Kajaani. It is somewhat longer than the direct route, but it is much more scenic. Travellers with less time may go straight on until they come into Road 5, where they should turn left for Kajaani.

45km
Kajaani

At a latitude of 64° 20', **Kajaani** is the northernmost point of the route, which now turns south through a region of dense, almost primeval forests. The Road 5 follows a straight track through the uninhabited Murtomäki region. The road is a good one, but there is virtually no human settlement in the area beyond the railway crossing about 25km south of Kajaani. One exception is the small village of Sukeva about half-way to Iisalmi, where there is another railway crossing. The road continues southward through the forest, partly following the

87km course of the Matkasjoki.
Iisalmi   **Iisalmi** (population 23,500) is delightfully situated in the middle
of a star-shaped lake system (the word *salmi* means a sound, or
channel between two lakes). Iisalmi is an important market town, with
a number of thriving wood-processing industries. It is well supplied
with hotels and tourist accommodation, and there is a camping site
(with sauna, of course) about 4km north of the town next to the
approach road from Kajaani.

The route carries on southwards along Road 5. Road and railway
run closely side by side, and drivers should beware the large number
of unmanned level crossings. The road first stays close to the shore
of the fjord-like Onkivesi, which clearly shows the north-west–south-
east orientation of the ridges formed by the ancient rock structures.
The lakes in this region are linked by rivers to the vast Saimaa lake
27km system 200km further south.
Lapinlahti   Soon after **Lapinlahti** (meaning 'Lapp bay'), the road leaves the
lakeside and begins to wind and twist through dense forests. The
landscape indicates that the region is more populated than further
34km north, with a number of cultivated fields along the roadside. There is
Siilinjärvi a railway junction at Siilinjärvi, where a branch line comes in from the
Koli region far to the east. Road 75 from Nurmes also comes in here
from the left.

⌘   The next part of the route is particularly delightful as the road picks
its way between the lakes along a number of causeways and islands.
Near **Toivala** the road forks: Road 17 goes left towards the North
Karelian capital of Joensuu, while the present route bears right along
✳   Road 5 to Kuopio. There is a monument near Toivala to the famous
battle of 1808, in which General Sandels and his troops fought
bravely against the Russian invaders.

To the left of the road is one of the many small airports that make
up the Finnish internal air network. It is easy to understand why air
transport is so vital in a country such as Finland. A Scandinavian
once said that the Finns moved from reindeer sledges to aeroplanes
without using railways, and that it is easier to meet a Lapp in the air
than on the tundra. In Finland the landscape can be so fragmented
by lakes that it is often difficult to build roads or railways through it.
22km This is vividly illustrated along the section of dual carriageway that
Kuopio leads into Kuopio.

Logging at Joensuu

Suoenenjoki — one of Finland's many large wooden churches

Lakeside forestry, Taivalkoski

Youth Hostel at Kurkkio

Finland's open countryside is ideal for pony-trekking

Kuopio (population 78,000) is one of the many towns to have been founded by the Swedish governor Per Brahe. He chose the site for its strategic importance rather than for its beautiful situation among the lakes. The rightness of his strategy is borne out by the many battles that have taken place in the area, such as the one near Toivala in 1808 (see above).

One place worth visiting is a hill called the Puijomäki (233m (764ft)), which lies 3km to the north-west of the town. The lookout tower at the top affords a magnificent panorama of the lakes and forests of the region. The view is particularly delightful in the early morning or towards evening. The tower also has a motel and a revolving restaurant at the top.

Kuopio is an ideal centre for visiting the lake country. With its modern theatre, university and concert hall, it forms a major cultural and commercial centre in the central part of Finland. The Orthodox Church Museum is unique in Western Europe. Also worth visiting are the cathedral and the Municipal Museum. The city has good hotel and guesthouse facilities, and a well-appointed camping and holiday centre.

26km   Road 5 continues southwards in the direction of Helsinki. After
Vehmasmäki   another 26km, at **Vehmasmäki**, the present route goes right along
48km   the E80/Road 9 to **Suonenjoki**. Five kilometres after Suonenjoki it
Rautalampi   turns right again along Road 69, bypassing **Rautalampi**. The next
ℬ   section of the route is particularly beautiful. The road winds through
              dense forests and along the shores of great lakes, climbing over a
              number of steep granite ridges on the way. The route goes via
              Konnevesi (by the lake of the same name) and **Laukaa** to
96km   Jyväskylä.
Jyväskylä   **Jyväskylä** (population 65,000) is an important road and railway
              junction, and the capital and cultural centre of the province of Central
              Finland. Thanks to its favourable position among the lakes and
              forests, it has developed into a flourishing centre for the timber-based
              industries. It has a university and several other specialist colleges.
⚓   Buildings of special interest include the neo-Gothic parish church
              and the Eastern Orthodox church. The many interesting museums
🏛   include the University Museum, the Museum of Air Flight and the
              Lyceum Museum.
                  Jyväskylä is an ideal centre for car or boat trips into the surround-
              ing lake country. There is daily boat traffic along the whole length of
              Lake Päijänne to Lahti. There are hotels and restaurants, and an
              excellent camping and holiday centre by the lake. Activities on offer
              include sports, folklore and cultural events. All in all, it is a highly
              desirable centre for the summer visitor to stay in. A more detailed
              description of Jyväskylä is provided on page 137.
                  The lakes in this area belong to the **Päijänne** lake system,
              Päijänne being the second-largest lake in Finland. They are just as
              vital for timber transport as the lakes in the Saimaa system, as is
              shown by the vast amounts of timber that can be seen floating along
              them.
Jyväskylä   The route goes south from Jyväskylä along the E4, and meets the
              wooded shore of Lake Päijänne near Korpilahti. The shoreline is
              extremely indented, and only a few of its inlets are visible from the
              road. The villages and towns along the shore are growing fast, being
              favourably situated for the development of modern timber-based
56km   industries.
Jämsä   At **Jämsä** there is a right turn along an unclassified road to
              Mänttä. Travellers with less time may prefer to go straight on to

Town Hall, Kuopio

Tampere along the E90/Road 9. Although shorter (100km) and far from uninteresting, the direct route to Tampere misses out some really beautiful scenery. So if time allows, travellers should turn off here for Mänttä. The road leads through the industrial suburb of Jämsänkoski and out into a delightful region of hills and forests.

46km
Mänttä

The village of **Mänttä** is closely followed by **Vilppula.** Vilppula is located at a point where a railway crosses a vital waterway, and is therefore an important timber-loading station. From here the route goes south-west through the village of Väärinmala. Following that, one should turn right along Road 66, which leads over a bridge across a lake to Ruovesi.

25km
Ruovesi

Ruovesi is a beautiful little village on the lake shore. It has a memorial to J. L. Runeberg, Finland's national poet, who taught here for a while. The boat trip from Ruovesi to Tampere along the 'Poet's Highway' is highly recommended. Car drivers can have their vehicles sent on to Tampere via a special pilot service.

✳

The road route returns over the bridge along Road 66. But instead of continuing straight on via Orivesi, one should bear right along an

Kuopio Market Place

unclassified road which goes to Tampere via Teisko. A short detour is recommended to the impressive **Murole Falls**, about 25km from Ruovesi. This is where the waters of the Palovesi empty via a broad channel into the Näsijärvi, while the 'Poet's Highway' is diverted through a lock.

There are plenty of other roads to the right leading down to the wooded lake shores, which offer countless opportunities for camping and bathing. There is a marvellous view across the lake from the road junction just after **Teisko**. The road passes Aitolahti to the right before eventually arriving at Tampere.

73km
Tampere

Tampere/Tammerfors

With a population of 175,000, Tampere is Finland's second-largest city, with a strong industrial base that rivals that of Turku. This highly modern city has grown particularly fast in recent decades. It is hemmed in by lakes and forests that come right into the centre, and the atmosphere is of trees interspersed by modern skyscrapers. Tampere is also a cultural metropolis; the five theatres include an

Secluded Lakeland holiday chalets

open-air theatre in which the auditorium can be moved around the stage. About 10,000 students attend the various academic establishments, including a university and a technical college.

Only a century ago Tampere was an insignificant little town. It was founded as Tammerfors in 1779 by King Gustav III Adolf of Sweden, and gained exemption from customs duties in 1821. Nowadays

Tampere — Finland's second-largest city

100,000 people are employed by the 500 companies that are based here. Most factories are built around the fringes so as not to spoil the parks around the centre. Tampere is best known as a centre for the manufacture of textiles, shoes and metal products.

The central hospital is the most modern of eight major hospitals in Finland. It was built in 1962, and has as many as 1,000 beds. Tampere has a wide choice of good hotels in all categories and some excellent camping sites. The Tourist Information and Congress Office provides ample information about city tours, boat trips and the hire of sailing and motor boats.

The city is built either side of the Tammerkoski — an impressive stretch of rapids linking the Näsijärvi with the Pyhäjärvi. The water from the Näsijärvi drops some 20m (66ft) within a distance of less than 1km, and provides enough hydroelectric power to satisfy the

Hämeensilta Bridge, Tampere

industrial and domestic needs of the area. The rapids divide the city into an eastern and a western half, which are linked by several road bridges and a rail bridge.

The **Hämeensilta** is the main central bridge in the centre of the town; it is decorated with sculptures by Väino Aaltonen. The square adjoining it to the west is the Keskustori, next to which are the town hall, a wooden church built by Engel in 1824, and the main theatre. Just to the north is the library and in front of it a statue of the great poet Aleksis Kivi. His best-known works are his comedy *The Heathen Cobbler* and the novel *The Seven Brothers.* The modern, new library building was designed by Pietiläs.

If one goes due west from the library past the tourist office one quickly comes to the Hämeenpuisto — a broad avenue with trees that runs between the town's northern and southern shores. At the

northern end are the hills bordering the Näsijärvi, where the **Häme**
Museum affords a marvellous view across the lake. It provides a
fascinating cultural and historical survey of the province of Häme.

An even better view can be obtained from the lookout tower. This
stands on a wooded peninsula called the **Särkanniemi**, which is
situated to the north-west beyond the railway and the north harbour.
With a height of 168m (550ft), it is the tallest tower in Finland, and was
completed in 1971. There is a magnificent view across the lake
country from the revolving restaurant near the top. The park surrounding the tower also contains an aquarium, a children's zoo and
a planetarium.

There are boat trips from the north harbour along the 'Poet's
Highway', which goes north through the Näsijärvi, past Ruovesi and
on to Virrat (see page 99). Its name recalls the poet Runeberg, who
taught at Ruovesi. (There is a similar boat link from the south harbour
called the Silver Line, which runs along the Pyhäjärvi to Hämeenlinna
— see page 106.)

At the southern end of the Hämeenpuisto is another park adjoining the Pyhäjärvi. The Pirkankatu is the main road leading off the
Hämeenpuisto to the west. It passes the **Alexander Church** in a
park on the left, and the Kustan Hiekka or **Goldsmith's Museum**
on the right. Further along are the **Museum of Art** and a square
called the Pyynikintori, where a colourful market is held every
morning.

Not far to the south is the **Museum of Modern Art**. Beyond that
in the **Pyynikki Park** is an open-air theatre with a revolving
auditorium. One can return to the Hämeenpuisto past the Workers'
Theatre and the Lenin Museum (Lenin lived in Tampere for a short
time in 1905). The town's southern bridge crosses the Tammerkoski
close to where it enters the Pyhäjärvi. Immediately to the east is the
Ratina Park, which contains an enormous stadium.

To the east of the Hämeensilta, the Hämeenkatu leads past the
post office to the railway station. If one turns north here, it is only a
short distance to the **cathedral**. This impressive granite structure
was built at the beginning of the present century. It contains some
lovely frescos and stained-glass windows, plus an altar screen by
Magnus Enckell. Further east beyond the railway is another park
called the Sorsapuisto ('Duck Park'), which includes a children's

Tampere Cathedral

♠ playground. Beyond that is the fifteenth-century **Messukylä Church**, which is the oldest building in Tampere.

The town contains many more interesting museums and collec-
⌂ tions, including the Museum of Finnish Education, the Technical Museum, the Natural History Museum and the Haihara Puppet Museum, plus numerous temporary exhibitions that are mounted in conjunction with conferences and other events held in Tampere.

Boat Trip to Hämeenlinna
This relaxing alternative is highly recommended for the next part of the journey. The Silver Line offers a choice of two routes. The first of these takes 7 hours, and runs along the Pyhäjärvi via Lempäälä and the Vanajanselkä. The other route takes 5 hours; it follows the Kaivanto Canal and the eastern branch of the lake system via Valkeakoski. There are facilities for car drivers to send their vehicles ahead via a special pilot service. Information on the services available can be obtained from the Silver Line offices near the embarkation point by the southern harbour.

Tampere The road route goes due south from Tampere past the airport and out along the E79/Road 3. This scenic route follows a new stretch of dual carriageway via Valkeakoski, and forms the quickest road link between Tampere and Hämeenlinna. Near **Valkeakoski** the road crosses the channel between the Mallasvesi and the Vanajanselkä. It does so via two bridges that take advantage of the islands in the middle of the channel. It continues towards Hämeenlinna past the 78km shore of the Lehijärvi and through a region of woods and heathland.
Hämeenlinna   **Hämeenlinna/Tavastehus** (population 42,500) is attractively situated at the southern tip of the Vanajavesi. It is the birthplace of Jean Sibelius, Finland's most famous composer. The town is over-
♜ looked to the north by Kronaberg Castle, which was founded by the Swedes under Birger Jarl in the thirteenth century. It was restored following Finnish independence, and turned into a national monument.

The town centre was completely rebuilt after the great fire of 1831, and most of the wooden buildings are in the Empire style that
✳ predominated at the time. Next to the Sibelius Square is a monument to the German soldiers who fell here during the Finnish struggle for

Old Church, Tampere

Hyvinkää Church

independence in 1918.

The town was primarily a cultural centre until World War II, since when it has become increasingly industrial. The chief industries are timber-related, including cellulose, paper and furniture. Hämeenlinna is also an important loading point for timber from the interior.

Ten kilometres to the north of the town is the village of **Hattula**, where the thirteenth-century church is full of original medieval wall paintings. This former pilgrimage church also contains two lovely wooden pulpits with some of the best carvings in the whole of Finland. There is a munitions museum nearby.

Hämeenlinna

Alternative Route to Helsinki (100km)

Visitors who wish to return to Helsinki should continue south from Hämeenlinna along the E79/Road 3. The route is a fast one through flat agricultural land that is relatively heavily populated. The villages often look Swedish rather than Finnish, and this reflects the fact that it was the first part of the country to be colonised by the Swedes. However, the scattered lakes and woodlands along the first part of the route preserve the Finnish character of the landscape.

The dual carriageway bypasses the main towns on the way, such as the glass town of **Riihimäki** (population 25,000) and the industrial town of **Hyvinkää** (population 38,500). Hyvinkää is also an important skiing centre, with numerous slalom courses in the hills around.

The rest of the journey is through the gentle hill country to the north of Helsinki, which is being increasingly encroached upon by the satellite towns around the capital. The road passes close to Helsinki Airport, and enters the capital via the Männerheimintie.

The route from Hämeenlinna to Turku goes right along Road 10, Hämeenlinna which quickly comes out of the Finnish lake country. It enters a more populous region that is heavily cultivated in comparison with the

lakes and forests of the interior. The scenery becomes somewhat
hillier, though the hills are never steep.

57km
Forssa
The road passes the industrial town of **Forssa** to the left. In recent
years Forssa has developed a flourishing textile industry. Soon after
Forssa there is a crossroads with Road 2, which forms the main road
link between Helsinki and Pori.

The land becomes flatter and more typical of the agricultural
regions of southern Finland. The Swedish character of the region
reflects the fact that it was extensively colonised by the Swedes —
so much so that a substantial minority of the population are still
Swedish-speaking.

The road follows the course of the Paimionjoki through cultivated
fields interspersed with woodlands that contain an increasing proportion of deciduous trees. The road is fast but busy as it approaches the
84km
Turku
city of **Turku/Åbo** (see page 63).

3 THE WEST COAST

The Gulf of Bothnia as Far as the Swedish Border

Turku • Mynämäki (Uusikaupunki) • Rauma • Pori • Lappfjärd (Kristinestad) • Vaasa (Jakobstad) • Kokkola • Raahe • Oulu • Kemi

What the Route Has to Offer

This route is ideal for combining with other routes, both in this volume and in the *Visitor's Guide to Sweden* (see below). It can be used for its own sake or to form a link between these other routes.

The journey goes through some of the oldest settled regions of Finland, whose west coast was colonised by Swedish settlers from across the Gulf of Bothnia. The gulf forms the northern arm of the Baltic Sea, and its moderating influence on the climate has encouraged the development of agriculture. Most of the food grown in Finland originates from these fertile coastal regions.

The economic changes since World War II have made a deep impression on these areas, which up to then were primarily agricultural except for the ports handling timber from the forests of the interior. The small market towns and the ports have now developed into centres of industry. Timber-based industries were the first to take root, but these were soon followed by other related forms of manufacture, such as that of machinery for the paper industry. Products such as these form a vital part of Finland's exports.

The new industry has enabled post-war refugees from the Russian-occupied territories to settle in towns along the coast, with the result that many of them have doubled or even trebled in size. This in turn has had a profound effect on the cultural and linguistic profile of the region. Whereas the original inhabitants were predominantly Swedish-speaking, these are now often far outnumbered by Finnish-speaking immigrants. But there still remain towns along the coast —

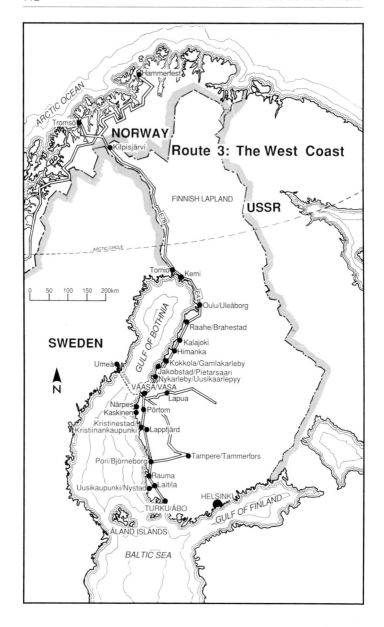

Nykarleby, for example — that are more Swedish than towns in Sweden itself. Few of the original buildings remain in the old ports, which, being mostly built of wood, have been frequently destroyed by fire. But where they do remain, they are usually grouped around a large market square that abuts onto the harbour. Local farmers would come here to offer their produce to the coastal fishermen.

Many of the town centres still show the influence of Finland's great architect Carl Ludwig Engel, a pupil of the Schinkel school of architecture in Berlin. They are now surrounded by the modern residential and industrial estates that have grown up during recent decades, but which have been carefully integrated with the landscape so as not to spoil it.

The route involves more than just the towns that it passes through on the way, for the scenery in between is equally interesting. It is a different Finland from that of the lakes and forests of the interior, and different from the wild expanses of the far north. The third face of Finland is the farms and fields that cover the south and west of the country. It is a picture that has been modified by the industrialisation of recent decades, especially in the busy ports along the coast.

Access Routes

This route is intended not so much as a tour in itself as for use in combination with other routes. The southern end of the route links with Routes 1b and 2, both of which end at Turku. Link roads to Routes 2 and 4 are described during the course of the journey.

The northern end at Kemi links with routes to the north along the Arctic Road (part of Route 4) and the Road of the Four Winds (Route 5). Travellers who continue along either of these routes are recommended to return via Norway. The Norwegian Arctic Road is summarised later in this book (see Route 7), but is described in much more detail in *The Visitor's Guide to Norway*. One can, of course, return through Finland, having already travelled up the Norwegian coast.

Finally, there are several ways of combining this route with a tour of Sweden. One may, for example, take a ferry to or from one of the ports along the way: Vaasa to Sundsvall or Umeå, or Jakobstad to Skellefteå. Or else one may continue from Kemi via Tornio and across the Swedish border. The routes through Sweden are described in *The Visitor's Guide to Sweden*.

Naantali Harbour

Length and Timing

The route described is roughly 750km long, but will vary according to which coastal detours or link routes are chosen. The road is a fast one, being dual carriageway for much of the way. It is also very busy, and there are opportunities for several more leisurely detours through small towns and villages on the coast. Travellers may also wish to take a short seaside break at one of the many coastal resorts on the way.

The Best Time to Travel

As with other routes in Finland, the best time to travel is the high summer, especially if the journey is to be continued northwards. But for hardier travellers, winter offers the exciting possibility of a return trip through the ice of the Gulf of Bothnia along one of the lanes opened up by icebreakers.

The Route

Turku The journey leaves **Turku/Åbo** (see page 63) along Road 8, which runs at some distance from the coast through the area first colonised by Swedish settlers. There are numerous side roads to small villages along the coast, which still preserve a number of old Swedish buildings.

8km
Raisio

There is a fourteenth-century church at **Raisio**, the first village outside Turku, which has almost been swallowed up by urban sprawl. One can go left here to the small bathing resort of **Naantali/ Nådendal** (10km), which is typical in having a holiday village and several camping sites. Naantali is linked by bridges with some of the offshore islands.

Just north of Raisio there is another left turn along a road which runs along the coast to the small holiday resort of **Taivassalo** (44km). From here one may continue along the coast to Uusikaupunki (another 36km — see excursion below).

Masku is the next village along the main road from Raisio. It is of similar historical interest, and has a fourteenth-century stone church. Not far away is the ancestral seat of the Horn family, who had such a great influence on the history of both Sweden and Finland.

25km
Mynämäki

The next town along Road 8 is the old town of **Mynämäki**. Once a Swedish port at the mouth of the Mynäjoki, it is now some distance from the coast. This is a common phenomenon along the coast of Finland, which has been continually rising since the melting of the glacial ice that once weighed it down. There is a thirteenth-century church in the old town centre. A turning to the right leads to a beautiful inland lake called the Pyhäjärvi.

27km
Laitila

The next town is **Laitila** on the banks of the Laajoki. There is a right turn here along Road 198 to the holiday resort of Säkylä by the beautiful Pyhäjärvi, and continuing inland towards Tampere.

Excursion to Uusikaupunki/Nystad (18km each way)
If one turns left at Laitila along Road 198, one quickly arrives at the old port and commercial centre of Uusikaupunki/Nystad (population 14,000).

The town was founded in 1617 by King Gustav II Adolf of Sweden. Its main claim to fame is the Treaty of Nystad, which was signed here in 1721. It laid down the division of the Baltic territories between Sweden and Russia. The Swedes kept Finland, while Russia established its claim to the provinces of Karelia, Estonia, Livonia and Ingermanland.

Uusikaupunki has suffered a similar fate to that of many other

Scandinavian towns. The wooden buildings needed heating in the cold winters, creating a danger of fire from sparks flying in the wind. The result was a series of major fires that have done as much damage as earthquakes in other parts of the world. Some buildings have nonetheless survived, including the old stone church, which now houses a museum of cultural history. The nearby Myllymäen Park contains four old windmills and a lookout tower.

Uusikaupunki is renowned as a centre for the processing and export of grey granite. It also boasts Finland's only car factory (Saab and Valmet), open to visitors Tuesdays and Thursdays, and also a car museum.

One can either return to Laitila via the same route, or else meander along the coast towards Rauma (50km), passing a number of resorts on the way.

Laitila
32km

Road 8 continues northwards in a straight line from Laitila at some distance from the coast.

Rauma

Rauma (population 31,000) has become a major port thanks to its harbour being free of ice for much of the winter. There are some remarkable shipyards here. Since World War II a variety of wood-processing industries have grown and prospered in the area around. Although the people are mostly Finnish-speaking, the old town is Swedish in origin. It is in a remarkable state of preservation, and includes a typical harbourside market place.

The old town hall is built in typical Classical Revival style with a tower. It is now a museum, with a historical section, plus collections of modern lace and old model ships. The annual festival at the end of July includes demonstrations of lace-making and folk music performances.

The old ruined church to the north is older than the town; it belonged to a fifteenth-century monastery that was dissolved in the Reformation. Rauma received its town charter in the fifteenth century, but in 1550 its Swedish-speaking inhabitants were forced to move to Helsinki on the orders of King Gustav Vasa of Sweden.

14km
Eurajoki

Road 8 continues northwards, crossing a number of rivers such as the Lappinjoki and the Eurajoki, which run out into the sea further west. **Eurajoki** is another example of a former port that is no longer on the coast. One can turn left here along a small road that meanders along the coast towards Pori. It takes much longer than the main road, but passes through some lovely little towns on the way.

Pori/Björneborg (population 81,000) lies on the banks of the Kokemäenjoki, the mouth of which is some distance to the west of where it previously was. This is due partly to the fact that the land has risen, and partly to the rubble and sediment brought down by the river, especially during the spring thaw, which has pushed the coastline further and further out.

36km
Pori

The site of the original eleventh-century town is as far as 30km further up-river. The town was subsequently resited on several occasions further down-river, mostly following its periodic destruction by fire. The present site goes back to 1558, when the city was built directly on the coast. But the sea has continued to retreat, and the town is now 10km from the coast. The nearest harbour is now 25km away at Mäntyluoto, which is situated at the end of an alluvial peninsula. This, together with the nearby island of Reposaari, is one of Finland's major ports.

The peninsula itself sports a number of magnificent beaches. Indeed, the bathing resort of **Yyteri** is one of the finest holiday centres in Scandinavia, with a beautiful beach lined by thick forests of trees. The island of Kirjurinluoto in the river mouth is the site for a regular summer jazz festival.

The old town centre was last rebuilt in the nineteenth century following a fire. It clearly shows the influence of the great Classical Revival architect Carl Ludwig Engel, whose buildings are to be found all over Finland, especially in Helsinki. Two examples of his buildings are the old town hall and the former corn exchange, which now houses the Museum of Art. To the south of the Kokemäenjoki is the Provincial Museum, which contains numerous replicas of old handicraft workshops.

The old town, with its theatre and its beautiful parks, is now surrounded by a modern industrial city. This phenomenon is typical of the post-war industrialisation that resulted partly from the Finnish response to demands for reparation. One consequence of this development is that the former Swedish-speaking majority is now far outnumbered by Finnish-speaking immigrants. The industries are primarily based on timber and its products, in particular paper manufacture. But textile manufacture has also become important.

Midsummer at the bathing resort of Yyteri

The town is an important road and rail junction, with three main road links apart from the main north–south coast road (Road 8). Road 2 links Pori with Helsinki via Kokemäki and Forssa (249km); though fast, it is also the busiest route. Road 11 goes due east to Tampere (112km), forming a link road to Route 2. Road 23 goes north-east, leaving Road 8 just to the north of Pori; it goes via Kankaanpää, Jyväskylä and Kuopio to Joensuu in the east of the country, forming another useful road link to parts of Route 2. Together with the railway that runs by its side, it forms a vital freight link with the forests of the interior.

Road 8 continues due north from Pori at some distance from the coast. The road is a good one, but also very busy. There is, however, an alternative route along the coast, leaving the main road at Lamppi, 15km north of Pori. This road follows the irregularities of the coast-line, and is therefore longer and much slower. But it passes through some lovely little villages along the way. There are several roads 96km leading back to the main road. The large Swedish-speaking village

Sauna cabins are often situated on the shores of a lake or a sea

of **Lappfjärd/Lappväärtti** is just north of where the coast road re- Lappfjärd
enters the main road, which now bypasses it.

Detour via Kristinestad/Kristiinankaupunki (15km)

If one turns left at Lappfjärd, it is only 5km to the small coastal town
of Kristinestad/Kristiinankaupunki (the rather long-winded Finnish
name is usually abbreviated to Kristiina). The town is approached via
a 350m-long (1,148ft) stone bridge across the river estuary. Like
many coastal towns, Kristinestad has grown fast in recent decades,
and now has a population of 10,000. Though previously exclusively
Swedish-speaking, its population is now equally divided between the
two linguistic communities.

The town was founded in 1649 by Per Brahe, the great Swedish
governor and benefactor of Finland, and was named after his wife
Kristina. Hans Eberhard Friedrich, author and expert on Finland,
describes the old town as 'the most Swedish of all Swedish towns,
including those in Sweden itself'. This is certainly the impression one
is given as one wanders though the narrow cobbled streets. By some
miracle the wooden buildings have escaped destruction by fire,
including the old wooden church with its leaning spire. The former
manor house has now been turned into a museum. On festival days
the people dress up in their brightly-coloured traditional costume.

Ski-race

Lappfjärd   The direct route along Road 8 from **Lappfjärd** is quicker though
13km   hardly any shorter than the detour route through Kristinestad, which
Pjelax   re-enters the main road just south of **Pjelax**.

Detour via Kaskinen and Närpes
A left turn at Pjelax along Road 67 brings one quickly to the old port
of **Kaskinen/Kaskö**, which was founded in 1785. It is situated on
an island, and is reached via a 100m-long (328ft) bridge that also
carries one of Finland's few railways. With a population of 2,000,
Kaskinen is Finland's smallest town. Its old wooden buildings are
mostly intact.
    The nearby village of **Närpes/Närpiö** is north of Kaskinen
across the bridge. This old Swedish-like village has preserved much
of its original atmosphere. The fifteenth-century stone church is surrounded by 200 stalls, where churchgoers from the surrounding area
once tied up their horses and carriages. Similar arrangements are
found in villages in the old Swedish province of Dalarna.
    Both Kaskinen and Närpes have become popular tourist resorts,
and provide suitable accommodation and camping facilities. A right
turn in Närpes brings one quickly back into Road 8.

North of Pjelax the main road retreats even further from the coast, Pjelax
with the old road often running parallel to the newly-built Road 8. It
goes through **Pörtom/Pirttikylä**, and comes to a junction with the
E79/Road 3 (the direct route from Tampere and Helsinki). This also
links with Road 16 running due east to Lapua and Kyyjärvi (see cross-
routes from Vaasa below). An airport to the right of the road indicates
that it is not much further to Vaasa.   80km

Vaasa/Vasa (population 55,000) has grown fast since World Vaasa
War II, and the Swedish-speaking native population has been joined
by large numbers of Finnish-speaking refugees from the Russian-
occupied eastern territories. The town played an important role in the
Finnish war of independence during World War I. It was the headquarters for General Mannerheim and government leader
Svinhufvud's campaign to free the country from Russian domination.

The town was originally founded in the seventeenth century, but
like other coastal towns it was continually resited as the coast
advanced. The frequent destructive fires often provided the opportunity for resiting the town. The last of these fires was in the nineteenth
century.

Like most Finnish towns, it is centred around a large market
square (Kauppatori). Its most interesting museums are the Os- 🏛
trobothnia Museum and the Brage Open-air Museum. The nearby
coastline is fragmented into numerous inlets, islands and skerries —
a paradise for all kinds of water sports. The nearest beach to the west
of the town has a camping site among other tourist facilities.

Vaasa is a major Finnish port. Situated at the narrowest point of
the Gulf of Bothnia, it provides the shortest freight and passenger
crossing to Umeå in Sweden. There are two longer ferry routes to
Örnskjöldsvik and Sundsvall respectively. Vaasa is also a provincial
capital and the administrative centre of one of Finland's most fertile
agricultural regions.

Cross-Routes from Vaasa/Vasa

The rest of the present route makes for fast driving, but is less
interesting than the part already covered. One possible variation is
to take the ferry from Vaasa to Umeå in Sweden, continuing northwards along the Swedish coast (see *The Visitor's Guide to Sweden*).
One can then cross back into Finland at Tornio, which lies at the

southern end of the Road of the Four Winds (see Route 5). It is only a short distance from Tornio to Kemi at the northern end of the present route. From Kemi one can continue towards the North Cape along the Arctic Road (see Route 4).

There is an eastward road link from Vaasa along Road 16, which turns left off the E79 Tampere road at Laihia. It goes via Isokyrö to the fascinating old village of **Lapua**, with its lovely wooden church built by Engel. It continues to Kyyjärvi, where it enters Road 13. This in turn runs south-eastwards and enters Road 4 beyond Saarijärvi, 250km from Vaasa and a short distance north of Jyväskylä (see Route 4).

Travellers who prefer to continue their holiday in Sweden can cross the gulf to Umeå or Sundsvall. From here they can either go south along the coast to Stockholm, or else make a tour of northern Sweden (see *The Visitor's Guide to Sweden*).

Vaasa | Road 8 continues north-east from Vaasa. A good straight road
113km | makes for a fast journey time, but there is little of scenic interest. The
Kokkola | 113km to **Kokkola** are quickly covered.

Detour via Nykarleby and Jakobstad (133km)

The alternative coast road leaves Road 8 about half-way between Vaasa and Kokkola, 11km beyond Oravais/Oravainen. It is 20km longer than the main road, but runs along a lovely stretch of coastline through old Swedish villages with stone churches.

The small Swedish town of **Nykarleby/Uusikaarlepyy** is followed by the larger port of **Jakobstad/Pietarsaari**. Jakobstad was the birthplace of Finland's national poet Johan Ludwig Runeberg. It is also the site of Finland's oldest tobacco factory, which was founded in 1762. There is a ferry link from here to Skellefteå in Sweden.

The road now crosses a series of offshore islands linked by bridges. It passes close to some lovely coastal resorts with camping sites, including Luoto, Bodö and Öja. It rejoins Road 8 at Kokkola.

Kokkola | **Kokkola/Gamlakarleby** (population 34,500) was founded in 1620, and has traditionally been a centre for the leather and fur industries. The town has grown enormously in recent decades, and the previous Swedish-speaking majority has been overtaken by Finnish-speaking immigrants. Post-war industrialisation has also

brought in a variety of new industries. There is a car ferry service from
Kokkola to Skellefteå in Sweden.

The town hall in the centre was built by Carl Ludwig Engel in 1842,
and is in his usual Classical Revival style. The wooden church nearby
was built somewhat later. In 1845, during the Crimean War, the
British attempted an invasion here to oust the Russian rulers. The
attempt failed, but the so-called English Park contains a memorial of
the event — a captured English boat that has survived the vicissi-
tudes of time.

The next part of the route is not particularly interesting. Road 8
now follows the coastline, but there is little of interest apart from the
view across the sea. On the other hand, the road is a very fast one,
and the 200km from Kokkola to Oulu are quickly covered — which is
certainly an advantage for travellers who plan to press on northwards
to beyond the Arctic Circle.

The road crosses a wide river at each of the towns along this
section of the route: the Lestijoki at **Himanka**, and the Kalajoki and
Pyhäjoki at **Kalajoki** and **Pyhäjoki** respectively. These rivers form
transport routes for timber from the forests and lakes of the interior,
and are normally accompanied by a road link. The towns themselves
have camping sites· and guesthouses providing simple but clean
accommodation. There are extensive sand dunes either side of
Kalajoki, with isolated beaches beyond.   127km

The next town is **Raahe/Brahestad** (population 19,000), which Raahe
is also an important timber loading point. As its Swedish name
suggests, it was founded by Per Brahe in 1649. The statue of its
founder in the market square is based on an original in Turku.

Detour via Olkijoki and Siikajoki (60km)
The coastal route is again longer and slower, but more interesting
than the direct route along Road 8. It turns left off the main road at
Raahe towards the small village of Olkijoki, whose chief claim to fame
is a treaty that was signed here between the Finns and the Russians
in 1808. The road continues through Siikajoki, which has a lovely
wooden church built at the beginning of the eighteenth century. It
rejoins Road 8 at Liminka (see below).

Raahe   From Raahe the main road turns inland again and goes eastwards
in a straight line towards Liminka. It crosses over Finland's main
north–south railway, which comes up from Helsinki via Tampere and
Kokkola and continues via Oulu to Tornio on the Swedish border.
Passengers and freight must be transferred at the border, because
48km   Finnish railways have the broad Russian gauge.

Liminka   **Liminka** is only a short way further on. It is situated at the
southern end of a long inlet. Road 8 comes to an end immediately
beyond Liminka, and the route turns left into the E4/Road 4, which is
Finland's main north–south artery. It comes up from Helsinki via
Jyväskylä, and continues north via Oulu to Kemi. The route becomes
much busier from now onwards, with the merging of traffic from both
roads. The E4 runs across the peninsula on which Oulu Airport is
situated. At **Kempele** it crosses the railway again, and soon enters
27km   the suburbs of Oulu.

Oulu   **Oulu/Uleåborg** (population 97,000) is the sixth-largest city in
Finland, and is situated at the mouth of the Oulujoki. The so-called
'White City of the North' received its town charter as early as 1605,
but it was already important by then, and had been fortified since
1590. The city owes its importance to the Oulujoki, which forms the
main east–west waterway through the northern forests of Finland.
The port of Oulu was once famous for the export of wood tar from the
hinterland, but in the last few decades it has become a prosperous
base for a variety of modern industries.

Like most Scandinavian cities, Oulu has been burned to the
ground on several occasions, because the wooden buildings caught
fire so easily. The last great fire was in 1822. The reader can of course
guess who replanned the town afterwards. Why, Carl Ludwig Engel
— who else?

The city is beautifully situated; it spreads out along both shores of
the river and across the islands in the middle, which are linked by
numerous bridges. The ruins of the castle are surrounded by parkland on the island of **Linnansaari**. The Oulujoki forms rapids as it
flows through the city; the Merikoski once merely constituted an
annoying hindrance to timber transport, but it now provides much-
needed hydroelectric power.

The town centre is formed by the market place on the city's
eastern waterfront to the south of the river. The architecture is varied,

Oulu

with modern buildings standing alongside the old warehouses along
the river bank. The cathedral was built by Engel in 1830, and was the
first important building to be completed following the great fire of
1822. The most northerly university in the world was founded here in
1960 — an outstanding example of the modern architecture that
prevails in the city centre. The Municipal Museum is especially
interesting, and includes a section on Lapland. The Turkansaari
Open-air Theatre is also worth seeing.

The E4/Road 4 continues due north from Oulu along the shores
of the Perämeri (the Finnish name for the northern part of the Gulf of
Bothnia). But the irregularity of the coast means that the sea is not
always visible. The road crosses several broad rivers such as the
Iijoki, the Olhavanjoki and the Kuivajoki, all of them important timber
transport routes. Small towns have grown up around the transfer
points at the coast — Haukipudas, Ii and Kuivaniemi, for example. At
Simo, 80km from Oulu, the road crosses the provincial boundary
into Finnish Lapland. It is now not much further to Kemi.

Kemi (population 28,000) lies at the mouth of the Kemijoki, which

107km
Kemi

is an important transport route for a large part of Finnish Lapland. As a port, Kemi naturally depends on the timber brought down from the hinterland. Following its destruction in World War II, it has been rebuilt on modern lines. But whereas previously it had been no more than a loading point for raw timber, it has now developed into a thriving centre for timber-based industries. These factories have changed the whole face of the town. They derive the power they need from the massive Isohaara hydroelectric plant, which is situated by the river bank to the north of Kemi. It also provides power for a large part of northern Finland.

Kemi was founded just over a century ago, and provides little of interest to visitors. It is, however, an important staging post on the way to the far north. There is a major road junction 6km to the north and just past the airport.

A left turn here along the E4/Road 21 brings one quickly to Tornio on the Swedish border. There are two possible routes from Tornio. One is to carry on northwards along the Road of the Four Winds towards Tromsø in Norway (see Route 5). The other is to cross the Swedish border to nearby Haparanda and continue the tour through northern Sweden (see *The Visitor's Guide to Sweden*).

The road that goes right at the junction north of Kemi is the continuation of Road 4, the Arctic Road. This goes north through Finnish Lapland, crossing the Arctic Circle at Rovaniemi. It continues northward until it eventually crosses into the Norwegian county of Finnmark. It thus forms the shortest route for travellers going from Finland to the North Cape (see Route 4).

FINNISH LAPLAND

Routes 4 and 5 both go through Finnish Lapland, and can of course be easily combined. One might, for example, go north along the Arctic Road to the North Cape (Route 4), returning through the Norwegian county of Finnmark (see Route 7) and along the Road of the Four Winds (Route 5). Or conversely one might follow the same roads in the opposite direction.

Finnish Lapland is sometimes called the 'other Finland', because it is so different from the rest of the country as to be worth considering separately. It is called Lappi in Finnish, and is Finland's northernmost

Lapland landscape

province. With an area of almost 100,000sq km, it is also the largest, covering nearly a third of the country's total land area. Apart from the area around Kemi on the Gulf of Bothnia, it lies mostly to the north of the Arctic Circle. It shares borders with Sweden, Norway and the Soviet Union. Up until World War II a small part of Finnish Lapland extended north as far as the Arctic Ocean. But this area was lost to the Soviet Union, and with it the ice-free harbour of Petsamo.

Lapland is Finland's mostly sparsely populated province, with a total of only 210,000 inhabitants; these include 4,000 Lapps. On the other hand, there are almost as many reindeer as people, numbering some 200,000 in all. The reindeer are herded by *poromies* or shepherd reindeermen who use motorsledges in winter and cars, motorcycles and even motorboats in the summer.

The population is concentrated in the southern part of the region, which is divided from the rest by a range of low mountains called *tunturi.* The word should not be confused with tundra, and normally indicates a bare rounded summit that rises up out of the forest. For the rest, the scenery consists of hardy coniferous forest interspersed with lakes and swamps.

The far northern region beyond the hills is called the Peräpohjola in Finnish. Apart from a few stunted pine and birch forests, it is mostly covered with barren tundra interspersed with rocky outcrops and swamps, with vegetation consisting primarily of moss and lichens.

The wedge of territory that extends north-west between Sweden and Norway is the only really mountainous part of Finland. It is a region of high plateaux covered with lakes and swamps, similar to the fjells of Norway. Indeed, the highest point in Finland, the Haltiatunturi (1,328m (4,356ft)), is directly on the Norwegian border.

The scattered communities of Finnish Lapland were largely destroyed during World War II. But the decades which followed saw a massive programme of reconstruction. The road network in particular was greatly improved, and is now extremely good for such an isolated region.

There are three main traffic routes: the E4 or Arctic Road, described in Route 4 below; the east–west route from Salla near the Soviet border via Kemijärvi and Rovaniemi to Tornio on the Swedish border (with a rail route running parallel); and the Road of the Four Winds, running north from Tornio along the Swedish border to Kilpisjärvi near the Norwegian border (see Route 5). The last of the three was named after the four-tasselled hats worn by the Lapps that live along the route.

Most of these and other roads have gravel surfaces. In the summer they are liberally sprinkled with a special kind of oil to keep them free of dust. They are also regularly rolled flat with special rolling machines, especially after rain, so as to keep the surface firm and even. They should therefore pose no problems for drivers, apart from the risk of damage from loose chippings. In winter the roads are kept firm by a permanent layer of ice and snow, but chains are only necessary in hillier regions. During the thaw, however, the side roads are difficult if not totally impassable.

In spite of the recent road-building programme, there are vast areas of wasteland that are not yet served by roads. Railways, moreover, are totally absent from the far north. Reindeer sledges to

Boating on the Oulujärvi lake system

Traditional ochre-painted house, Kemi

Sodankylä Church — many centuries old

Float plane at Inari

be seen are likely to be there as a tourist attraction. Most Laplanders use cars, motorised sledges, motorcycles and motorboats (see page 127).

Visitors are always amazed at how far north the forest extends in Finnish Lapland — much further north than in the corresponding regions of Norway and Sweden. The main reason for this is the fact that most of the region is low-lying. The few hills and mountains rarely exceed 600m (1,968ft), and these merely form bare rounded summits above the surrounding forest.

The woodland becomes continually sparser as one travels northward, until eventually it consists purely of hardier pines and birches. There are no more pines north of the shores of Lake Inari, and from here onwards the only trees are small bushes and weirdly-shaped birches with tiny leaves. But the vegetation flourishes on even the thinnest of soils. During the short summer season, the tiny shrubs are covered with a bright carpet of flowers and berries, including many rare (and therefore protected) species.

It is said that the people of Finnish Lapland went straight from reindeer sledges to aeroplanes. And it is certainly true that the aeroplane has become commonplace in a region of such vast distances. In the summer, seaplanes can use the lake surfaces to land on. In the winter the same planes are provided with special runners for landing on ice.

There are really only two seasons in Lapland: the winter, during which the land is covered in snow for between 6 and 8 months; and the short summer with its long hours of daylight. Winter turns to summer in a matter of a few days, during which nature explodes into life. The 2 months of high summer from June to July are often characterised by almost permanent daylight (see page 43).

Winter, on the other hand, includes a period of permanent darkness in areas north of the Arctic Circle. In the most northerly regions the sun never rises for the whole of December and January, and the most one can expect is a brief period of dusk. It is the middle of January before the situation begins to improve. However, the cold, clear nights of winter are the ideal setting for the northern lights or aurora borealis (see page 47).

The snow starts to melt at the beginning of May, and nature suddenly springs into life. It reaches its zenith in mid-June, when the lakes and rivers are scarcely clear of ice. The warmest period is from mid-July to mid-August, when temperatures of up to 30˚C (86˚F) are possible.

The leaves turn red, yellow and brown with the first night frosts in late August or early September, one of the most beautiful sights in Finland. The first snowfalls occur in October, and the ground is then covered with snow from mid-November to the end of April. During this period the temperature can drop as low as −30˚C (4˚F).

The fauna of Lapland consists mostly of birds. Virtually the only large animals are the semi-domesticated reindeer. The commonest animals are smaller species such as squirrels, hares, foxes and martens. The elk is very rare, as are also the bear, the wolf, the lynx and the glutton, which can only be found in isolated regions, in special nature reserves or, rarely, in south-eastern parts of Lapland.

One remarkable animal phenomenon is the migration of the lemmings, most commonly called *sopuli* in Finnish. Every few years they undergo a population explosion, and migrate in their thousands across the countryside until they eventually 'commit suicide' in some lake. They are naturally pursued by large numbers of birds of prey and small carnivorous mammals.

Reindeer are rare in southern Lapland, where at most they are found in small zoo-like enclosures. But they are common in the north, where they often leap out of the forests onto the roads, surprising motorists. In the winter the herds are gathered together and divided among their owners; the young deer are then marked on the ears according to the owner. The great 'division of the herds' is one of the most important events of the winter.

4 THE ARCTIC ROAD

From Helsinki to the Arctic Ocean

Helsinki • Lahti • Jyväskylä (Saarijärvi) • Pihtipudas • Oulu • Kemi • Rovaniemi (Kemijärvi) • Sodankylä • Ivalo • Inari (Menesjärvi) • Kaamanen (Utsjoki) • Norwegian border • Karasjok • Lakselv • Olderfjord • North Cape

What the Route Has to Offer

There are said to be three faces of Finland: the agricultural south-west, the lake country of central and south-eastern Finland, and the northern tundra of Lapland.

The present route goes through all three types of scenery. It passes through a small part of the fertile south between Helsinki and Lahti, and crosses the lake country from Lahti via Jyväskylä to Pihtipudas. Then the short coastal section along the Gulf of Bothnia is reminiscent of Sweden. But the most distinctive part of the route is the section beyond Rovaniemi on the Arctic Circle. From here onwards the forests become progressively sparser until they eventually give way to bare tundra that extends northwards to the Arctic Ocean.

The people that one meets along the way are equally varied: the hardworking farmers who till the fertile soils of the south, the coastal dwellers, who are largely of Swedish descent, the hardy forest-dwellers, the dour northern Finns, and the cunning but friendly Lapps. North of Rovaniemi there are few towns, churches or museums to speak of. But many of the things that one sees will probably themselves be museum pieces within the next decade or so. They include the huts and summer camps of the Lapps, the old wooden churches of the north, and the colourful markets in the small towns along the Arctic Circle.

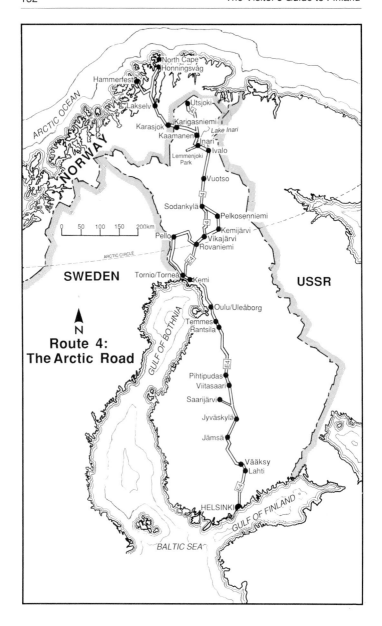

Route 4:
The Arctic Road

Quite apart from the people and the scenery, there is the magic of the midnight sun, when the sun never sets for days on end. Summer here is a time when nature explodes into life, and the people are full of joy and celebration.

Campers and caravanners will experience the northern summer all the more intensely. The camping sites in the north are much quieter and more spacious than those in the south, but they sometimes lack the extra facilities that one might expect in more popular areas. The same applies to the huts and chalets that can be found wherever one travels. Unnecessary comforts are anathema to the Finns when they are trying to get away from it all. The only luxury they require is a sauna, where they can relax in the heat and recover from the exertions of the journey. There are however, increasing numbers of hotels, motels and holiday/ski resorts springing up all over Lapland. Facilities for skiing holidays are now quite considerable. Slalom-slopes with electric ski-lifts have been built all over and tracks for cross-country skiing are excellent. Booking of hotels in advance is recommended especially between February and mid-April.

Finnish Lapland has yet more to offer. Anglers need only pay a small fee to fish in some of the world's best salmon rivers. Apart from that king of fishes, they are teeming with trout of all kinds, and with other fish such as pike, perch and eel.

The journey is a long one, involving some 6,000km of driving. But the rewards are well worth the wear and tear on the car, which will return with a thick layer of dirt and possibly a pair of reindeer antlers tied to the roof rack. Apart from the usual souvenirs, Lapland has experiences to offer that can be found nowhere else in Europe.

A strong, healthy vehicle is an essential for the trip, with plenty of equipment for dealing with breakdowns (punctures and broken windscreens are a particular hazard). A spare can of fuel is another must for a journey that goes such a long way from civilisation. The Finns are extremely accommodating and helpful to anyone unlucky enough to be stranded along the way. The overland buses, which account for most of the traffic along northern roads, will stop immediately if the driver sees a vehicle that appears to be in trouble. The northern end of the E4 may not be such a good road as its E-designation might lead one to expect, but it is nonetheless quite safe to drive on provided one observes the necessary precautions.

Access Routes

The route begins at Helsinki, and the same access routes apply as those for Route 2: by air to Helsinki, or the longer land and sea route via Danish, German and/or Swedish ferry ports.

Route 4 is not intended as a round tour, but for use in combination with other routes. One possibility is a continuation along the Norwegian Arctic Road (see Route 7), maybe returning along the Road of the Four Winds (see Route 5). Alternatively, one might prefer to continue the whole length of Norway to Oslo or Bergen (see *The Visitor's Guide to Norway*).

The route can also be combined with Route 3 along the west coast from Oulu, and even with parts of Route 2 via a cross-route from Oulu to Kajaani (using Road 22). Finally, the Swedish coast road (E4) forms a good access and/or return route, crossing the Finnish-Swedish border between Tornio and Haparanda (see *The Visitor's Guide to Sweden*).

Length and Timing

The route measures some 1,400km from Helsinki to Lakselv, ignoring the detours and excursions along the way. The return route via the Road of the Four Winds is some 600km further. The journey through Norway is even longer, amounting to some 5,000km, and making a total journey of well over 6,000km. If one drives up through Sweden, the distance travelled will be shorter, but the amount of driving involved will be much the same.

Most of the roads are fully surfaced these days, but there are several sections north of the Arctic Circle that are still laid with oiled gravel. These are passable with care and attention to the dangers of loose chippings. Moreover, the lack of traffic makes for a good steady travelling speed. The roads further south are better surfaced. But they are often much busier, and are made slower by the terrain. The road is frequently forced to climb over small but sharp undulations, which being of granite are difficult to cut through. This results in a large number of twists and switchbacks.

The return route through Norway poses problems of a different kind. Though well surfaced, it is often narrow and twisty, especially towards the northern end. Waiting time must also be allowed for the ferries along the route.

Rukatunturi on the Kemijärvi road is a skier's paradise

All in all, this is a time-consuming trip, especially if one is to spend time along the way. Four weeks is the absolute minimum to allow, and if possible 6 weeks is preferable.

The Best Time to Travel
The only practicable period for travelling in the far north is from mid-June to 20 August. Before then night frosts are still common, while autumn sets in immediately afterwards. The midnight sun is best at the beginning of this period in areas north of the Arctic Circle (see page 43).

The midges that plague the tundra regions of Finland and Norway are commonest in July and August. Stories of them are, however, often exaggerated, and one can always buy various preventative preparations before setting out. A pharmacist will be able to advise on suitable insect-repellent creams, antiseptic ointments and (if necessary) anti-allergy preparations. Moreover, one or two insect-repellent sprays form a small but essential part of the holiday luggage.

The Route

Helsinki The route leaves **Helsinki** along the E4/Road 4/5, which is sign-posted for Lahti. The road is of motorway standard, and runs out through the sprawling suburbs of the city. The villas include some interesting examples of modern architecture. The motorway soon comes out into the countryside, which at this stage is heavily cultivated and distinctly 'un-Finnish' in character. The route 38km bypasses Kerava, and the motorway section ends just before Järvenpää **Järvenpää.**

22km The E4 continues to **Mäntsälä**, where there is an important Mäntsälä crossroads with Road 55. Mäntsälä is in the middle of a fertile region covered with glacial deposits. The ice sheet pushed up a great heap of material in front of it, which it left behind when it melted. The result is a moraine: a range of hills that has dammed back the lakes to the north. This particular moraine is called the Salpausselkä.

The E4 continues through countryside that is heavily cultivated by Finnish standards. The landscape is wooded, but less so than one might expect. Those expecting forests should not feel disappointed at this stage, as there are plenty of forests to follow. The road also passes the first of many lakes — the Hunttijärvi — on the left. It 66km remains dual carriageway as far as Lahti.

Lahti **Lahti** (population 94,000) lies at the south-eastern end of the Vesijärvi. It straddles the boundary between the fertile glacial soils of the Salpausselkä to the south and the endless forests of the Finnish lake country to the north. It is a bustling town full of ultra-modern apartment blocks that contrast strangely with the landscape around. Lahti received its municipal charter only 80 years ago, when it was no more than a small market town. The decades since then have seen an enormous expansion, thanks mostly to modern industrial development. Furniture manufacture is the town's chief industry. But Lahti is best known as a winter skiing resort, with annual ski races and ski-jumping competitions from the 90m-high (295ft) Olympic ski-jump. The Historical Museum in Kirkkokatu presents a good historical survey of the province of Häme. Other places of interest include the Museum of Art in Vesijärvenkatu, and the Radio Museum at the radio station.

The route continues northwards from Lahti along the E4. The first 25km section to Vääksy is thickly wooded, but is also fairly populous. At

Hotel complex, Jyväskylä

Vääksy the road crosses the channel that links the Vesijärvi to the south with the great Lake Päijänne to the north. Lake Päijänne has an area of 1,000sq km, and extends as far north as the town of Jyväskylä (see below).

The road carries on northwards at some distance from the lake shore via Kuhmoinen to **Jämsä**. The nearby paper mill at Kaipola on the lake shore is the largest of its kind in Scandinavia. The E4 goes north-east from Jämsä, passing several long inlets of Lake Päijänne, until it eventually arrives at Jyväskylä.

Jyväskylä (population 65,000) is the cultural and administrative centre of the province of Keski-Suomen (Central Finland). Situated at the northern end of Lake Päijänne, it is the oldest town in Central Finland. But even so it was founded only 150 years ago, and a century ago had a population of less than 1,000. Since then it has expanded rapidly, especially since World War I, when newly-independent Finland began to mobilise its own resources. Jyväskylä nowadays is a flourishing industrial town. Its lakeside position has favoured the development of timber-based industries. But it is also an important centre for the manufacture of chemicals, metals and

Vääksy

90km
Jämsä

55km
Jyväskylä

textiles, not to mention a flourishing printing trade.

The town is equally important in the cultural sphere. The first-ever Finnish-language secondary school was founded here in 1858. This was followed in 1863 by the first Finnish-language teacher-training college, which became a university in 1934. The modern university buildings are of particular architectural interest. They were designed by the internationally famous architect Alvar Aalto, who was born in Jyväskylä.

Jyväskylä is famous for its so-called summer universities, which have been in existence for some 60 years. They run courses throughout the summer holidays for interested students of all ages. Between June and August they are patronised by as many as 2,000 students.

The parks overlooking Jyväskylä provide magnificent views of the town and of the surrounding lakes and forests. Buildings of interest in the town include the neo-Gothic parish church and the Eastern Orthodox church. The many interesting museums include the University Museum, the Museum of Air Flight and the Lyceum Museum.

The Museum of Central Finland (Keski-Suomen Museo) is of particular interest, providing a detailed and comprehensive survey of the province. Central Finland is a varied region of vast forests and countless lakes linked by fast-flowing rivers. The main traffic artery is the E4, commonly known as the Arctic Road, which at this stage is mostly dual carriageway. This road has been instrumental in opening up the interior of Finland, and one can often find cultivated fields adjoining it. The local economy still depends for the most part on forestry, which since World War II has favoured the development of numerous related industries. Sawn timber, chipboard, paper, cellulose, furniture and prefabricated chalets are just some of the products that are exported from the region.

Jyväskylä is an ideal centre for car, coach or boat trips into the surrounding lake country. It has hotels and restaurants, a motel and an excellent camping and holiday centre by the lake. Activities on offer include sports, folklore and numerous cultural events, making it a highly desirable centre for the summer visitor to stay in. Many farms in the area provide excellent guesthouse facilities. Detailed information about tourist facilities in Jyväskylä and Central Finland can be obtained from the Central Tourist Office, Vapaudenkatu 38.

Wildwater trail on the Saarijärvi

The youth hostel is housed in the same building.

The route continues north along the E4 through a varied landscape of lakes and forests. After about 20km it passes Jyväskylä Airport on the left. The road is a fast one, and bypasses most of the small towns along the route. There is **Äänekoski** (population 10,000), for example, which has a significant timber industry.

40km
Äänekoski

Excursion to Saarijärvi (28km each way)
If one turns left off the E4 along Road 13 just before Äänekoski, it is only a short distance to Saarijärvi. This small town is a good base for the Pyhä-Häkki National Park, famous for its virgin forests, deep wells and chasms, and its wildwater trail running past no less than twenty-two sets of rapids.

The main route follows the shore of Lake Keitele, and eventually comes to the lovely little village of **Viitasaari**. Viitasaari is in a glorious island setting between two parts of Lake Keitele. The road

58km
Viitasaari

42km continues northwards through a typically Finnish landscape to the
Pihtipudas small town of **Pihtipudas**, which is in a beautiful forest setting,
⌘ sandwiched between two lakes called the Alvajärvi and the
Kolimajärvi.

52km The E4 runs north along the shores of several more lakes until it
Pyhäjärvi eventually reaches the **Pyhäjärvi** at the northern fringe of the
Finnish lake country. There is a town of the same name on the
opposite shore.

From now on the landscape consists more exclusively of forest as
68km the road continues through villages such as **Kärsämäki** and
Pulkkila **Pulkkila**. It runs along the bank of the Siikajoki and through more
villages such as **Rantsila** and **Temmes**. The E4 soon becomes
straighter but correspondingly busier as it approaches the junction
with Road 8 coming up from the Gulf of Bothnia. It is now only a short
96km distance to the city of Oulu.
Oulu **Oulu/Uleåborg** (population 97,000) is the sixth-largest city in
Finland, and is situated at the mouth of the Oulujoki. The so-called
White City of the North received its town charter as early as 1605, but
it was already important by then, and had been fortified since 1590.
The city owes its importance to the Oulujoki, which forms the main
east–west waterway through the northern forests of Finland. The port
of Oulu was once famous for the export of wood tar from the
hinterland, but in the last few decades it has become a prosperous
base for a variety of modern industries.

Like most Scandinavian cities, Oulu has been burned to the
ground on several occasions, because the wooden buildings caught
fire so easily. The last great fire was in 1822. The reader can of course
guess who replanned the town afterwards. Why, Carl Ludwig Engel
— who else?

The city is beautifully situated; it spreads out along both shores of
the river and across the islands in the middle, which are linked by
Ꮵ numerous bridges. The ruins of the castle are surrounded by parkland on the island of **Linnansaari**. The Oulujoki forms rapids as it
flows through the city. The Merikoski, as they are called, once merely
constituted a hindrance to timber transport, but now provide much-
needed hydroelectric power.

The town centre is formed by the market place on the city's
eastern waterfront to the south of the river. The architecture is varied,

Fishing in Finnish Lapland

with modern buildings standing alongside the old warehouses along the river bank. The cathedral was built by Engel in 1830, and was the first important building to be completed following the great fire of 1822. The then most northerly university in the world was founded here in 1960. (There is now a more northerly university at Rovani- 🏠 emi). It is an outstanding example of the modern architecture that prevails in the city centre. The Municipal Museum is especially 🏛 interesting, and includes a section on Lapland. The Turkansaari Open-air Theatre is also worth seeing.

The E4/Road 4 continues due north from Oulu along the shores of the Perämeri (the Finnish name for the northern part of the Gulf of Bothnia). But the irregularity of the coastline means that the sea is not always visible. The road crosses several broad rivers such as the

Iijoki, the Olhavanjoki and the Kuivajoki, all of them important timber transport routes. Small towns have grown up around the mouths of these rivers. They include Haukipudas, Ii and Kuivaniemi. At **Simo**, 80km from Oulu, the road crosses the provincial boundary into Finnish Lapland. From here it is not much further to Kemi.

108km
Kemi

Kemi (population 28,000) was founded just over a century ago. It lies at the mouth of the Kemijoki, which with a length of 512km is the longest river in Finland. It also forms an important transport route through Finnish Lapland. The port of Kemi depends very much on the timber that is brought down-river from the hinterland. Following its destruction in World War II, it has been rebuilt on modern lines. But whereas previously it had been no more than a loading point for raw timber, it has now developed into a thriving centre for timber-based industries. Its many modern factories have changed the whole face of the town. They derive their power from the massive Isohaara hydroelectric plant, which is situated by the river bank to the north of Kemi, and which also provides power for a large part of northern Finland.

Kemi itself provides little of interest to visitors, but is an important staging post on the way to the far north. There is a major road junction 6km to the north and just past the airport. The present route goes right here along Road 4 (see below). A left turn here along the E4/Road 21 brings one quickly to Tornio on the Swedish border. From Tornio there are two possible routes. One can either carry on northwards along the Road of the Four Winds towards Tromsø in Norway (see Route 5), or else cross the Swedish border to nearby Haparanda and continue the tour through northern Sweden (see *The Visitor's Guide to Sweden*).

Detour via Tornio and Pello (about 270km)

This detour is longer and more difficult than the direct route from Kemi to Rovaniemi, but is also very interesting. It first follows the E4/Road 21 (see above) to the border town of **Tornio/Torneå**, which is linked via a causeway to the Swedish town of Haparanda. Finland's only rail link with Sweden crosses the border here. But all freight and passengers must be transferred to a different train at Tornio, because the Finnish (and Russian) railways have a different gauge from those in the rest of Europe. Tornio, which is described in more

detail on page 156, has been a port since the early Middle Ages. The
seventeenth-century wooden church contains a number of interesting carvings.

The route turns north along the E78/Road 21, known as the Road
of the Four Winds (see Route 5). This runs along the river that forms
the border between Finland and Sweden: the Tornionjoki, or in
Swedish the Torneälv. This world-famous salmon river offers especially good fishing at Kiviranta just north of Tornio, and 14km further
north at the Kukkola Rapids.

The valley is surprisingly densely populated. The road goes
through Karunki and several other small settlements that were rebuilt
following their destruction in World War II. Soon before **Kauliranta**
there is a hill with a lookout tower called Aavasaksa (242m (793ft)).
It overlooks the mouth of the Tengeliöjoki, and affords a wide
panorama of the surrounding area, extending far into Sweden. About
13km after Kauliranta, the road crosses the Arctic Circle.

The route leaves the E78 Road of the Four Winds at the border
town of **Pello**, turning east along Road 83. After 10km there is a left
turn along a road signposted to Marrasjärvi, which comes out at
Meltaus. From here one turns south-east again to follow the course
of the Ounasjoki, which forms a busy timber transport route. It is
another 55km to Rovaniemi (see below).

The main route goes direct from Kemi to Rovaniemi along Road 4, Kemi
which now follows a different course from the E4. It runs along the
west bank of the Kemijoki through a densely populated valley with a
large number of timber-based industries. The railway runs parallel to
the road as it passes near to Tervola and continues via Petäjäskoski
and Muurola towards Rovaniemi.

The scenery changes noticeably as one moves inland from the
gulf. Many people imagine that Finnish Lapland consists solely of flat
tundra wastes. But this is far from the case in the southern part of the
region, where the undulating terrain is covered with vast pine forests,
occasionally interrupted by areas of swamp.   118km

Rovaniemi (population 32,000) is the capital of the Finnish Rovaniemi
province of Lapland. The town is a small one, but covers an
administrative area of at least 7,500sq km and does have its own
university. Rovaniemi lies at the confluence of Finland's longest river,

the Kemijoki (512km), with its third-longest river, the Ounasjoki (340km). Both rivers form vital timber transport routes, without which the local forestry could never have become economically viable.

Rovaniemi itself is the main market town for the area, serving a vast number of tiny settlements scattered across the region. It is the best place to prepare for the long journey across the wastes of Lapland. Drivers, for example, are recommended to have their vehicles serviced here, and all travellers should buy in reserve supplies of food and other essential items.

The town was destroyed in 1944, but had been rebuilt by 1952. There is little of great architectural interest, apart from the Danish Church, so-called because it was built from donations received from Denmark. Its most remarkable feature is an enormous wall painting 14m (46ft) high.

It is worth taking a wander through the market place, which is full of local life and colour. The Lapps from the area around come here to buy and sell their wares. There is also a regular fur market, which is especially worth visiting. The nearby shores of the Kemijoki are lined with pleasantly laid-out gardens.

One of the few buildings to have survived the last war is the famous Marttiini knife factory, which provides a fascinating permanent exhibition. The main product is a Lapp dagger known as a *lapinleuko* or *puukko*, which is inscribed with the monogram of J. M. Marttiini. This blade is much sought-after, and makes a lovely souvenir. It is slightly bent in shape, and is made of high-quality steel with a birchwood handle and a leather sheath. No self-respecting Lapp is without his trusty blade. It is sold in a variety of sizes, ranging from a heavy woodcutting tool to a small souvenir knife that can be used as a letter-opener.

The town is overlooked by a hill called the Ounasvaara. From the hut at the top there is a magnificent view of the town and its two rivers, and northwards into the land of the midnight sun. There is tourist centre nearby and a popular winter sports centre.

Also of interest is the open-air museum at **Pöykkölä**, 4km outside the town. It provides insights into the lifestyle of the Lapps.

There is a large German cemetery 15km to the north, next to the shores of the Norvajärvi. It is the last resting place for 2,500 soldiers who fell in the Lapland and Oulu provinces. They are buried in one

The Arctic Circle — land of snow and souvenirs

enormous vault, above which are eight rows of memorial stones bearing their names and dates. The entrance hall to this impressive red granite structure contains a modern sculpture entitled *Mother and Son*.

Further information about Rovaniemi and its environs can be obtained from the Municipal Tourist Office, Aallonkatu 2C. The town offers accommodation of all kinds, together with a number of restaurants and a choice of two camping sites.

The route continues from Rovaniemi along Road 4, known as the Arctic Road, which crosses the Ounasjoki past the rapids that form the confluence of the two rivers. Soon after that one can see Rovaniemi Airport on the left. Visitors who fancy a trip in a small plane may go on a round trip from the airport, and gain a vivid impression of the vast wastes of Finnish Lapland. The railway turns east here, and continues via Kemijärvi to Salla and the Soviet border.

✳   It is not long before Road 4 crosses the **Arctic Circle**, known in Finnish as the Napapiiri. It is not easy to miss, as it is indicated by large signs. There is a large colony of buildings, including a restaurant, a large souvenir shop, a post office and a Lapp camp that has an unfortunate resemblance to a zoo. There are all sorts of souvenirs available, including car stickers, postcards with special postmarks, items of Lapp handiwork, and certificates stating that one has crossed the Arctic Circle.

28km   A few kilometres further on, the road comes to a junction by the
Vikajärvi shores of the **Vikajärvi**. Road 4 continues northwards, while Road 80 goes east towards Kemijärvi.

Detour via Kemijärvi and Pelkosenniemi (170km)

Although longer and slower than the direct route to Sodankylä, this
✇ detour passes close to the beautiful Pyhätunturi. This wooded hill country provides some of the best scenery in southern Lapland.

The route follows Road 80 eastwards, parallel to the railway but at some distance from it. The area is completely uninhabited. Small side roads lead off to tiny goods stations along the line. Here, as elsewhere in Finnish Lapland, passenger transport is mostly confined to the infrequent but regular bus services that run along the roads. Further north they are replaced by sledge buses during the

60km   winter.
Kemijärvi   It is 60km to **Kemijärvi** (population 12,600), which is not only Finland's most northerly town, but also its most widely scattered. It is an important centre for timber industries, and the main market centre for the surrounding area. There is accommodation available in hotels and chalets, and the camping site by the lake is provided with a sauna.

From Kemijärvi it is possible to make a road or rail excursion to **Salla**. This winter sports centre near the Soviet border is close to the Oulanka National Park, with its wooded hills and lakes full of fish.

The route turns north from Kemijärvi along an unclassified road which, though not particularly good, is nonetheless quite driveable. It runs due north along the valley of the Kemijoki towards Pelkosenniemi. After about 35km, just past a lone forester's hut called Vuostimo, there is a small turning to the left leading up into the

Pyhätunturi. This beautiful wooded hill country is a popular area for ⌘
winter sports and walking holidays in the summer. The road leads up
to a small inn on the highest summit (540m (1,771ft)).

Shortly before Pelkosenniemi, there is another road off to the left
leading to the lovely Pyhäjärvi — a tiny lake nestling among the ⌘
woods along the northern fringe of the Pyhätunturi. The small market
village of **Pelkosenniemi** provides hotel, guesthouse and camping
facilties.

51km
Pelkosen-
niemi

The road continues down through the woods to the banks of the
Kemijoki. It soon comes to a fork, where the present route goes left
for Sodankylä. The road continues its lonely course through the
forests, passing numerous tiny lakes and settlements. The scenery ⌘
is typical of southern Lapland, the region known to the Finns as the
Perä-Pohjola.

59km
Sodankylä

The road eventually enters Road 4 at **Sodankylä** (see below),
where the present route rejoins the main route.

The main route goes due north from Vikajärvi through an undulating
region that is mostly uninhabited. The road first follows the banks of
the Raudanjoki, which forms lakes in several places. At **Käyrämo**
there is a small road to the left leading into the hills and forests of the
Käyrästunturi.

Vikajärvi
40km
Käyrämo

There is less and less evidence of human settlement. The peaks
of the Pyhätunturi (540m (1,771ft)) become visible in the distance to
the right. At Vuojärvi a side road comes in from Kemijärvi. Then at
Torvinen there is a small road to the right leading to the summit of the
Luostotunturi (510m (1,673ft)).

44km
Aska

Soon after **Aska** the road meets the fast-flowing Kitinenjoki. Near
Tähtelä on the approach to Sodankylä, it passes the Geophysical ✳
Observatory of the Finnish Scientific Academy. Those specially
interested are welcome to pay a visit, but must make an appointment
beforehand.

16km
Sodankylä

Sodankylä is one of the coldest and most scattered villages in
the whole of Finnish Lapland. The administrative district stretches as
far as the Soviet border, and covers an area of about 20,000sq km.
There has been a settlement at Sodankylä since the late Middle
Ages. It serves as a market centre for the scattered homesteads
along the Arctic Road.

The village itself consists of no more than a cluster of buildings. The wooden church was built in 1689, and is the oldest surviving church in Lapland. The stone church next to it was built in the mid-nineteenth century. These old buildings are in stark contrast to the modern bus station, which is a vital stopping-off point for the region's far-flung transport services. The village offers overnight accommodation, and also has a camping site.

Road 4 continues northwards from Sodankylä through an uninhabited region of forest and swamp. Car drivers are advised to set off with a full tank of fuel and a spare can with enough fuel for at least 100km. Filling stations in the north are few and far between. To the left are the hills of the Kaarestunturi. The road follows the course of the Kitinenjoki, which it crosses at **Peurasuvanto**.

45km
Peura-
suvanto

Soon the peaks of the Nattastunturi (544m (1,784ft)) become visible to the right. The road eventually passes through the village of **Vuotso**, which is linked via a side road to several other tiny villages. A short way further on there is a side road leading off to the Nattastunturi. Travellers are recommended to make a short excursion to the inn at the summit (544m (1,784ft)), from which there is a marvellous view.

45km
Vuotso

⌘

The road now enters the Laanila region, with its famous gold station of **Tankavaara**. At one time this was a gold-prospecting area, and many visitors still try their luck here. However, anglers are very much more likely to meet with success. The region's rivers are famous among anglers, and can be guaranteed to yield some of their bounty. Fishing permits can be obtained from local forestry offices.

Saariselkä, between Tankavaara and Kaunispää consists of dozens of high-class redwood-log houses, most of them belonging to Finland's leading companies. During the skiing season this is the place to see and be seen — 'everybody' goes there including the president and his guests.

⌘

Another worthwhile excursion is to the Kaunispää (438m (1,436ft)). The road to the top of this beautiful wooded hill is well signposted off the main road. The name actually means 'beautiful head'. The lookout tower at the summit was built for firewatching purposes, and commands a magnificent view to the south-east. There is a bus terminal here, and a restaurant with a few guest rooms and other facilities.

Inari Church

Continuing along the main road, it is not long before Ivalo Airport _{72km} appears on the left. **Ivalo** was once an important crossroads, with Ivalo roads leading off into the former Finnish territory of northern Karelia. The former Arctic Road used to go north-east from Ivalo along the eastern shore of Lake Inari, and eventually came out at the Arctic port of Petsamo. Now that the Petsamo region has been lost to the Soviet Union, the road comes to an end at the Soviet border.

For many years Ivalo was no more than a crossroads, but in the eighteenth century a few settlers came here from southern Finland. A small settlement grew up around the crossroads. Ivalo now has the most northerly airport in Finland. It serves as a centre for the Lapps who live in the area around, with a modern hospital, a shopping centre, several boarding schools and an Eastern Orthodox church.

Road 4 continues north-west from Ivalo. There is a marked change in the landscape as the road enters the region of Arctic Lapland. The sparse northern forests with their small trees are now interrupted by large areas of bare and often boggy plateau. The tundra is scattered with huge blocks of granite and weirdly-shaped dwarf pines and dwarf birches.

⌘   **Lake Inari** soon comes into view. With an area of 1,300sq km,
it is the third-largest lake in Finland. It possesses an air of wild,
untamed beauty that is further emphasised by its 3,000 islands,
some of which are little more than rocks. It is frozen over for nearly
half the year, and there are few roads to speak of along its shores.
So the few (mostly Lapp) fishermen that inhabit the lonely huts along
its shores rely on boats and sledges as their chief mode of transport.
In traditional Lapp religion, Lake Inari is looked on as a special holy
lake.

The road continues its meandering course through the wild
Lapland scenery. About half-way to Inari the road passes the
⌘   Karhunpesäkivi or 'Bears' Den Rock'. This rock is full of caves that
40km   were indeed once inhabited by bears.
Inari   The small settlement of **Inari/Änar** is situated at the westernmost point of Lake Inari, where the Juutuanjoki enters an inlet called
the Ukonselkä. Inari is the centre of an administrative district with an
area of over 17,000sq km, but with a population of only 7,000. The
village itself has only about 100 residents, most of whom are Lapp.
Inari looks amazingly friendly and hospitable as one approaches it
across the wild tundra. The village was destroyed at the beginning of
World War II, and was rebuilt on modern lines. It is centred around
a lovely wooden church.

On the nearby island of **Pielpajärvi** there is an old wooden
church built in the early eighteenth century. It was built for the Lapps
when they were converted to Christianity (a process which was never
quite completed) on the site of a former pagan temple. The church
can be reached by boat, but the only services held there are to
celebrate the birth of St John the Baptist at midsummer. Not far away
is another island called **Ukonkivi**, which means 'God's Rock'. This
was the site of another Lapp temple.

⌂   The Lapp Open-air Museum is of particular interest at Inari. It
includes a Lapp village, reindeer stables, a herdsmen's camp and a
fishing village. The village provides hotel, guesthouse and chalet
accommodation. Anglers can get a permit from the forestry office for
fishing in local waters, which are full of fish. The Juutanjoki flows out
of the Paadarjärvi, which in turn is filled by other famous fishing rivers
such as the Lemmenjoki and the Vaskojoki. In the summer there are

frequent boat trips, both along the rivers and to different parts of the lake.

Excursion to the Lemmenjoki National Park

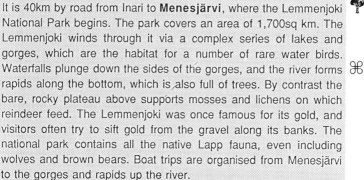

It is 40km by road from Inari to **Menesjärvi**, where the Lemmenjoki National Park begins. The park covers an area of 1,700sq km. The Lemmenjoki winds through it via a complex series of lakes and gorges, which are the habitat for a number of rare water birds. Waterfalls plunge down the sides of the gorges, and the river forms rapids along the bottom, which is also full of trees. By contrast the bare, rocky plateau above supports mosses and lichens on which reindeer feed. The Lemmenjoki was once famous for its gold, and visitors often try to sift gold from the gravel along its banks. The national park contains all the native Lapp fauna, even including wolves and brown bears. Boat trips are organised from Menesjärvi to the gorges and rapids up the river.

Road 4 goes due north from Inari, and soon arrives at the tiny village of **Kaamanen**. Kaamanen is situated just off the road, and consists of no more than a few houses, a large Lapp school and a post station.

Inari
30km
Kaamanen

Kaamanen is the main supply centre for the Skolt Lapps that live scattered across the Sevettijärvi region to the north-east of here. They are all refugees from regions which were occupied by the Soviet Union. Their Eastern Orthodox faith is not the only feature that distinguishes them from other Lapps. Their costume, appearance and customs are also different. The community has just one church, where an itinerant priest holds a service just twice a year. Sledges are the chief mode of transport in the winter, when the post is delivered from Kaamanen in a 'snow-bus' — a large vehicle like a caterpillar tractor. During the thaw the region is cut off from the outside world.

A few kilometres north of Kaamanen the road forks. The right fork leads along Road 98 to **Utsjoki** (95km), which is Finland's most northerly community. Utsjoki lies to the south of the Tenojoki (in Norwegian Tana), which forms the border with Norway. There is no way across the river, but a road leads along the south bank, parallel to the Norwegian Road 92 on the opposite shore. After Nuorgam it crosses the Norwegian border, and joins Road 6 at Skipagurra (see

The Visitor's Guide to Norway).

The main route, however, follows the left fork north of Kaamanen. Road 4 continues through the uninhabited tundra wastes, past occasional groups of crippled birches and Lapp settlements. It also passes close to some famous fishing rivers such as the Kaamasjoki and the Kielajoki. Drivers should beware of reindeer, which often graze on the roadside and wander across the road.

65km
Norwegian
border

Karigasniemi is the Finnish customs post on the Norwegian border. It lies immediately below the Ailigas (623m (2,043ft)), the holy mountain of the Lapps. The border is formed by the Tenojoki (in Norwegian Tana), which is spanned by a bridge. Road 4 now becomes the Norwegian Road 96, but it is another 7km to the Norwegian customs post at Elevemunningen. (The route from now on is also described in *The Visitor's Guide to Norway.*)

18km
Karasjok

The road soon arrives at the Lapp settlement of **Karasjok** on the banks of the Karasjokka. The village has a post office and tourist accommodation. The region is so cold that the ground often remains frozen throughout the year. Only the narrow surface layer thaws, in spite of more than 2 months of continuous daylight in the summer.

Soon after Karasjok there is a right turn along Road 92. This runs back to the Finnish border, which is formed by the River Tana/ Tenojoki. But instead of crossing the border, the road follows the north bank of the river all the way to Tana bru, where it enters Road 6 to Kirkenes.

Road 96 continues north-westwards across the tundra. The road is unmetalled in places, but is nonetheless quite driveable. After another 19km it arrives at Nattvatnstua — a tourist hut that is prettily situated by a lake. About 10km later there is a wonderful view of the mountains, which become gradually closer as the road carries on northwards. Some of the more northerly mountains are over 1,000m (3,280ft) high, and are covered in snow throughout the summer. The road also passes numerous lakes and wide rivers.

75km
Lakselv

At **Lakselv** (population 2,200) the road finally enters the Norwegian Arctic Road (Road 6) at the point where it rounds the southern end of the Porsangerfjord. Lakselv is situated at the mouth of the river of the same name (*lakselv* actually means 'salmon river'). The town provides a camping site and simple overnight accommodation.

If one goes straight on at Lakselv, one simply comes out at the

Brown bears, to be found in the Lemmenjoki National Park

airport. A right turn along Road 6 leads north-east out of Lakselv, and carries on towards Kirkenes (about 340km). But the present route goes left along Road 6, which runs due north along the western shore of the Porsangerfjord.

The road stays close to the shore, passing a few tiny settlements and isolated homesteads. There are some lovely views of the islands in the fjord. After 54km the road turns west along a small side-branch of the fjord called the Olderfjord. In clear weather there is a marvellous view along the Porsangerfjord to the bird island of Store Tamsøy and the Arctic Sea beyond.

64km
Olderfjord

It is another 10km to **Olderfjord** at the end of the fjord. At this point the Arctic Road (Road 6) turns southwestwards and carries on down the west coast of Norway towards Trondheim (see Route 7). But the present route turns right along Road 95, which goes north in the direction of the North Cape.

This road soon arrives at **Russenes**, which was once the ferry port for the North Cape. Because of this it provides a small amount of tourist accommodation and a camping site. Like many settlements along this route, it is too amorphous to be called a village as such, consisting mostly of a few scattered buildings.

Road 95 keeps close to the shore of the Porsangerfjord as it continues due north towards Kåfjord. During the first 25km to the Lapp encampment at Svartvik, the road goes through a 3km-long tunnel and climbs up the cliffside to a height of 250m (830ft). After another 10km the road draws level with the bird island of Store Tamsøy, which is also a nature reserve. It is unfortunately often obscured by sea mists. The road passes close to the pier at Repvåg, from which boats also used to go to the North Cape.

70km Kåfjord

It is another 25km to the present ferry port of **Kåfjord**. The ferry to Honningsvåg runs ten times daily. It takes 45 minutes, and there are excellent facilities on board. In the high season it runs throughout the 'night' — if one could call it that during the period of the midnight sun! Visitors may either take their cars across or else go as foot passengers and continue by bus. As the ferry takes only eighteen cars and 200 passengers, the latter option is usually preferable in view of the possible queues. Moreover, there is an alternative foot ferry service taking only 20 minutes, and the roads on the island are very steep and narrow.

Honningsvåg (by ferry)

✳

The fishing port of **Honningsvåg** (population 4,000) on the island of Magerøy has a large frozen-fish factory and a national school of fisheries. The pilot station is important for boats, and the picturesque harbour has a number of interesting features. The island is inhabited by groups of Karasjok Lapps who between them own more than 3,000 reindeer.

⌘

The road to the North Cape runs across a steep neck of land to **Nordmannsett**, where there is a large Lapp encampment and a reindeer exhibition. Fishing trips are organised to the nearby Skipsfjord. The road runs alongside the Skipsfjord and climbs steeply to the highest point of the route (312m (1,023ft)). There is a marvellous view of the North Cape and of the rest of the island of Magerøy. It is now only another 17km to the North Cape. The road passes a turning to **Skarsvåg**, which is the most northerly fishing village in the world.

33km North Cape

The **North Cape** (in Norwegian Nordkapp) rises 307m (1,007ft) above the sea below, at a latitude of 71° 10' 21". Most visitors find it rather disappointing: a bare, rocky headland like many others along this irregular stretch of coastline. Strictly speaking it is not quite the most northerly point of Europe, the nearby Knivskjelodden being at 71° 11' 8". This is inaccessible by land, but in clear weather it is visible to the west of the North Cape.

The local climate is such that clear, sunny days are a rare event here. Too often the only reward for the long journey is a thick bank of sea fog that obscures everything. But for visitors who are lucky enough to find clear weather, especially during a midsummer night, the experience is quite unforgettable. It is true that the midnight sun can be equally attractive from other parts of the same coast, but this in no way diminishes its beauty at the North Cape. The midnight sun lasts here from 14 May to 30 July.

One must also note the Nordkapphalla: an attractive building of undressed local stone, with large picture windows for admiring the view from indoors. It is full of souvenir stalls selling some of the most incredible junk, such as a certificate stating that one has visited the North Cape. One can buy photos or transparencies of the midnight sun at the Cape — which is especially useful if the weather has ruined one's chances of taking a good picture oneself. And surely everyone will want to take home a picture of the famous signpost at the northernmost tip of· the cape, where the Lapps once set up a sacrificial altar.

5 THE ROAD OF THE FOUR WINDS

Along the Swedish Border and into Norway

Kemi • Tornio • Pello • Muonio (Pallastunturi) • Palojoensuu • (Enontekiö) • Kaaresuvanto • Kilpisjärvi • Skibotn

What the Route Has to Offer

This route provides an alternative to the second part of Route 4 through Finnish Lapland. It runs along the Finnish–Swedish border, and passes through Finland's only true mountains before crossing into the Norwegian county of Finnmark. The route can be used in combination with Routes 3, 4 and 7, whether in whole or in part. One possible option is to continue northwards to the North Cape along the Norwegian Arctic Road (see Route 7), then return south again via the Finnish Arctic Road (see Route 4). There are other possible ways of combining this route with a trip through Norway and/or Sweden (see also *The Visitor's Guide to Norway* and *The Visitor's Guide to Sweden*).

The Route

Kemi The route goes north from **Kemi** along the E4/Road 4. Six kilometres out of Kemi, and just past the airport, there is a major road junction: Road 4 goes right towards Rovaniemi (see Route 4), while the present route goes left along the E4/Road 21 towards the border

28km town of Tornio.

Tornio **Tornio/Torneå** is linked via a causeway to the Swedish town of **Haparanda**. The two towns lie either side of the mouth of the Tornionjoki/Torneälv. Finland's only rail link with Sweden crosses the border at this point. However, freight and passengers have to be transferred onto a different train at Tornio, because the Finnish (and

156

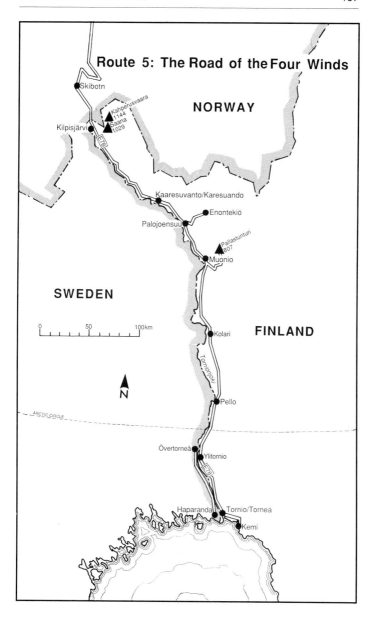

Russian) railways have a different gauge from those in the rest of Europe. Tornio has been a port since the early Middle Ages. The seventeenth-century wooden church contains a number of interesting wood carvings. The modern town and its Swedish counterpart have almost grown together. There are several camping sites and holiday settlements to the north of the town, which are mostly patronised by anglers.

The route leaves Tornio along the E78/Road 21, or Road of the Four Winds, which runs along the Finnish bank of the river. The road was given its name by the Lapp poet Yrjö Kokko, presumably after the cap worn by the local Lapps. As with other groups of Lapps, their costume has a special feature that distinguishes it from that of other groups. In this case it is a four-tasselled cap that is supposed to represent the four winds — hence the name of the road.

The Road of the Four Winds has been much improved in recent years, but is still unmetalled in places. It mostly runs close to the Finnish–Swedish border, which is always formed by a river, whether by the Tornionjoki or by its tributary. A more minor road runs parallel along much of the Swedish side of the border as far as Kaaresuvanto/ Karesuando. A railway also runs parallel as far as just beyond Kolari — the most northerly railway in Finland.

The Tornionjoki/Torneälv is a famous salmon river. Anglers come to fish its waters from all over the world. The two most popular angling sites are at the Kiviranta Rapids just north of Tornio, and 14km further north at the Kukkola Rapids.

The valley is surprisingly densely populated. The E78/Road 21 goes through **Karunki** and several other small settlements, all of which were badly damaged at the end of World War II. Most of them are linked to a 'twin' settlement with an almost identical name on the Swedish bank of the river — Karungi, for example. Most of these names are of Lapp origin. Ferries and other boats cross the river between corresponding villages. The border traffic is subject to no customs formalities between Scandinavian countries. However, the ferries are not usually suitable for motor vehicles.

74km
Aavasaksa

Soon before Kauliranta, and opposite the Swedish village of Övertorneå, there is a hill with a lookout tower to the right of the road. It is called **Aavasaksa** (242m (794ft)), and affords a wide panorama of the surrounding area, extending far into Sweden. At midsummer

Pallastunturi Fell

the midnight sun shines at the top of the hill, even though it is south of the Arctic Circle. This is in fact the most southerly point in Finnish Lapland from which the midnight sun can be seen.

The river is now narrower, and forms several stretches of rapids. Near Juoksenki, about 13km beyond Kauliranta, the route crosses the **Arctic Circle**, or in Finnish the Napapiiri. The road crosses the railway several times, and passes through a number of small settlements.

The next border crossing to Sweden is at **Pello**. Only 12km from here is the lovely old village of **Konttajärvi**, with its beautiful old wooden houses. It is one of the few local villages to have been spared the ravages of World War II.

55km
Pello

After Pello the E78 begins to run at some distance from the border river. The forests become increasingly wilder as the road approaches the village of **Sieppijärvi**. This is a market centre for the scattered homesteads and settlements in the area around, many of which are inhabited by Lapps.

The next place of any size is **Kolari**, where there is another border

62km
Kolari

crossing to Sweden. There are road connections from here to the
Swedish mining district of Kiruna (see *The Visitor's Guide to Sweden*). Shortly after Kolari the railway comes to an end. The landscape
quickly becomes more mountainous. The often bare, rounded peaks
⌘ (*tunturi*) rise like beacons above the forest. They include the
Yllästunturi (718m (2,355ft)) and the Lainiotunturi (635m (2,083ft)),
80km both of which are visible to the right of the road.

Muonio   At **Muonio** there is a major road junction, where Road 79 comes
in from Rovaniemi and Meltaus.

Excursion to the Pallastunturi

Muonio is a good centre for excursions into the Pallastunturi — the
nearby mountain range with peaks over 800m (2,624ft). The approach road turns left off Road 79 at Särkijärvi; it comes to an end at
the Pallastunturi Tourist Hotel, which stands on the tree line at an
altitude of 425m (1,394ft).

⌘   There are numerous marked pathways through the surrounding
forests to the many lakes in the area. Visitors should note that they
are in a nature reserve. Camping is only allowed in the immediate
vicinity of the hotel. There is further accommodation available in the
tourist huts that are built along the roadside.

♨   The hotel also has a small museum attached, with displays
showing the minerals, plants and animals of Finnish Lapland. There
is also information on things to do in the area. The mountains are a
popular region for winter sports, while in summer the many lakes and
rivers are a paradise for anglers.

Muonio   The Road of the Four Winds continues north-westwards from Muonio
✳ through a mostly uninhabited region. It passes the lovely old village
50km of **Ylimuonio**, which is typical of traditional Lapp settlements. After
Palojoen- 50km the E78 comes to another major junction at **Palojoensuu**,
suu with a road going off to Enontekiö.

✳ **Excursion to Enontekiö** (28km each way)
The village of Enontekiö is situated to the north-east of Palojoensuu.
It is one of the most beautiful of all Lapp villages, lying between the
meadows and the forest on the northern shore of the Ounasjärvi.
Enontekiö is an important religious and commercial centre for the

Church at Kemijärvi on the Arctic Circle

Muonio from the river banks

Lapp by her encampment near Enontekio

Lapps in the area around. On special occasions they assemble here in their traditional costume to stage a folk festival, though this usually happens outside the main tourist season. There are several small roads leading to outlying Lapp settlements such as Nunnanen (42km). The Lapps in this area are mostly involved in reindeer herding. In the summer they follow their herds across the Norwegian border and north towards the Arctic Ocean.

The Road of the Four Winds carries on from Palojoensuu to the border village of **Kaaresuvanto**, with its Swedish 'twin' Karesuando on the opposite bank of the river. The two villages together form a market centre for the local Lapps, who pay little heed to national frontiers. There are road connections from here to the towns of Jokkmokk and Kiruna in Swedish Lapland (see *The Visitor's Guide to Sweden*). *Palojoensuu 40km Kaaresu- vanto*

The E78 again runs close to the Swedish border, following the course of the small border river through the mountains of Hirvasvuopio. There is no longer a road on the Swedish side of the border, and the countryside is uninhabited apart from a few isolated homesteads along the way such as Kelottijärvi and Itto. The scenery becomes more mountainous, with summits over 1,000m (3,280ft).

The road eventually arrives at **Kilpisjärvi**, which is the final outpost of Finland. It is situated next to a lake of the same name, and overlooked by the Saanatunturi (1,029m (3,375ft)), the holy mountain of the Lapps. Kilpisjärvi lies close to the point where the Finnish, Swedish and Norwegian borders meet. Finland's highest mountain, the Haltiatunturi (1,328m (4,356ft)), is some distance to the north of here. *112km Kilpisjärvi*

The road crosses the Norwegian border immediately beyond the Siilastupa tourist hut, which is in the Mallan National Park. The Norwegian customs post is 12km further on at Gardeborre next to Lake Galgo. The E78 descends along the valley of the Skibotnelv to **Skibotn**, where it comes into the E6, or Norway's Arctic Road. One can follow this in either direction (see Route 7). *44km Skibotn*

6 ÅLAND/AHVENANMAA

These islands effectively form a bridge between Finland and Sweden. There are 6,554 of them in all, amounting to a total land area of 450sq km distributed over a sea area of more than 10,000sq km. The 23,000 inhabitants live on only eighty of the islands, while some of the others are often little more that nameless rocks or skerries.

The islands can be reached by ferry from Finland or Sweden. The main port of Mariehamn/Maarianhamina is served by ferries from Turku/Åbo and Naantali/Nådendal on the Finnish mainland, and from Stockholm, Norrtälje and Kapellskär in Sweden. There is a further service from Grisslehamn to Storby on the island of Eckerö. For more details about ferry services, please turn to page182.

From a geographical point of view, the islands straddle the entrance to the Gulf of Bothnia. The channel between Åland and Sweden is known in Swedish as Ålands Hav. The main nucleus of the archipelago is on the western side towards Sweden, while the eastern side towards southern Finland consists mostly of smaller islands scattered across a wide area of sea.

The main nucleus to the west includes the largest of the islands, known as Fasta Åland or 'mainland Åland', because it was the original island after which the whole group was named (Åland means 'water-land'). The only town, Mariehamn, is also situated on the main island, which is linked by bridges to the other islands that form the nucleus. These islands are well served by roads, and are the only ones to have been opened up to tourism, apart from the Pargas-Korpo group near Turku/Åbo, which are easily accessible from the Finnish mainland. The smaller inhabited islands are served only by local ferries, which are rarely suitable for carrying motor vehicles.

Åland is a paradise for holiday boats of all kinds, including motorboats and yachts, with innumerable island moorings to choose

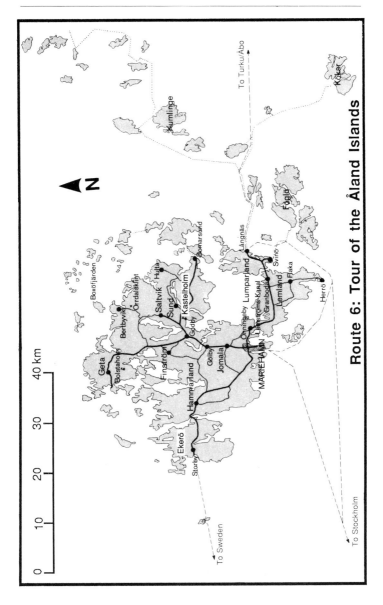

Route 6: Tour of the Åland Islands

from. Car drivers may take a vehicle plus trailer to Mariehamn, and are recommended to take their cars if they plan to stay for any length of time. Visitors on short stays can happily leave their vehicles behind, as the main islands and villages are well served by buses.

Åland is the ideal destination for the visitor who seeks solitude and who also likes the sea. The main islands provide fertile agricultural land interspersed with meadows, leafy woodlands and massive red granite cliffs. The richness of the vegetation owes much to the moderating effect of the sea on the climate, which even allows orchids to grow here. Only 4km north of Mariehamn, there is a fascinating nature reserve: an area of open woodland with an amazingly varied flora.

Åland was the earliest part of Finland to be settled. The first settlers from Sweden arrived in historical times, though there is archaeological evidence of human habitation going back as far as 3,000 years. The islands were very important during the heyday of sailing ships, when deep-water vessels brought grain to Europe from Australia.

The inhabitants are almost exclusively of Swedish origin. Swedish is therefore the main language and the official medium of communication. The province of Åland is to a large extent self-governing. It even has its own flag and its own stamps. This goes a long way towards satisfying the people's strong desire for independence.

Åland belonged to the Swedish Crown for many centuries, but fell to the Russians in 1809, when they took over the Finnish mainland. After World War I Åland was handed over to Finland against the wishes of its inhabitants, who had stronger leanings towards Sweden. It was, however, granted a special constitution. It was demilitarised, and the people were exempted from military service.

Detailed tourist information about Åland is available from Ålands Turistförening, Norra Esplanadgatan 1, Mariehamn.

Mariehamn/Maarianhamina

With a population of 9,500, Mariehamn is the only town in Åland. It is prettily situated on a peninsula on the southern coast of the main island, flanked on either side by two outstanding natural harbours. The two harbours are linked by a kilometre-long avenue of lime trees,

Wooden fishing huts, Åland

and the town is often known as the 'town of a thousand lime trees'.

Mariehamn forms the transport headquarters for the whole archipelago. It has an airport, and several boats a day make the 6-hour voyage to either Stockholm or Turku/Åbo. There are good bus routes to the villages on the main islands, and smaller boats to the other inhabited islands further east. The roads on the main islands are in excellent condition.

Mariehamn has several first-class hotels — the only ones on the islands — plus guesthouses and other tourist accommodation. It is also well supplied with camping sites and marinas.

The town belongs to the old parish of Jomala, and was founded as late as 1861 by Swedish settlers under Tsar Alexander II. It soon took over from the former island capital of Sund, 40km to the north, which diminished in importance following the Crimean War, with the destruction of the nearby Russian fortress at Bomarsund by British and French fleets.

There is little of great historical value in this town, which is reminiscent of southern Sweden. But the houses are often pretty and stylish, with lush, well-kept gardens and innumerable lime trees. The profuse vegetation is encouraged by the relatively mild island climate. The 24m-high (79ft) Badhusberg is topped by a water tower with a viewing platform, affording a lovely view of the town and the sound together with the nearby islands.

The Åland Museum at Mariehamn was voted the best museum in Europe in 1982. It chiefly contains archaeological and historical collections illustrating the history of the islands. Also worth seeing is the Maritime Museum, which documents the history of the great sailing ships that once made Åland so important. It recalls the great sailor Gustav Erikson and the intrepid sea captains who made the islands so famous throughout the maritime world.

The local shipping companies bought and used ships from all over the world, including famous vessels from the Hamburg Flying P Line such as the *Pamir* and the *Passat*, which was later sold back. The most famous of these ships is the *Pommern*, an old four-master, which remains as a living witness to the great days of sailing. It lies at anchor in the West Harbour, and has been turned into a museum. The Navigator's Monument on the nearby promenade is dedicated to the many sailors that still live here.

Just north of the town towards the airport is the Ramsholmen Nature Reserve (see above). Further information about this can be obtained from the local tourist office.

Going West from Mariehamn

There is a major crossroads just to the north of Mariehamn. All the main overland routes lead off from here, making the town a good starting point for touring Åland. Visitors without cars will find that all the main radial routes are well served by buses. Moreover, none of the distances involved are very great.

A left turn at the crossroads brings one quickly out to the west. The first small village of **Näfsby** is just 20km from Mariehamn. It is closely followed by **Hammarland**, where the thirteenth-century stone church is typical of Åland. For the islands were settled and converted to Christianity very much earlier than the Finnish mainland.

The road continues westwards, crossing the Marsund via a bridge onto the island of **Ekerö**. It passes a similar thirteenth-century church at the village of the same name. Ten kilometres from

Windmill, Mariehamn

Hammarland on the west coast of Ekerö is the ferry port of **Storby**, which is the main village on the island. The ferry crosses from here to Grisslehamn on the Swedish coast in only $2^1/_2$ hours, making it by far the shortest crossing to Sweden.

Storby was once famous as the last post office on the way to Sweden. The fishermen and farmers of Ekerö were responsible for getting post across the channel to Sweden. The task was not an easy one, and in winter it often involved a trek across the ice. The post office is a rather pretentious-looking building, erected under the Tsars to spite Sweden.

Storby provides plenty of holiday accommodation and a camping site. The harbour is as popular with anglers and fishermen as the waters close to Hammarsund and Ekerö.

Going North from Mariehamn

If one carries on due north from the crossroads north of Mariehamn,
one soon comes to the village of **Jomala** (10km). The twelfth-
century stone church is the oldest on the island. The parish, to which
Mariehamn also belongs, is also the oldest on the island. For this is
where the first Swedish settlers put down their roots. There is also
evidence nearby of much earlier habitation, including dolmen tombs
from the second century BC.

Further north at **Gölby** the road forks. The turning to the right
leads across a long inlet to **Godby**, where there is another fork. A left
turn here leads due north again to **Finström**, where the thirteenth-
century stone church contains some fascinating medieval frescos
and sculptures.

Another 15km further north is **Geta**, the most northerly village on
the island, which also has a medieval stone church. To the north of
the village is the Getaberg, which at 107m (351ft) is the second-
highest point on the island, with cliffs dropping sheer into the sea.
There is a road to the restaurant at the summit, from which there are
paths leading down to the interesting caves nearby. To the south of
Geta is Bolstaholm Castle. The large, irregular inlet south of here is
the Hammarsund, around which there are several popular seaside
resorts.

If one goes right instead of left at Godby (see above), the road
leads across another inlet, after which there is yet another fork. A left
turn brings one to **Saltvik**, with its thirteenth-century stone church.
It is surrounded by early and prehistoric remains, including a Viking
settlement. The road north of here runs through hills covered in fields
that are typical of Åland. It comes out at the highest point of the island,
the Orrdalsklint (130m (426ft)), from which there is a marvellous view
of the nearby islands across the Boxöfjärd.

If one goes right instead of left before Saltvik (see above), one
quickly comes across Kastelholm Castle on the right. This was built
in the fourteenth century on the site of a previous ruin, and the
Swedish governor of Åland resided here until 1634. One wing of the
castle was later restored, and was used by the Swedish kings as a
summer residence and hunting lodge. It now contains a cultural and
historical museum.

Further east, the old village of **Sund** is picturesquely situated by

Kastelholm Castle near Saltvik

an inlet, and is built around the famous Wenni Cross. The medieval church contains some fascinating stone paintings. Sund appears to have been important in the early Middle Ages before the arrival of Christianity. For the Viking fortification of Borgboda to the north is one of the largest-known sites of its kind in the whole of Scandinavia. Sund and its immediate environs have become a popular holiday area.

Not far away is the open-air museum of Jens Karl Gården. This reconstructed medieval farm with all its side buildings contains a comprehensive collection showing the peasant culture of the time.

Ten kilometres further east is **Bomarsund**, where the Russians built a large fortification and anchorage point for their fleet in the early nineteenth century. It was intended to guard the entrance to the Gulf of Bothnia, but was completely destroyed in 1854 during the course of the Crimean War. As a result of this the older town of Sund gave way to the new settlement of Mariehamn as the administrative centre of the islands. The old castle ruins are a popular tourist spot, with a beach and a good large camping site close by. There is also a good viewing point on the nearby 'Devil's Hill'.

Kökar Church

Going East from Mariehamn

The road that goes right at the crossroads north of Mariehamn leads via Önningeby to a bridge over the Lemström Canal. The canal was built between 1880 and 1882 to link Ålands Hav with Lumparen Sound. It changed Lemland from a peninsula into an island, but considerably shortened the sea journey from Mariehamn to Turku.

Sixteen kilometres south-east of Mariehamn is the village of **Lemland**, where there is a ruined stone chapel on top of the nearby Lemböte Hill. It was built around 1200, probably on the site of a pre-Christian temple, and close to the largest Viking cemetery on the islands.

There is a small road going south off the main road. It runs partly along the coastline and partly through extensive woodlands, and goes via Flaka to Herrö, the most southerly point of the island. Though of strategic importance in both World Wars, it is now completely deserted.

A few kilometres beyond Granboda, the main road crosses via a bridge to the island of **Lumparland**, where it soon arrives at **Svinö**.

Both Svinö and **Långnäs** to the north of it provide small ferry services to the rocky islands further east.

The most interesting of these islands are probably **Föglö**, Kumlinge and Kökar, with their old churches and scattered farmsteads. **Kökar** to the south has become popular with artists in recent years. A fascinating Bronze Age village has also been unearthed on this bare, rocky island. The fifteenth-century church on **Kumlinge** contains some beautiful decorations. All three islands are famous for their summer festivals.

Just north of Kumlinge is **Enklinge**, which has a small open-air museum with buildings from the eighteenth century. Finally there is **Sottunge**, which with a population of 150 is the smallest parish in Finland.

Other Islands

The many scattered islands to the east of the archipelago provide a multitude of beautiful sites for a boating and/or camping holiday. Those of them that are inhabited provide friendly if modest accommodation.

The main islands to the east form a 60km-long east–west chain. They are linked by ferries, both to each other and to the coastal island of Pargas/Parainen next to Turku/Åbo. The main islands in the chain (from east to west) are **Nagu/Nauvo**, **Korpo/Korppoo** and **Houtskär/Houtskari**. The ferry from Korpo to Houtskär crosses the Kyrkfjärd, which is the main shipping lane to the port of Turku. There are several beaches and camping sites on the islands of Korpo and Nagu, which also provide ample accommodation for yachts.

7 RETURN ROUTE THROUGH NORWAY

The Norwegian Arctic Road from the North Cape to Trondheim

Strictly speaking this route does not belong in a book on Finland. It does, however, provide a possible return route for visitors who have travelled north along Route 4. Parts of it can also be used in conjunction with Route 5, or by drivers combining both of these routes through Finnish Lapland. The whole of this route is of course described in more detail in *The Visitor's Guide to Norway*.

The route follows the Norwegian Arctic Road for most of its length. This road is very much better than it used to be. It is nearly all metalled, and the worst of the bends have been made smoother and more manageable. New bridges have been built to avoid long detours around fjords and time-wasting ferry crossings. The ferries in particular made it difficult to plan the journey ahead, and were sometimes rather expensive. The few ferry crossings that remain are much shorter. Extra boats have been laid on, made available when other ferry routes became redundant, and this has shortened the waiting times considerably.

The Route

The first part of the route merely retraces the last section of Route 4 between the **North Cape** and **Olderfjord** (see page 153). At Olderfjord it turns west along Road 6, which it follows for the rest of its course. The first section is rather bare of vegetation as it is well beyond the tree line.

At **Skaidi** there is a right turn along Road 94, which goes via Repparfjorddalen and across the Kvalsund to **Hammerfest** (57km). Hammerfest is the most northerly town in the world, and is very much worth an excursion. It was rebuilt on modern lines following its destruction at the end of World War II.

North Cape
103km
Olderfjord

13km
Skaidi

Road 6 continues south-west through a typical fjell landscape —
a boggy plateau, where one may meet wandering Lapps following
their reindeer herds through their summer haunts.

87km
Alta

After 87km the road arrives at **Alta** (population 3,000). This port
next to the Altafjord is a market centre for the Lapps, and at one time
was a whaling station. There is a left turn here along Road 93, which
leads south through the uninhabited mountains to the Finnish village
of Enontekiö, eventually coming out into the Road of the Four Winds
at Palojoensuu (see Route 5). This road is only partly made up; it is
isolated and steep in places, and is only suitable for the more
adventurous driver.

Road 6 goes north along the western shore of the Altafjord before
turning west again along the Langfjord to **Langfjordbotn**. Shortly
afterwards it crosses the county boundary from Finnmark into Troms,
and continues south-west via Alteidet, Burfjord and Badderen. Then
there is a new bridge across the **Sørstraumen**, a narrow fjord
entrance with strong tidal currents like those of a fast-flowing river.

82km
Langfjord-
botn

97km
Nordreisa

The road continues, partly along the coast, to **Nordreisa**. It then
arrives on the eastern shore of the Lyngenfjord, which it follows south
to **Oldendalen**. Travellers once had to wait ages here for a ferry to
Lyngseidet, where the old road continues south along the opposite
shore. The new road along the east shore to Skibotn bypasses this
ferry. At **Skibotn** it meets the E78 Road of the Four Winds, which
comes over the mountains from Finnish Lapland (see Route 5).

50km
Oldendalen

63km
Skibotn

Road 6 is now the E6 as well. It continues along the shore to
Oteren at the end of the fjord, where it rejoins the old road from
Lyngseidet. It then crosses a neck of land to Nordkjosbotn at the end
of another long fjord. The E78 goes right here for **Tromsø** (73km),
the famous whaling and seal-hunting station.

46km
Nordkjos-
botn

The E6 soon leaves the fjord, and continues inland over several
moderate passes to **Elverum** at the entrance to the Bardu Valley,
which the road then follows. The mountains on either side rise to
heights of well over 1,000m (3,280ft). The road carries on via
Brandvoll to **Fossbakken**, where the road comes into a wild valley
called Spansdalen. The scenery is particularly impressive along the
next section of the route to **Bjerkvik**, where the road meets the
Herjangsfjord. The E6 soon approaches Narvik, making a wide loop
around the Rombak, which was the site of a famous battle in 1940.

69km
Elverum

50km
Fossbakken

32km
Bjerkvik
⌘

35km   **Narvik** (population 15,500) is the most important iron-ore port in
Narvik Europe. The ores are brought over from the Swedish mining region
of Kiruna via the famous Ofot Railway to be loaded onto ships at
Narvik. Thanks to the warming effect of the Gulf Stream, the harbour
is ice-free in winter, just like others along the Norwegian coast. Narvik
was in the centre of fierce fighting in 1940, and thousands of German
and Allied soldiers are buried in the military cemetery here. The most
✳   interesting part of Narvik is the Malmkai, where the iron ore is loaded
onto ships throughout the day and night.

The section which follows was once littered with ferry crossings,
but most of these have now been either replaced or shortened by
means of new roads and bridges. The E6 runs south-west along the
shore of the Ofotfjord, crossing from Grindjord to Skærvik via a new
bridge. The road crosses a neck of land to another fjord, where the
former ferry from Forså to Sætran has also been replaced by bridges.

83km   Fifteen kilometres further on, there is a 35-minute ferry crossing
Skarberget from **Skarberget** to **Bognes**. Any delays nowadays are fortunately
minimal. The road continues southwards through the mountains via
107km   a series of steep passes and fjords; it is very twisty in places. The ferry
Bonnåsjøen crossing from **Bonnåsjøen** to **Sommarset** is still unavoidable, but
Sommarset is much shorter than it used to be thanks to a new road along the
(by ferry) eastern shore of the Sørfoldafjord. The previous ferry journey to
Sørfold was made even worse by the long waiting times involved.

48km   The Arctic Road continues mostly along the shore of the fjord to
Fauske **Fauske**, from where it is possible to make a short excursion along
Road 80 to **Bodø** (63km), the chief port of the Lofoten fishermen.

72km   The E6 meanwhile continues southwards via Rognan and Saltdal
Storjord to **Storjord**. The next section is very wild as the road carries on up
the Lønsdal, passing a number of Lapp settlements along the way.
Road and railway run closely parallel at this stage. Immediately after
40km   the station at Stødi, the road crosses the Arctic Circle (66° 33').
Bolna   Ten kilometres further on at **Bolna**, the E6 at last meets the tree
line again, which is marked by a rather stunted birchwood. The road
descends steeply along the Dunderlandsdal, passing a famous 20m-
72km   high (66ft) waterfall called the Reinfoss. It soon arrives at the modern
Mo i Rana town of **Mo i Rana**, with its broad, open streets. Mo has grown up
around an enormous smelting works based on ores brought down
from the Dunderlandsdal.

The E6 runs through delightful scenery along the shore of the ⌘
Ranafjord as far as Finneidfjord, then climbs and twists up the valley 41km
to **Korgen**. Korgen Power Station is the biggest in Norway, with an Korgen
output of about a quarter of a million kilowatts. It depends for its power
on the mighty Røssåga, which plunges down into the valley at this
point.

The E6 bears right up the hillside. It passes the mighty
Smedsengfjell (over 1,000m (3,280ft)) to the left, and crosses a
famous salmon river called the Fusta. It eventually comes down to 54km
the industrial port of **Mosjøen**, which depends for its livelihood on Mosjøen
aluminium smelting and timber shipment.

The road goes inland up the Bjorndal, and in places runs parallel
to the railway. After about 30km it passes a 16m-high (52ft) waterfall
called the Laksfoss. A salmon ladder has been constructed nearby
so that the salmon can climb past the waterfall. The next village is 44km
called **Fellingfors**; there was once a silver mine here.   Fellingfors

The E6 continues to climb as far as Majavatn, then begins to 95km
descend again. It goes through Brekkvasselv and carries on down Brekkvasselv
the Namsdal towards Grong, passing several waterfalls that have 56km
been harnessed for hydroelectricity. At **Grong** there is a right turn for Grong
the coastal port of Namsos.

Nine kilometres beyond Grong there is a famous waterfall called 9km
the Formofoss. At this point there is a left turn along Road 74, which Formofoss
runs east across the Swedish border. The E6 continues south-west, ✳
and runs along the shore of the Snåsavatn, one of Norway's largest 78km
inland lakes. The next town is Steinkjer, which is an important timber Steinkjer
port with a number of timber-related industries.

The E6 crosses a peninsula, and arrives on the shores of the 42km
Trondheimsfjord. After **Levanger** it goes inland again through the Levanger
hills, but returns to the shore at **Størdalshalsen**. The E6 then runs 50km
along the shore towards Trondheim via a number of seaside and Størdals-
industrial towns.   halsen
                                                                        33km
Trondheim (population 135,000) is the first large town on the Trondheim
route. There are several ways of continuing south from here, most of
which are described in *The Visitor's Guide to Norway*. The most
direct route, however, is to carry on along the E6 via Dombås
(200km) and the famous Gudbrandsdal, eventually arriving at Oslo
after another 321km. The road is excellent throughout.

8 ADVICE TO TOURISTS

The information on the pages which follow has been updated and revised to take account of changes. However further changes are always liable to occur. Complete accuracy cannot therefore be guaranteed and such information should be used for general guidance only.

Preparing for the Holiday

Travel Documents
A current valid passport is needed by visitors from the UK, USA and Canada, but no visa is required (the same applies to all Scandinavian countries) for a stay of up to 3 months. Spouses and children under sixteen may travel with their husband or wife and/or parents using a family passport.

Car Documents
A current driving licence from one's own country is quite sufficient for driving in Finland. Third-party insurance is compulsory, but proof of this is no longer required. The Green Card is now only optional but all visitors are recommended to take this additional protection. In the case of accident it provides immediate proof of insurance cover. No special permits are needed for a caravan or a boat.

Car Hire
There is a comprehensive network of car-hire services available all over the country. They are provided by both local and international firms. The major ferry and airline companies provide car-hire facilities from the port or airport of arrival. Cars can also be hired at some hotel receptions. If you are renting a car, all you need is a valid driver's licence.

176

Customs Regulations

These need not cause any problems. A verbal declaration is sufficient in most cases. Hand luggage is rarely searched, and customs officers usually act generously. Visitors are normally questioned by customs officers on entering Scandinavia. Questions normally concentrate on the importation of alcohol and tobacco. Normal holiday essentials are allowed in without question.

Boats and water-sports equipment such as outboard motors are also allowed free entry upon presentation of a certificate from a recognised water-sports organisation. Hunting equipment and fire-arms (though only for hunting) require a hunting permit from the local police authority at the place of arrival.

Finland is outside the EEC. An adult from a European country entering Finland may bring in the following quantities without paying duty: 200 cigarettes, or 100 cigarillos, or 50 cigars or 250g other tobacco goods; 2 litres of beer and 1 litre of wine(minimum age 18) plus 1 litre of spirits (minimum age 20); other luxury goods up to a value of 1,000mk (upon presentation of receipts). Customs officers are normally generous about camping equipment. For travellers from non-European countries, restrictions regarding drink are the same but an adult may bring in 400 cigarettes or 500g of other tobacco.

Pets

The import of all live animals and plants is basically forbidden. It is possible to bring a dog in with a special licence from the Finnish Consulate, but this is only granted on condition that the animal is vaccinated against rabies and kept in quarantine (at the cost of the owner) for a minimum of 4 months.

Postal Services

These are very good in Finland. Long-distance post is automatically sent by airmail without extra charge. It costs 2.30mk to send a postcard or a letter under 20g to a European country outside Scandinavia (1 January 1987). The outside Europe air rate is 2.80mk for a letter, 2.30mk for a postcard and it costs 1.70mk to send a postcard or letter under 20g within Scandinavia (1 January 1987). Poste restante letters are always delivered to the nearest main post office.

Telephone Services

When consulting a Finnish telephone directory, it is important to remember that the letters , **ä**, **ö** and **å** (in that order) come at the end of the alphabet after **z**. Local calls within an exchange in Finland cost a standard rate of 1mk (1987).

In Finland it is almost always possible to dial direct when making telephone calls abroad. The international code from Finland to the United Kingdom is **99044**; the code for the USA or Canada is **9901**. These should be followed by the dialling code for the exchange (minus the initial **0**) and then the number.

The international dialling code for Finland is **010 358** from the United Kingdom and **011 358** from the USA or Canada. This should be followed by the dialling code for the exchange (minus the initial 9) and then the number.

Currency and Exchange

The Finnish unit of currency is the Finnish Mark (*markka*, mk, fmk or Fmk), which is made up of 100 *penniä*. (The plural of *markka* is *markkaa*.) The exchange rate fluctuates continually, but on 5 May 1987 it stood as follows:

£1=7.43mk   US$1=$4.45mk
1mk=£0.13   1mk=US$0.22

The following coins are in use at present: 1 and 5 *penniä* (copper); 10, 20 and 50 *penniä* (brass); 1mk and 5mk (silver). The following notes are in current use: 5mk (new notes not made any longer), 10mk, 100mk, 500mk and 1,000mk.

There is no limit to the amount of Finnish or other currency that may be imported into Finland. A traveller resident abroad may export any amount of currency which he can prove to have brought in with him on arrival in Finland.

Exchange rates are so variable that it is impossible to say whether it is cheaper to change currency at home or on arrival in Finland. The best policy is to find out about the current situation from one's bank or travel agent.

Opening Hours

Shops in Finland are generally open from 8.30am to 5pm, department stores until 6pm and many markets until 8pm, weekdays. Some specialist shops in towns do not open until 9am. The normal closing time on Saturdays is 4pm. One exception is a shopping street near the main station in Helsinki, in which the shops are open at weekends until well into the night. Post offices are open from 9am to 5pm, and are closed on Saturdays and Sundays. Banks are generally open from 9.30am to 4pm. Filling stations are usually open from 7am to 9pm.

Cheques and Credit Cards
Eurocheques and travellers' cheques are normally accepted throughout Finland. The same is true of the main credit cards.

Health Care
Finland is a country of great distances, and although medical care is always available, it can often involve long journeys and waiting times. Visitors are therefore recommended to take a certain amount of self-medication with them, based on the advice of a doctor. It is, however, reassuring to know that the Finns are extremely clean and careful about hygiene.

Medical care is free for all Finnish citizens, and is subsidised for foreign visitors. A doctor or an ambulance can be obtained in cases of emergency outside normal surgery hours by telephoning the emergency number. This is usually **008** or **000**, but it is different in some parts of Finland.

UK residents should apply to the DHSS for a leaflet which gives details of reciprocal arrangements for medical treatment and contains application form E111 for certificate of entitlement.

Other visitors who are not covered by arrangements of this kind should take out short-term full-cover medical insurance.

Electricity
Electricity is the chief form of energy available in Finland, and its cost is relatively cheap. An electrical socket is normally available on camping sites at no extra cost. 220V AC at 50Hz is the norm, apart from a very few exceptions. Good hotels will normally provide adaptors. But the best way to overcome this problem is to take an extension lead and fit it with a Finnish plug on arrival in Finland.

Maps

A good map is essential for visitors who wish to drive around Finland. This is particularly important for those travelling in the far north of the country. One can either buy or order a good map from the nearest bookshop at home, or else buy one immediately on arrival in Finland. There is an excellent selection of maps on sale at the Surveyor-General Office Mapshop, (Maanmittaushallituksen), Karttakeshus, Etelä-Esplanadi 4, Helsinki, near the ferry harbour.

Clock Time

Finland has so-called Eastern European Time (EET), which is 2 hours ahead of Greenwich Mean Time (GMT). When Daylight Saving Time (DST) is in effect (29 March-27 September (1987)) time in Finland is 3 hours ahead of GMT. The difference between Eastern US Standard Time and Finnish Standard Time is 7 hours. To avoid confusion, clocks and watches should be reset to the new time prior to arrival in the country. Note also that arrival and departure times are always given in the time used at the place they refer to.

Rules and Regulations

Finland is a very free and liberal country, in which hard work has enabled its citizens to overcome the economic difficulties of the past. There are relatively few 'no entry' or prohibition signs in Finland, and these normally only affect traffic. Traffic signs in Finnish are usually totally incomprehensible to the foreign visitor, but most of them are explained in a document available at most customs entry points.

All prohibition signs should be strictly observed, especially those in border areas. Finland's policy of openness towards other countries means that it must observe the Soviet Union's demands for restricted access to border zones.

Most land outside built-up areas is the property of the state, and is free for everyone to use. Lakes are similarly open to all, and the only permits required are for hunting and fishing. However, visitors should be extremely careful not to disturb or damage the environment in any way.

Open fires are strictly forbidden on all open land. This is perfectly understandable considering the enormous damage that could result from a forest fire. Many of the lay-bys on Finnish roads provide covered seating and a protected fire-grate with firewood available. This is for the use of tourists, who should place a small contribution in the 'trust-the-motorist' box provided. Any fire must be carefully extinguished before leaving the lay-by where there is normally an unlimited supply of drinking water.

The Finns take enormous care of their environment. They are modest and unassuming in character, and foreign visitors should always make allowances for this. Loud or uproarious behaviour is viewed with suspicion, and can sometimes lead to tourists being refused service or even being thrown out of restaurants. The same applies to people who are drunk.

Shopping in Finland

Shopping is by no means cheap in Finland, but there are some things which are particularly recommended as souvenirs. Some of the best souvenirs are various items of woodcraft, including carvings and wickerwork. Finnish glass products in particular are renowned throughout the world. A large variety of these is available at reasonable prices in the big city department stores. Another speciality is silverware of all kinds, from the traditional to the modern.

The best places for buying food and everyday goods are the large stores and hypermarkets that are growing up around the edges of the cities. Campers and other self-catering visitors should note that not every village is provided with a general store. Even larger camping sites do not always have a shop on site.

Public Holidays

In Finland, as in other Scandinavian countries, the main public holidays coincide with religious festivals: Good Friday, Easter Monday, Ascension Day, Whit Monday, Christmas Day, Boxing Day and New Year's Day; All Saints' Day is celebrated on the first Saturday in November, and Epiphany on 6 January or the following Saturday.

May Night (*Vappu*) on 30 April takes the form of a spring festival, with carnivals and other celebrations lasting through the night into May Day, especially in university towns. Midsummer Night is celebrated on the Friday nearest 24 June, and again lasts into Midsummer Day on the Saturday. Independence Day is on 6 December.

School summer holidays throughout Finland are from 1 June to 18

August. They are the longest in Europe, and are observed by all types of educational establishment, including universities.

Sea Ferry Connections

There are no direct sea routes between the United Kingdom and Finland. Travellers wishing to go by road and ferry must first travel to Germany, Denmark or Sweden before continuing along one of the many Baltic routes.

Travellers with more time might possibly consider a combined Swedish and Finnish holiday, using one of the shorter ferry connections across the Gulf of Bothnia. The main Baltic Sea routes to Finland are listed in the section below.

Another possibility is to begin or end the holiday with a leisurely cruise along the Baltic. Some of the ships are equipped with such luxuries as a swimming pool, a sauna and a variety of restaurants. Sleeping accommodation varies from a rest-chair to a first-class cabin. The prices vary enormously, and the number of combinations is vast. So travellers who are contemplating this method of transport should seek the advice of travel and tourist agencies.

Ferry Services from Germany and Denmark

Travemünde–Helsinki
Finlines (Finnjet): 3–4 times weekly (22 hours)
TT Lines: weekly (39 hours)
Copenhagen–Helsinki
Finlines (Finnjet): daily (33 hours)

Direct Services from Sweden

Stockholm–Helsinki
Silja Lines: daily (14 hours)
Stockholm–Turku/Åbo
Silja Lines: daily (12 hours)
Sundsvall–Vaasa/Vasa
Oy Vaasa–Umeå AB: twice daily (9 hours)
Umeå–Vaasa/Vasa

Oy Vaasa–Umeå AB: 4 times daily (4 hours)
Skellefteå–Jakobstad/Pietarsaari
Jakob Lines: daily (5 hours)

Services from Sweden via Åland

Stockholm–Mariehamn–Turku/Åbo
Silja Lines: daily (7½ hours and 6½ hours)
Norrtälje–Mariehamn–Turku/Åbo
Silja Lines: several times daily (4½ hours and 6½ hours)
Kappellskär–Mariehamn–Naantali/Nådendal
Viking Line: daily (3½ hours and 8 hours)
Grisslehamn–Storby (Ekerö)
Ekerö Lines: daily (2½ hours)

Travel Within Finland

Finland is virtually an island from the point of view of public transport.
For in spite of its long borders with Sweden, Norway and the Soviet
Union, there are no major public transport routes across any of these
borders. Thus a Finnish holiday usually begins with an air flight or a
sea voyage.

Rail Travel
Finland has barely 6,000km of railways, belonging to the Finnish
State Railways (VR), which is surprisingly little for a country that
measures 1,160km from north to south. Only the south of the country
is well served by railways, and the network effectively ends at the
Arctic Circle. The one minor rail route into Sweden is marred by the
fact that the track gauge is different in the two countries. On the other
hand the prices are low, with a wide range of family reductions and
roundabout tickets that can also be used on some of the shipping
routes.

Air Travel
Finland's international airline company is Finnair, and there are
regular international flights to Helsinki. There are twenty airports
served by the internal air network, and inland air fares are astonish-

ingly low. Apart from the regular flights, there are special summer and winter excursions for tourists, plus a number of holiday packages combining air, bus and ferry. The system is further augmented by charter-plane (air-taxi) services and private aeroplanes, which are particularly important in the sparsely populated northern regions.

Boat Travel

Boats are an important means of transport, especially in the lake regions. The southern part of the country has a vast number of ferry routes linking the main towns via the major lake systems. Of particular interest are the so-called Silver Line linking Tampere with Hämeenlinna via two quite delightful routes, and the 'Poet's Highway' running north from Tampere along the Näsijärvi.

Both lines provide a parallel car-transfer service, whereby the car is carried separately and is ready to be picked up at the destination point. This so-called auto-pilot service is also provided for many of the other internal ferry routes including the waterbus (*vesibussi*) service from Lahti to Heinola.

The Saimaa lake system has a vast network of ferry services linking the many towns and resorts that border it, such as Lappeenranta, Savonlinna, Mikkeli, Kuopio, Joensuu and Punkaharju. There is also a special boat tour of the lake system lasting several days; cabin accommodation and catering facilities are provided on board. Inari in the far north provides a number of waterbus services across Lake Inari, enabling visitors to see parts of the lake that are totally inaccessible by road.

All in all, the number of lake tours and excursions available throughout Finland is far too vast to be enumerated. They vary enormously in length and in the size of boat used. For sea ferry services, please turn to page 182 above.

Road Travel

The Finnish road system was once considered a driver's nightmare, but has been greatly improved in recent years. In the more populated south the road network is fairly tightly drawn. The major long-distance routes are partly dual carriageway, and form motorways in the neighbourhood of cities such as Helsinki, Turku and Tampere.

The roads are much fewer in the sparsely populated northern

regions, but the main roads are good and well maintained. The few unsurfaced roads are regularly flattened by enormous rolling machines, especially after rain. Those that are more heavily used are regularly drenched with oil to keep them free of dust. But vehicles should nonetheless be driven with great care in view of the danger of loose chippings.

The major long-distance routes are plied by regular coach services. The timetables are arranged to include meal breaks and even overnight stops on the way.

In winter the roads are generally driveable, provided that the vehicle is fitted with suitable tyres. Though the snow is not cleared, it is quickly compressed by traffic into a firm layer of ice. Spikes and snow chains are allowed from 16 October to 15 April in southern Finland, and from 1 October to 30 April in central and northern Finland.

Advice to Drivers

Finland has most of the usual international traffic regulations, but there are some extra rules to be observed. The traffic drives on the right (as in all European countries apart from the United Kingdom and Ireland). As in the United Kingdom, seat belts are compulsory for the driver and the front-seat passenger. Vehicles must also be driven with at least the side lights on.

Main roads which are indicated as such have priority over minor roads. Where no priority is indicated, then the vehicle coming from the right has priority. Using the horn is prohibited in towns except in cases of danger. Outside built-up areas a driver must use the horn to indicate his intention of overtaking. The vehicle being overtaken should then reply with a hoot to indicate that the way past is clear.

According to the new speed regulations, 80km/h (50mph) is the standard speed limit on all roads outside built-up areas where no other speed limit is displayed. Other (indicated) speed limits range from 60km/h (37mph) to 120km/h (75mph) on motorways. In built-up areas the usual speed limit is 50km/h (31mph).

Parking on the street is only allowed if a parking place is specifically indicated (make sure it is not a bus stop), or if one can see at least 100m (328ft) in both directions.

The Finns tend to drive cautiously, especially in built-up areas. Driving while under the influence of alcohol or drugs is punished severely. The permitted blood-alcohol limit is very low, and conviction can lead to a prison sentence.

The Finnish roads are being continually improved, and most of the main roads are fully surfaced. Unmetalled surfaces are uncommon, and are mostly confined to side roads or a few main roads in the far north. These are usually kept free of dust by the application of oil, but there is always a danger of loose chippings being thrown up by the vehicle in front.

Emergency services are well organised in Finland as in other Scandinavian countries, and will quickly deal with a smashed windscreen. Shell garages in particular are windscreen specialists, and will provide a replacement from one of two central depots. Specialist garages are to be found all over Finland.

Some Important Traffic Signs

TIETYÖ — roadworks

AJA HITAASTI — drive slowly

KOKEILE JARRUJA — try your brakes

KELIRIKKO — frost damage

KAPEA SILTA — narrow bridge

LOSSI — ferry jetty

IRTOKIVIÄ — loose chippings

TIE SAVETTU — new road surface (danger of skidding)

HEIKKO TIENREUNA — beware soft verges

PAANNE — danger of skidding

AJO SALLITTUU OMALLA VASTUULLA — road used at driver's own risk

ALUERAJOITUS — regional speed limit

Accommodation

Hotels

Like other Scandinavian countries, Finland has a system of hotel cheques. The so-called *Finncheque* covers one person for one night's bed and breakfast in a double room. Children under four can stay free. In category-III hotels a modest lunch is also included. More than 130 hotels now belong to this scheme. Only the first night can be booked in advance, but further bookings can be made on arrival. Hotel cheques are valid from 1 June to 31 August, and a minimum of four cheques must be bought in advance of the departure date. They can be obtained through travel agents.

With the growth in the tourist trade, numerous motels and holiday homes have sprouted up in areas bordering the lakes and coasts. Lappeenranta even has a special holiday village with ample tourist accommodation. Visitors are recommended to book in advance. Information is available from the various tourist agencies

University towns offer yet another kind of board: the so-called summer hotels. These are student hostels that are let to visitors during the summer holidays. They are clean, simple and modern, and are normally self-catering. The rents are very reasonable.

The growth of tourism has also brought about an increase in the private guesthouse accommodation available. Houses with rooms to let are usually indicated by signs in several different languages.

Farm Holidays
This form of holiday has been available in Finland for many years, and is perhaps one of the cheapest and friendliest ways of getting to know the country and the people. Many farms offer self-catering accommodation in a building that is separate from the farm. Rowing boats are usually available, and a sauna is of course included in the price. Other farms can provide full or half board. More detailed information is available through tourist offices and travel agents.

Youth Hostels
Finland's 160 or so youth hostels are not just restricted to young people. They are clean and simple, and are available to adults provided there is space. They can, however, be full in the high season. It is advisable to obtain an international youth hostel card before going on holiday. Finnish youth hostels, known as *retkaily-maja*, carry the international youth hostel symbol of a blue-and-white triangle with the letters SRM inside it.

Camping

Camping is a national pastime in Finland. There are more than 360 camping sites distributed all over the country. Many of them have excellent facilities, and all of them provide a sauna. The more northern sites have fewer facilities than most Europeans would expect, but at the same time are usually very cheap. Camping sites are signposted according to the international convention. Many of them are listed in international camping guides available from motoring and travel agents.

It is also possible to pitch camp on open land on a suitable site — by a lake or a stream, for example. If the site is clearly on private land, it is normal etiquette to ask the permission of the landowner. An open fire is strictly prohibited.

At one time caravans were not allowed to be wider than the vehicle towing them. Though some brochures still state this, the present regulation is different. Nowadays an overall width limit of 2.4m (7.8ft) is imposed on all caravans and trailers.

Food and Drink

Finnish cuisine has often been summarised as 'mixed', reflecting the strong influences exerted by both Sweden and Russia during the course of the country's history. One notable Swedish import is the famous *smörgåsbord* or buffet meal, which is available in large restaurants and on Finnish ships. The Finnish version, known as *voileipäpöytä*, is possibly less refined but more substantial than the original Swedish version.

In addition there are a large number of local specialities that are served in country restaurants. Visitors are recommended to ask what the local specialities are, and preferably to have them explained as well.

One summer custom that has become almost universal in Finland is the crayfish platter. The crayfish season begins on about 20 July and lasts for 2 months. There are restaurants all over the country that specialise in this delicacy, known in Finnish as *rapuja*. They are clearly indicated by a large sign or a flag with an enormous crayfish on it. The whole thing has developed into an elaborate ritual, for which the cook must don a special red crayfish apron. The way the crayfish are eaten rather clashes with normal Western forms of etiquette. For according to the Finns, a crayfish meal is not finished until there is a fringe of empty claws all around the edge of the plate. What is more, every claw should traditionally be accompanied by a tot of clear schnapps, though nowadays this would mean saving up one's alcohol rations for months on end. If the reader is invited to a crayfish meal, he will now have some idea of what is expected of him! In recent years, however, the ritual has become a rather expensive luxury, as most crayfish must now be imported from outside Finland.

The other main Finnish speciality is the reindeer, of which the liver and the tongue are treated as particular delicacies. Reindeer meat (in Finnish *poronliha*) is prepared in all sorts of ways, and is either roasted, broiled or smoked.

In north-eastern Finland the Russian influence is evident in the excellent *borsch* and *piroshki*. *Borsch* is a soup made from broth, beetroot and soured cream, while *piroshki* consists of pasta cases (in Finnish *piirakka*) filled with meat, vegetables or rice. One speciality of central Finland in the area around Kuopio is *kalakukko*, a kind of rye bread baked with pieces of meat and fish. Visitors to Lapland should not leave without trying some of the game, either roasted or smoked. One special delicacy is ptarmigan (*riekkoa*), with a sauce made from a northern fruit called the *lakkoja*, which is a light-coloured version of the blackberry.

Seafood and fish dishes are particularly good in coastal towns, where the majority of the indigenous population is of Swedish origin. It is therefore not surprising that most of these local dishes are similar to those found in Sweden. One favourite which is sold at fish markets is fresh-boiled shrimp, which can be eaten straight out of the packet. Fresh salmon is especially good during the salmon season, whether grilled or steamed. Pickled or red smoked salmon can be equally delicious. Restaurants in the lake regions serve various freshwater fish in a variety of different forms. The favourites are pike, eel and trout, including some delicious local preparations.

The Finns are great coffee drinkers, consuming large quantities of the beverage at every opportunity. The beans are more lightly roasted than in many parts of Europe, which many British coffee drinkers prefer. The second most popular drink is *olut*: a light beer with a very low alcohol content, which is nonetheless carefully graded. the sale of stronger varieties such as *A-olut* is restricted to specially authorised outlets at certain times of day.

The sale of all other alcoholic drinks is controlled by a state monopoly, and is subject to severe restrictions. They are sold exclusively at specially authorised shops with the label Oy *Alkoholiliike*. These exist in towns and other larger places, and have no advertising or displays. Finnish citizens over the age of twenty are allowed a limited ration of spirits. Foreign visitors are free from such restrictions on the presentation of a passport. However, spirits and imported alcoholic drinks are extremely expensive.

Restaurants

Known in Finnish as *ravintola*, these are common all over Finland, and are often the focal point of scattered country communities. They in many ways combine the role of restaurant and public house. Some are very traditional and elaborate, while others are simpler and more original in style.

Restaurants are officially classified in five categories: E for elite-class restaurants, followed by categories I to IV. Restaurants attached to hotels are normally classified E or I. The category is always displayed on the outside of the restaurant.

These categories also affect licensing to sell alcoholic drinks. The licensing laws are very complicated, but the higher licensing categories are subject to fewer restrictions. Licensing categories are also displayed outside every restaurant. Nearly all E- or I-category establishments have an A-category licence, which allows for almost unlimited sale of alcoholic drinks. A B-licence involves considerable restrictions on such sales, while C-licence restaurants may only sell light beers. Anyone who is under twenty or drunk may not be served at a Finnish restaurant. The service charge is included in the prices, but cloakroom charges are extra. The term *baari* applies to cafés and snack bars that are not licensed to sell alcohol.

Finnish meal times are similar to those in other Scandinavian countries. They eat a light lunch at some time between 11am and 2 or 3pm. Dinner is the main meal of the day, between 4 or 5pm and 7pm; it normally consists of several hot dishes. There is sometimes a light supper before bedtime.

Sporting Activities

The first Finnish sportsman that people usually think of is Paavo Nurmi, the famous runner who won five Olympic golds. But it would be wrong to forget all the other great sportspeople who have earned this small country a world reputation as a sporting nation. Athletics is the field in which Finns have achieved the most world records and Olympic medals, but they have also excelled in weightlifting and combat sports.

Given the cold winter climate, it is not surprising that winter sports are very important. The Finns are at the top of the European league in all winter sports, but especially in cross-country skiing and ski-jumping. They have similarly produced some brilliant performances in speed skating, while ice hockey is popular throughout Finland.

The emphasis that the Finns place on sport generally is reflected in the great variety of sports which they pursue. For such a small country, they have achieved success in a surprisingly large number of different areas. They are admittedly outclassed in certain popular European sports such as football, but this merely reflects their very strict interpretation of amateur status.

Sport is pursued enthusiastically at all levels of Finnish society. Physical conditioning was considered important here long before it became fashionable elsewhere. One very popular Finnish sport combines orienteering with cross-country running; this attracts large numbers of people of all ages out into the forests.

Finland is represented internationally by the Finnish Sports Federation (SVUL). One of the main sports organisations inside Finland is the so-called Workers' Sports Federation (TUL). Sports are financed both by the state and by the income from football pools. The universities of Turku and Jyväskylä both have sports faculties, and there is further educational backing from the National Sports College at Vierumäki.

Visitors to Finland have the opportunity to take part in all sorts of sports. Foreigners tend to be be particularly interested in activities that are appropriate to the local environment. Walking and rambling, for example, are especially popular, whether on one's own or in guided parties under the auspices of one of the many interested tourist organisations.

The innumerable lakes of the interior provide opportunities for every kind of water sport. There are few restrictions on the use of motorboats, and yachting seems to be allowed almost everywhere. Boats of all sizes are available for hire, both for longer and for shorter periods. Information on what is available can be obtained from the various tourist offices.

Hunting

Hunting in Finland is less attractive than the forested landscape might lead one to imagine. Red deer are relatively uncommon in the kinds of forest that are found in Finland, while intensive hunting has depleted other game populations.

The only special animal worth hunting is the elk, which, however, is much more common in Sweden. The elk season lasts from 16 October to 15 December. If one is invited to hunt elks in Finland, whether by a hunting club or by a private individual, one must first obtain an elk-hunting permit from the Finnish Embassy by 31 May prior to the hunting season. A shooting test is also compulsory for anybody using a hunting rifle. Most hunting groups request it yearly although by law it is valid for 3 years.

There are a number of specific regulations governing the use and disposal of equipment, firearms and captured quarry. Hunting weapons may be brought into the country, but a licence must be obtained from the police authority at the place of arrival. Hunting dogs are virtually impossible to bring in because of the strict quarantine regulations (rabies vaccinations and 4 months' quarantine).

Fishing

Finland is a paradise for anglers. A permit is necessary for fishing in Finnish waters, but this can be easily obtained from the local tourist office on arrival, or even at the hotel or local post office.

Sea fishing is most popular around the islands of Åland, where the commonest fish caught are cod and sea trout. There are countless opportunities for fishing in the Finnish lakes, the best areas being around the great lakes of central and south-eastern Finland, and also in Finnish Lapland. All forms of freshwater fish are present in abundance, including salmon, river trout, pike and perch.

Fishing boats are available for hire in most angling areas. Detailed information on angling opportunities is available from the various tourist agencies.

The Sauna

Part of the Finnish Way of Life

As far as the Finns are concerned, the sauna means more than just a steam-bath, an aspect of hygiene, a way of keeping fit or a medical procedure: it is part of the Finnish way of life. The origins of the sauna are lost in the mists of time. The custom probably goes back as far as 2,000 years, and was brought over by the early Finns from central Asia. Perhaps it is one of the keys to the survival of this resilient people in the face of both climatic and political adversity.

The Greeks and Romans also had steam-baths, but these, like the first bathrooms, were purely for the use of the upper classes or the wealthy gentry. The sauna, on the other hand, has always been available to the whole of Finnish society. Everyone, from the tribal chief down to the lowliest hunter or servant, could relax in the sauna after a hard day's grind.

The sauna was, no doubt, originally no more than a hole in the ground covered with moss and soil, in which a pile of stones was heated up. Water was regularly poured over the stones to produce steam. The bathers sat in the steam and whipped themselves with birch twigs to improve their circulation and further encourage perspiration. This relaxed the muscles and made the body more able to cope with the country's harsh and often extreme climate. It also improved hygiene, thus preventing the spread of infectious diseases.

Every modern Finnish family has a sauna, and even the smallest and most basic of houses is equipped with one. The Finns still practise the custom with almost religious fervour. No one in Finland sees anything immoral in nude bathing; it is simply part of everyday life. Nowadays the sauna is usually arranged so that members of the opposite sex only bathe together within the family or among close friends. At public saunas, men and women bathe at different times or in separate rooms. There are estimated to be over a million saunas in Finland as a whole.

The Finnish Sauna Today

The classic Finnish sauna consists of three rooms: the dressing room, the washroom and the sweating room or sauna proper. The dressing room usually contains cupboards or lockers where the bathers can leave their clothes, and couches where they can lie down and relax before beginning the sauna. Larger or more luxurious saunas have separate rest rooms.

The bathers then go into the washroom and wash themselves down thoroughly before going into the sauna proper. No self-respecting Finn goes dirty into the sauna. The layout of the washroom varies enormously, from a simple room with a slatted wooden floor and a wooden bucket full of lake or spring water, to a tiled bathroom with hot and cold water and a fully adjustable shower.

The sweating room is always lined with natural wood (any colour or treatment would not survive the heat and the steam). The most important feature is the stove, which was previously walled in with tiles, but is now usually covered with an iron mantel. The stove is filled with stones or bricks, which are heated up to a high temperature. The heat is usually produced by a wood furnace outside, and is circulated though the stones via ducts in the floor of the stove.

In the old days a fire burned in the sauna itself. When the stones reached the right temperature, the smoke was drawn off and the remains of the fire were removed so that the sauna could begin. The sauna chamber was then also used for smoking meat, fish and other items of food for the winter.

The sauna still has ventilators near the ceiling and ducts near the floor to allow fresh air to come in. This ensures that the air remains clean and free of the smell of sweating bodies. A modern sauna is also equipped with a thermometer, a hydrometer and a sand glass, this being the only timing device that works accurately in such hot and humid conditions.

The furniture consists of benches made of well-planed natural wood. If possible they are constructed without nails or screws, which can cause burns. They are usually made of spruce wood, which neutralises the heat most effectively. They are arranged in step formation so that bathers can work their way up from the 'cooler' zones at the bottom to the hottest bench at the top. For reasons of hygiene each bather takes in a 'bench cloth' to sit or lie on; this also prevents burns.

The next essential item is a ladle and a bucket full of water, which is poured at regular intervals onto the stones to create steam. In the old days the ladle was always carved out of wood, while the bucket was often beautifully fashioned from copper. Nowadays the bucket and ladle are often made out of some heat-resistant plastic.

Finally there is the *vihta* — a switch made of birch twigs, which is used to stimulate circulation and encourage sweating. Nowadays there are some sauna experts who prefer just to let the body sweat naturally, while others use a hard brush of some sort. In the old days the making of a *vihta* was an art in itself. The birch twigs could only be collected during the main growing season at midsummer. They were dried according to a special procedure, and salt was used to help preserve them. They were then often frozen to keep them fresher. But every individual has his own special method of making a *vihta*.

How the Sauna Works

The benefit of the sauna lies in the high temperatures to which the body is subjected. For a short period the air temperature rises to around 100°C (212°F), while the body temperature reaches about 40°C (104°F).

The body sweats profusely in order to cope with the heat. The skin surface is cooled as the sweat evaporates, while the internal organs are warmed by the circulating blood. Meanwhile the blood circulation is increased without any accompanying physical stress. However, a heavy meal should be avoided before a sauna, as the consequent blood shortage in the digestive organs will disturb the blood circulation.

The profuse sweating is also beneficial, as it opens the pores and allows the skin to be thoroughly cleansed. The cooling-off period afterwards makes the body more resilient, and improves its resistance to colds and flu. During the final period of relaxation, the bather feels pleasantly drowsy as the body's energy resources are regenerated.

Most people are fully capable of withstanding a sauna, even those with a slightly weak heart. However, anyone with heart or circulation problems should seek the advice of their doctor before embarking on a sauna. It is a mistake to imagine that a sauna helps one to lose weight. It is true that an intensive sweating session can produce a temporary weight loss of as much as two kilos. But this is only due to loss of body fluids, and these are quickly replenished afterwards.

There are two types of sauna — the dry sauna and the wet sauna. In a dry sauna it is the hot air only that affects the body, causing it to sweat profusely; the sweat then evaporates, allowing the body to cool again. In a wet sauna, water is regularly poured over the heated stones in the oven, creating a cloud of steam and increasing the humidity level. The evaporation actually has the effect of cooling the air, but the steam makes it feel hotter, and the increased humidity apparently causes the body to sweat even more profusely. There are advocates for both types of sauna, and it is very much a matter of personal taste. However, experience suggests that a wet sauna is better for people who do not sweat very easily.

In the Sauna

Having washed and dried themselves thoroughly, the bathers then enter the sauna proper, equipped with a bench cloth. The air temperature is between 80° and 110°C (176° to 230°F), and at first it quite takes the breath away. As the bathers sit or lie down on the lowest bench, they are already sweating profusely. If anyone does not sweat within the first minute or so, he should throw some water on the stove. In Finland nothing is added to the water apart from a few birch leaves — unlike communal saunas elsewhere in Europe, where various aromatic products are added to freshen the air.

After the first good sweat, one should try whipping oneself with birch twigs or a hard brush to see if it helps the skin. One can also begin to climb up to the higher benches, where the air is much hotter and the sauna is all the more effective. Beginners can make this process easier by lying on the bottom bench and raising their legs. This is because the legs cope better with the heat than the head does. Many Finnish saunas have bars installed expressly for this purpose.

Depending on one's capacity, one should stay in the sauna for between 10 and 20 minutes before returning to the washroom for a wash in lukewarm and then cold water. A cold shower or a quick plunge in a cold pool then helps to make the body more resilient. After a rest of about 10 to 15 minutes, one can return for a repeat performance, or maybe even two.

The final sweating session should be followed by an extra thorough wash and cold shower. Bathers should then lie down in the rest room for at least 15 minutes, wrapped up in a towel. Beginners in particular tend to sweat again during this period, in which case a lukewarm shower is the best remedy. The end of a sauna is accompanied by a feeling of physical tiredness and wellbeing, which quickly gives way to renewed vigour and energy.

A final massage is of course the best ending for a sauna, ensuring complete physical relaxation. Many communal saunas in Finland have a woman in charge, who is usually of mature years. She will perform the task of soaping down and showering the bathers before and after sweating sessions, and will often administer the final massage. The Finns see nothing strange or indecent in this. On the contrary, a rub-down after a sauna is like the final icing on a cake.

Sauna Customs

Anyone staying with a Finnish family can be certain of being invited at least once to take part in a sauna. If one is unsure of the procedure, one can always confide in one of the members of the family, who will explain it carefully. Traditionally it is the menfolk who go into the sauna first.

A family sauna is usually followed by a good snack. This satisfies the hunger pangs and replenishes the salts and fluids that have been lost in the sweat. One favourite is a kind of ham sausage; it is taken into the final sweating session, where it bubbles and swells.

Foreign visitors can do their hosts a great favour by providing a few bottles of imported beer or something stronger. Though easy for the foreigner to buy, such luxuries are strictly rationed to Finnish citizens, who will therefore appreciate the gesture all the more.

The Finnish Language

Finnish is the mother tongue of 92–93 per cent of the population of Finland, while 7–8 per cent are primarily Swedish-speaking. The Swedish-speaking minority live mostly along the western and southern coasts, where towns and villages usually have a Swedish and a

Finnish name. Swedish maps give only the Swedish name, but Finnish maps often have both names, giving priority to the language that is spoken by the majority in that place.

There are two other tiny minorities: about 3,000 Lapps speak their own separate language, and there are a very few Russian-speakers along the Soviet border in Karelia.

Many Finns are at least bilingual, speaking Swedish as well as Finnish. A large number speak English or German too, so it is not necessary to learn Finnish to make oneself understood.

Finnish is a hard language to learn, partly because of its difficult grammar, and partly because it is unrelated to most other European languages, the majority of which are of Indo-European origin. Finnish belongs to the Finno-Ugrian family of languages. It is closely related to Estonian, and has a clear affinity with Lapp, though it is not known how much this is due to common roots and how much to geographical proximity; Hungarian is probably also distantly related. These few scattered languages are believed to have originated beyond the Urals, and their only affinity with other European languages is in the few words that have been borrowed.

Foreign visitors cannot be expected to learn such a difficult language as Finnish. The noun structure is particularly complicated, with as many as fifteen cases (compared with six in Latin and four in German), often taking the place of prepositions. The complex grammar means that the words tend to be very long, but there are also fewer of them. There are no articles ('a' or 'the'), and unlike most European languages (apart from English) there is no grammatical gender.

Finnish is, however, relatively easy to pronounce. It has few consonants and is highly phonetic, being spoken very much as it is written. This makes it fairly easy for the foreigner to look up words in a dictionary and repeat them aloud. One need not be put off by all the double consonants and double vowels. The pronunciation is much easier than the strangeness of the words suggests.

The consonants **b**, **c**, **d**, **f**, **g**, **w**, **x** and **z** are found only in foreign words and proper names, except for the combination **ng**, which is pronounced as in the English 'si**ng**'. The consonants **k**, **l**, **m**, **n**, **p**, **r**, **t** and **v** are rather weaker; **s** is like a weak form of the English **s** in 'si**ng**'; **h** occurs only in the middle of words, and is like the Scottish

ch in 'lo**ch**'. Double consonants are pronounced double as in Italian, but have no effect on the length of the vowels.

Of the vowels **i**, **e** and **o** are similar to English, though they are pronounced rather closer; **y** is like the German **ü** or the French **u**, while **ö** is like the German **ö** or the French **eu**; **u** is as in 'p**u**t', not as in 'p**u**tt'; **ä** has a quality like that of the southern English short **a** (as in 'p**a**t'), while **a** has a quality rather like the southern English long **a** (as in 'f**a**ther'); thus the two dots affect the *quality* and not the length of the vowel. Single vowels are all short, while double ones are pronounced very long. Diphthongs are made up of the constituent vowels, and are pronounced very clearly, as in Italian. The Finnish *Europa*, for example, is pronounced rather like 'eh-oo-ropa'.

Useful Words and Phrases

English — Finnish
Britain — Iso-Britannia
USA — Yhdysvallat
Canada — Kanada
Denmark — Tanska
Finland — Suomi
Norway — Norja
Sweden — Ruotsi

Do you speak . . . — puhutteko . . .
English — englantia
I do not understand — en ymmärrä
yes — niin, kyllä
no — en, ei
please — oikaa hyvä
excuse me — pyydän
thank you — kiitos
thank you very much — kiitoksia paljon
good morning — hyvää huomenta
good day — hyvää päivää
good evening — hyvää iltaa
good night — hyvää yöta
goodbye — näkemiin

man — herra
woman — nainen, rouva
girl — neiti

Where is . . . — missä on . . .
. . . Street — . . . katu
. . . Square — . . . tori
the road to . . . — tie . . .
the church — kirkko
the museum — museo
when? — milloin?
open — auki
the Town Hall — kaupungintalo
the post office — postikonttori
a bank — pankki
the station — rautatieasema

a hotel — hotelli
I should like — haluaisin mielelläni
a room — huoneen
single — yhdenhengen huone
double — kahdenhengen huone
with bath — kylpyhuoneella
without bath — ilman kylpyä
the key — avain
the lavatory (bathroom) — käymälä
a doctor — lääkäri
to the right — oikealla
to the left — vasemmalia

FURTHER INFORMATION

The following information is for general guidance only as it is subject to change. Continually updated information is available from banks, travel agents, the Finnish Tourist Board and embassies.

Museums and Art Galleries

Alajärvi

Nelimarkka Museum
62900 Alajärvi
☎ (9) 66–2129
Paintings of Eero Nelimarkka. Finnish art from nineteenth century to present.
Open: 15 May-31 August, weekdays 11am–7pm, Saturday 11am–4pm, Sunday 12noon–6pm; 1 September-15 May, Wednesday-Friday and Sunday 12noon–6pm, Saturday 12noon–4pm.

Åland Islands/Ahvenanmaa

Åland Art Museum
Stadshusparken
Öhbergsvägen 1
Mariehamn
Mostly modern art.
Open: Tuesday-Sunday 11am–4pm, Tuesday 6–8pm.

Åland Museum
Stadshusparken
Öhbergsvägen 1
Mariehamn
Relics from the Stone Age. Archaeological and historical collections.
Open: Tuesday-Sunday 11am–4pm, Tuesday 6–8pm.

Maritime Museum
Mariehamn
Relics of seafaring history of the islands.
Open: weekdays 9am–5pm, Sunday 10am–4pm.

Dragsfjärd

Söderlångvik Museum
25870 Dragsfjärd
☎ (9) 25–4662
About 200 works of Finnish art from the 1930s and 1940s.
Open: 1 June-15 August 11am–6pm.

Ekenäs/Tammisaari

Ekenäs Museum
Gustav Wasas gata 13
☎ (9) 11–14 600 /14 111
Open: mid-May – mid-August, Tuesday-Sunday 12noon–5pm.

Espoo/Esbo

Automobile Museum
Pakankylä
☎ (9) 0–855 71 78
Open: summertime, 10am–8pm.

Gallen-Kallela Museum
Tarvaspää
☎ (9) 0–513 388
Painter Akseli Gallen-Kallela's
stone studio, built 1911–13.
Original furnishings, tools,
paintings, sculptures and graphics.
Open: 16 September-14 May,
Tuesday-Saturday 10am–4pm,
Sunday 10am–5pm; 15 May-15
September, Tuesday-Thursday
10am–8pm, Friday-Sunday
10am–5pm.

Espoo Museum Glims
Bemböle
☎ (9) 0–862 979
Farmhouse and furnishings from
nineteenth century.
Open: 10 May-30 September
12noon–6pm; 1 October-11 May,
daily 12noon–4pm, Wednesday
12noon–6pm.

Evijärvi

Väinöntalo House Museum
62540 Vasikka-aho
☎ (9) 67–53 160/67–51 311
Displays of peasant culture, handicrafts, hunting, fishing.
Open: May-August, daily
10am–7pm.

Hämeenlinna/Tavastehus

Hämeenlinna Art Museum
Viipurintie 2
☎ (9) 17–202 669
Finnish art.

Open: weekdays 10am–7pm,
weekends 12noon–6pm, Thursday
also 7–8pm.

Hämeenlinna Historical Museum
Lukiokatu 6
☎ (9) 17–22 826
History of Hämeenlinna and province of Häme.
Open: Monday-Saturday
12noon–4pm, Sunday
12noon–6pm.

Medieval Hämeenlinna Castle
Linnantie 6
13100 Hämeenlinna
☎ (9) 17–26 820
Guided tours in English, German
and Swedish, May-August every
hour.

Hamina/Fredrikshamn

Town Museum
Kadettikoulunkatu 2
☎ (9) 52–40 212
Open: Tuesday-Saturday
11am–3pm, Sunday 12noon–3pm.

Harjavalta

Emil Cedercreutz Museum
Museotie
29200 Harjavalta
☎ (9) 39–740 356
Early twentieth-century Finnish art.
Open: all year, 11am–5pm plus
5–8pm Tuesday and Thursday.

Hartola

Eastern Häme Museum
19600 Hartola
☎ (9) 10–61 252
Cultural history.
Open: 12noon–4pm.

Heinola

Town Museum
Kauppakatu 14
Open: Tuesday-Saturday
12noon–4pm, Wednesday also
4–8pm.

Helsinki

Amos Anderson Art Museum
Yrjönkatu 27
☎ (9) 0–640 221
Twentieth-century Finnish art,
European art.
Open: weekdays 11am–5pm,
weekends 12noon–5pm.

Art Museum of the Ateneum
Kansakoulukatu 3
☎ (9) 0–694 59 33
Open: 1 June-31 August, weekdays 9am–5pm, Wednesday also
5–8pm, weekends 11am–5pm;
1 September-31 May,
Monday–Saturday 9am–5pm, also
5–8pm, Sunday 11am–5pm.

Helsinki City Art Collections
Tamminiementie 6
☎ (9) 0–484 044
Finnish and French art from the
twentieth century, photography etc.
Open: Wednesday-Sunday
11am–6.30pm.

Helsinki City Museum
Karamzininkatu 2
☎ (9) 0–169 34 44
Art, furniture, literature etc.
Open: Sunday–Friday
12noon–4pm. Thursday also
4–8pm.

Military Museum
Maurinkatu 2
00170 Helsinki
☎ (9) 0–177 791

Collection of over 60,000 objects of
militaria.
Open: Sunday-Friday 11am–3pm.

Museum of Applied Arts
Korkeavuorenkatu 23
☎ (9) 0–174 455
Industrial art and design, artistic
handicrafts.
Open: Tuesday-Friday 11am–5pm,
weekends 11am–4pm.

Museum of Finnish Architecture
Kasarmikatu 24
☎ (9) 0–661 918
Pictures, archives, records.
Open: daily 10am–4pm.

Museum of Technology
Viikintie 1
00560 Helsinki
☎ (9) 0–797 066
Open: May-September, Tuesday-
Sunday 11am–5pm; October-April,
Wednesday-Sunday 12noon–4pm.

National Museum
Mannerheimintie 34
☎ (9) 0–40 251
Prehistory, history, ethnology.
Open: October-April, Monday-
Saturday 11am–3pm, Tuesday
also 6–9pm, Sunday 11am–4pm;
May-September, Monday-Sunday
11am–4pm, Tuesday also 6–9pm.

Seurasaari Open-air Museum
Seurasaari Island
☎ (9) 0–484 712
Complete manor and farm
buildings from all over Finland.
Open: 1 June-31 August,
Monday-Sunday 11.30am
–5.30pm, Wednesday until 7pm;
May and September,
weekdays 9.30am–3pm,
weekends 11.30am–5pm.

Sports Museum
Stadion
00250 Helsinki
☎ (9) 0–407 011
Open: Tuesday, Wednesday,
Friday 11am–5pm, Thursday
11am–7pm, weekends
12noon–4pm.

Zoological Museum
Pohjoinen Rautatiekatu 13
00100 Helsinki
☎ (9) 0–40 271
26 million specimens.
Open: June-August, weekdays
9am–2pm; September-May, weekdays 9am–3pm, Sunday
12noon–4pm.

Iisalmi/Idensalmi

Museum of Musical Instruments
Mansikkaniemi
Open: 1 June–31 September, daily
11am–3pm and 4–8pm.

Iittala

Iittala Glass Factory Museum
Iittalan lasikeskus
14500 Iittala
☎ (9) 17–55 055
Open: May-September 9am–8pm;
October-April 9am–6pm. Guided
tours of factory, weekdays
11am–1pm and 3pm.

Ilmajoki

Yli-Laurosela House Museum
60800 Ilmajoki
☎ (9) 64–546 719
Example of Pohjanmaa lifestyle
and buildings.
Open: May-September 11am–5pm;
October-April, Sunday-Friday
10am–4pm.

Imatra

Imatra Art Gallery
Honkaharju 7
Open: Tuesday-Friday
12noon–6pm, weekends 2–6pm.

Inari

Inari Lappish Museum
99870 Inari
☎ (9) 697–51 107
Open-air museum.
Open: 1 June–10 August
8am–10pm; 11-31 August
8am–8pm; 1-20 September,
9am–3.30pm.

Järvenpää

Ainola
04400 Järvenpää
☎ (9) 0–287 322
Home of Jean Sibelius.
Open: May-August, Tuesday-
Sunday 10am–6pm, Wednesday
12noon–8pm; September,
Tuesday-Sunday 11am–5pm;
October weekends 11am–5pm;
March, Sunday 12noon–3pm; April,
weekends 11am–5pm.

Joensuu

Joensuu Art Gallery
Kirkkokatu 23
☎ (9) 73–201 698
Finnish art from nineteenth and
twentieth centuries.

Northern Karelia Museum
Siltakatu 1
☎ (9) 73–201 634
History and culture of north Karelia.
Open: Tuesday, Thursday, Friday
12noon–4pm, Wednesday
12noon–8pm, Saturday
10am–4pm, Sunday 10am–6pm.

Jyväskylä

Alvar Aalto Museum
Seminaarinkatu 7
☎ (9) 41–294 176
Aalto's sketches, drawings,
designs and furniture plus town art
collection.
Open: Tuesday 12noon–8pm,
Wednesday-Sunday 12noon–6pm.

Central Finland Museum
Ruusupuisto Park
Handicrafts, ethnographical
collection.
Open: Tuesday-Sunday
12noon–7pm.

Finnish Handicrafts Museum
Seminaarinkatu 32
☎ (9) 41–294 066
Open: Tuesday-Sunday
12noon–7pm.

Museum of the Jyväskylä Lyceum
Open: Sunday 12noon–4pm.

Museum of Jyväskylä University
Open: Tuesday-Sunday
12noon–3pm.

Kajaani/Kajana

Kainuu District Museum
Asemakatu 4
☎ (9) 86–1551
Cultural history, art.
Open: Tuesday-Saturday
12noon–3pm, Sunday and
Wednesday 12noon–6pm.

Kemi

Kemi Art Museum and Cultural
Centre
Pohjoisrannankatu 9–11
☎ (9) 80–299 437
Open: June-August, Tuesday-

Friday 10am–5pm, Saturday
10am–2pm, Sunday 2–6pm;
September-May, Tuesday-Friday
10am–7pm, Saturday 10am–5pm,
Sunday 12noon–7pm.

Kemijärvi

Kemijärvi Museum
Sepänkatu 2
☎ (9) 692–21 494
Ethnographic.
Open: summer, daily 10am–6pm.

Keuruu

Keuruu Museum
Pitäjäntuvantie 6
42700 Keuruu
☎ (9) 43–11 820
Open: June-August, Tuesday-
Sunday 10am–7pm; September-
May, Tuesday-Sunday
12noon–6pm.

Kotka

Imperial Fishing Lodge
by Langinkoski rapids
Open: May-August, daily
10am–7pm.

Kymenlaakso Museum
Kotkankatu 13
☎ (9) 52–12 220
Objects connected with naval battle
of Ruotsinsalmi.
Open: Tuesday-Friday
12noon–6pm, weekends
12noon–4pm.

Karhula Glass Museum and Shop
☎ (9) 52–292 021
Antique and modern art,
glass.
Open: June-August, daily
12noon–5pm.

Kristinestad/
Kristiinankaupunki

Lebell Residence
Rantakatu 51
64100 Kristinestad
☎ (9) 62–12 159
Merchant's house (1750–1840)
restored to original style.
Open: May-September, Tuesday-
Sunday 12noon–4pm.

Kuopio

Kuopio Art Museum
Kauppakatu 35
☎ (9) 71–182 611
Modern and older art.
Open: weekdays 9am–4.30pm,
Sunday 11am–6pm.

Kuopio Museum
Kauppakatu 23
Open: weekdays 9am–4pm,
Sunday 11am–7pm; in summer
also, Saturday 10am–4pm,
Wednesday 6–8pm.

Orthodox Church Museum
Karjalankatu 1
☎ (9) 71–122 611
Unparalleled in western Europe.
Open: May-August, Tuesday-Sunday 10am–4pm: September-April,
weekdays 10am–2pm, weekends
12noon–5pm.

Lahti

Lahti Historical Museum
Lahti Manor
Lahdenkatu 4
☎ (9) 18–182 228
Ethnographical and cultural history.
Open: Tuesday-Sunday
12noon–4pm, Tuesday also
6–8pm.

Lapinlahti

Emil Halonen Museum
73100 Lapinlahti
☎ (9) 77–32 288
The sculptor's original plaster
models, sketches, works in bronze
and marble.
Open: Tuesday-Sunday
10am–6pm.

Lappeenranta/Villmanstrand

Southern Karelia Museum
Kristiinankatu 2 in Fortress
(Linnoitus)
☎ (9) 53–518 514
Art, folk costumes etc.
Open: in summer, weekdays
10am–6pm, weekends 11am–5pm;
winter, Tuesday-Sunday
11am–5pm.

Lieksa

Pielinen Open-air Museum
Pappilantie 2
☎ (9) 75–20490
Eighteenth and twentieth-century
farm buildings.
Open: 15 May-15 September
10am–6pm.

Mikkeli/St Michel

Mikkeli Art Museum
Ristimäenkatu 5A
☎ (9) 55–1941
Open: Tuesday-Friday and Sunday
12noon–6pm, Saturday
12noon–3pm.

Church Museum
Porrassalmenkatu 32A
Stone chapel, built 1320.
Open: 15 May-31 August, daily
11am–5pm.

Mustasaari

Stundars Handicraft Village
65460 Sulva
☎ (9) 61–440 282
Thirty-five buildings — tinsmith's,
cobbler's, carpenter's etc.
Open: 15 May-15 August
12noon–6pm.

Mäntsälä

Sepänmäki Handicrafts Museum
04680 Hirvihaara
☎ (9) 15–88 070
Workshops representing the
trades.
Open: May-September
12noon–6pm.

Mänttä

Museum of Gösta Serlachius
  Fine Arts Foundation
Joenniemi Manor
35800 Mänttä
☎ (9) 34–412 111
Finnish, Flemish, Spanish and
Italian art.
Open: May-September, Tuesday-
Friday 12noon–5pm, weekends
10am–5pm; September-April,
weekends 12noon–5pm.

Naantali/Nådendal

Naantali Museum
Katinhäntä 1
In three wooden houses.
Open: 15 May-31 August, daily
12noon–6pm.

Nivala

Nivala Museum
Katvala
85501 Nivala
☎ (9) 83–42163

History, trade etc.of Nivala.
Open: June-August, Tuesday-
Sunday 12noon–4pm.

Oulu/Uleåborg

Northern Ostrobothnia Museum
Ainola Park
☎ (9) 81–12 624
Shipping, tar burning and trade,
silver, glass, porcelain, weapons.
Open: May-15 September,
Monday, Tuesday, Thursday
11am–6pm, Wednesday
11am–8pm, Saturday 11am–3pm,
Sunday 12noon–6pm; 16 Septem-
ber-30 April, Monday, Tuesday,
Thursday, 11am–4pm, Wednesday
11am–7pm, Saturday 11am–3pm,
Sunday 12noon–6pm.

Turkansaari Open-air Museum
Turkansaari Island
Can be reached by boat.
Open: 20 May-15 August, daily
11am–9pm, 16 August-
30 September, daily 11am–7pm.

Pori/Björneborg

Pori Art Museum
Etel äranta
☎ (9) 39–412 220
Modern art.
Open: Tuesday-Sunday
11am–6pm.

Porvoo/Borgå

Porvoo Museum
Välikatu II
☎ (9) 15–140 589
Cultural history of the region.
Open: May-August, daily
11am–4pm; September-April,
Tuesday-Saturday 12noon–3pm.
Sunday 12noon–5pm.

Rovaniemi

Rovaniemi Art Museum
Lapinkävijäntie 4
☎ (9) 60–299 822
Open: Tuesday, Thursday, Friday,
Sunday 12noon–6pm, Wednesday
12noon–8pm, Saturday
10am–4pm.

Museum of the Province of Lapland
Lappia House
Hallituskatu 11
☎ (9) 60–299 483
Objects connected with the Lapps,
with exhibitions showing the natural
history of Lapland.
Open: June-August, Tuesday-Sunday 10am–6pm; September-
December, Tuesday-Sunday
12noon-4pm.

Saarijärvi

Paavo Museum
Paavontie 6
43100 Saarijärvi
☎ (9) 44–21 045
Local history museum.
Open: 1 June-15 August, Tuesday-
Friday 12noon–5pm, weekends
11am–5pm.

Savonlinna/Nyslott

Savonlinna Museum
(with museum ships *Salama*,
Savonlinnan and *Mikko*)
Open: 1 January-31 August, weekdays 11am–7pm, weekends
11am–5pm; 1 September-
31 December, Tuesday, Thursday-
Sunday 11am–3pm, Wednesday
11am–8pm.
During opera festival in July, open
daily 10am–8pm.

Tampere/Tammerfors

Art Museum of Tampere
Puutarhakatu 34
Finnish nineteenth- and twentieth-
century art.
Open: daily 11am–7pm.

Tampere Technical Museum
Itsenäisyydenkatu 21
Automobile and aviation displays.
Open: Tuesday-Sunday
12noon–6pm.

Häme Museum
Näsilinna
Ethnography, cultural history of
Tampere and Häme province.
Open: Tuesday-Sunday
12noon–6pm.

Varala Gymnastics Museum
Varalankatu 36
Open: June-August, Tuesday
6–8pm, Sunday 1–4pm.

The Workers' Museum of Amuri
Makasiininkatu 12
☎ (9) 31–111 633
Museum block of workers' housing
of the nineteenth and twentieth
centuries.
Open: 15 May-31 August, Tuesday-Sunday 12noon–6pm.

Tankavaara

Gold Prospecting Museum of
  Tankavaara
99690 Vuotso
☎ (9) 693–46 171
Open-air museum; buildings
relocated from gold prospectors'
community in Lapland.
Open: 1 June-15 August, daily
9am–6pm; 16 August-30 September 10am–5pm; October-May
10am–4pm.

Tornio/Torneå

Torniolaakso District Museum
Keskikatu 22
☎ (9) 80–42 831
Ethnographical material, furniture,
handcrafts.
Open: Tuesday-Friday
12noon–7pm, weekends
12noon–5pm.

Turku/Åbo

Wäinö Aaltonen Museum
Itäinen Rantakatu 38
Archives and library of sculptor
Wäinö Aaltonen (1894–1966).
Open: weekdays 10am–4pm and
6–8pm, Saturday 10am–4pm,
Sunday 10am–6pm.

Sibelius Museum
Piispankatu 17
Musical instruments, manuscripts
of Jean Sibelius and other Finnish
composers.
Open: May-September, Tuesday-
Sunday 11am–3pm, Wednesday
also 6–8pm; October-April,
Tuesday-Sunday, 12noon–3pm.

Qwensel House and Pharmacy
  Museum
Läntinen Rantakatu 13
Open: May-September, daily
10am–6pm; October-April daily
10am–3pm.

Luostarinmäki Handicraft Museum
Vartiovuorenkatu 4
Eighteen artisan buildings from
eighteenth century with home
interiors and workshops.
Open: May-September, daily
10am–6pm; October-April, daily
10am–3pm.

Vaasa/Vasa

Brage Open-air Museum
Hietalahti
Relocated peasant buildings.
Open: weekdays 4–7pm,
weekends 1–4pm.

Ostrobothnia Museum
Museokatu 3
History of the town of Vaasa,
Italian, Dutch, Flemish, German
art.
Open: weekdays 12noon–8pm,
weekends 1–6pm.

Virrat

Virrat Folk Village
Herranen
34800 Virrat
☎ (9) 34–56 509
Open: all year.

Churches and Cathedrals

Åland Islands/Ahvenanmaa

Granite churches, dating back to
earliest period after the advent of
Christianity, are among the most
impressive historical monuments of
the province.

Ruins of Lemböte Chapel, date
from 1200s. The ruins stand on
summit of Lemböte in parish of
Lemland.

Grey stone church at Finström
about 25km from Mariehamn in the
Åland Islands. Begun thirteenth
century. Medieval objects and
atmosphere.

Ekenäs/Tammisaari

Granite church built in the 1650s.
Also church in Snappertuna, one
of the oldest wooden churches in
Finland, built 1688.

Espoo/Esbo

Espoo granite church with
medieval frescos.

Hamina

Hamina Church, Raatihuoneen-
tori, opens daily from 9am–3pm.

Peter-Paul's Orthodox church in
the same street. Open: Tuesday-
Sunday 11am–3pm.

Hattula

Church of the Holy Cross, built of
brick 1320–50. Chalk murals date
to early sixteenth century. Open
in May, daily 9am–6pm; June–15
August, daily 10am–6pm;
16 August–6 September,
12noon–4pm.

Heinola

Heinola Church, octagonal
wooden church and a campanile
designed by Engel 1842. Open
1 June-31 August, daily
11am–2pm, 4–6pm.

Helsinki

Temppeliaukio (rock) Church
(1969). Open: 10am–9pm daily,
except Sunday 12.30–4pm,
6–9pm.

Uspensky Cathedral: Open:
1May-30 August, weekdays
10am–4pm.

Iisalmi/Idensalmi

Wooden cruciform church from
the 1770s, open in summer
1–6pm.

Kerimäki

The world's largest wooden
church, accommodates 5,000
people; enormous dual cross
interior and Byzantine atmosphere.

Jyväskylä

City Church, open: 10am–5pm.
Taulumäki Church, open in
summer, daily 9am–3pm.

Lohikoski Church, open in
summer, daily 10am–5pm.

Kajaani/Kajana

Paltaniemi Church — pictures
worth seeing, built 1726.

Kokkola/Karleby

Kaarlela Church, built 1460,
about 2km from centre.

Kotka

Orthodox church of St Nicholas,
built 1795, open in summer,
Tuesday-Sunday 12noon–2pm.

Kuopio

Cathedral (1815) open in
summer, daily 10am–5pm; in
winter 10am–3pm.

Lappeenranta/Villmanstrand

Lappee Church (1794), open in
summer, daily 12noon–5pm.

Virgin May Church (1785) in the Fortress, the oldest Orthodox church in Finland, open in summer, Tuesday-Sunday 10am–6pm.

Lohja/Lojo

St Lauri's Church, a medieval granite church from the fourteenth century, with famous sixteenth-century paintings, open Monday-Saturday 10am–7pm, Sunday 11.30am–6.30pm.

Mikkeli/St Michel

Lutheran cathedral (1897). Open: daily 11am–7pm.

Naantali/Nådendal

Convent church from fifteenth century, open from 2 May-15 May, Monday-Saturday 11am–6pm, Sunday 12noon–6pm; 1 June-15 August, as above; 16 August-30 September 12noon–4pm; 1 October-1 May, Sunday 12noon–3pm.

Oulu/Uleåborg

Cathedral, built 1770–6, burnt 1882, renovated. Open in summer, daily 10am–7pm.

The oldest wooden church in Finland (1634) is at Muhos (30km east).

Pargas/Parainen

Granite church from the 1300s.

Pori/Björneborg

Central Pori Church (1863) between the two bridges crossing the River Kokemäenjoki.

Porvoo/Borgå

Cathedral (1418), open May-September, Monday-Saturday 10am–6pm, Sunday 2–5pm; October-April, Tuesday-Saturday 12noon–4pm, Sunday 2–4pm.

Rauma/Raumo

Church of the Holy Cross, fifteenth-century, belonged to a Franciscan monastery. Also the ruins of Church of the Holy Trinity, a monastery church in the fourteenth century.

Savonlinna/Nyslott

Cathedral (1879), open May-September, weekdays 10am–4pm, Sunday 9am–7pm.

Tampere/Tammerfors

Cathedral (1907), open May-August, daily 10am–6pm; September-April 11am–5pm. Interesting altarpiece and frescos.

Messukylä Old Church (fifeenth-century) is the oldest building in Tampere. Open summer 10am–6pm.

Eastern Orthodox Church, Tuomiokirkonkatu 27, open May-August, weekdays 10am–3pm, is the only neo-Byzantine church in Nordic countries; its church bells are the biggest in Finland.

Tornio

Tornio Church (1686), Kirkkotie, open 1 June-15 August, weekdays 9am–5pm.

Alatornio Church (1797) is the biggest church in northern Finland.

Turku/Åbo

Cathedral (thirteenth-century), open June-August weekdays 9am–7pm, Saturday 9am–3pm; September-May 10am–4pm, Saturday 10am–4pm, Sunday 2.30–4.30pm all year.

Uusikaupunki/Nystad

Old Church (1629), Rantakatu 39, open 1 June-15 August, Monday-Saturday 11am–3pm, Sunday 12noon–4pm.

Vaasa/Vasa

Old Vaasa (6km from centre) includes the ruins of St Mary's Church from the fourteenth century.

Vantaa/Vanda

Granite church (1494) in the village of Helsinki parish.

Other Places of Interest

Aiskainen

Louhisaari
about 30km from Turku.
Example of Dutch Renaissance manor house, built 1655.

Forssa

Spinning Mill
Founded 1847; brick factory buildings and wooden dwellings for workers.

Hämeenlinna/Tavastehus

Aulanko National Park:
Aulanko Tower and café
☎ (9) 17–120 314
Open: 1 May-31 August, daily.

Hanko

Water Tower
Open: summertime, daily 10am–1pm.

Helsinki

Parliament House
Mannerheimintie 30
For entrance hours:
☎ (9) 0–169 37 57
(City Tourist Office)

Helsinki Zoo
Korkeasauri Island
☎ (9) 0–170 077
Specialities include snow leopard, amur tiger, pandas, reindeer etc.
Open: daily, May 10am–8pm; June/July 10am–8pm; September 10am–7pm; October-February 10am–4pm; March 10am–5pm; April 10am–6pm.

Suomenlinna Fortress
island near harbour
☎ (9) 0–668 154/668 341 (summer)
Eighteenth-century fortifications, museums, parks, beach, restaurant.
Open: May-September.

University Botanical Gardens
Unioninkatu 44
☎ (9) 0–650 188/83
Open: daily 7am–9pm.

Sibelius Monument
Sibelius Park
off Mechelininkatu

Unusual monument of steel pipes (1967) by Eila Hiltunen.

Stadium Tower
Eläintarha
☎ (9) 0–440 363
Lookout tower of Olympic Stadium.
Open: daily 9am–5pm; 1 June–30 August, weekdays 9am–8pm. weekends 9am–5pm.

Jaala

Verla Groundwood/Paper Mill
60km from Lahti
Power plants from nineteenth century. Museum.

Jakobstad/Pietarsaari

Viexpo
Strengbergsgatan
☎ (9) 67–13 100
Permanent exhibition of export goods.
Open: weekdays 8am–4pm, weekends 11am–2pm.

Karjaa

Mustio Manor
60km east of Helsinki
Built in 1780s, converted into hotel 1986.

Korka

Sunila Sulphate Cellulose Mill
Built 1936–9 and 1951–4.
Designed by Alvar Aalto.

Kotka

Haukkavuori Look-out Tower
Memorial to naval battle of Ruotsinsalmi (1790).
Open: 1 May-31 August, daily 11am–9pm.

Kuopio

Puijo Tower
75m-high (245ft), revolving restaurant, observation decks.
Open: 1-31 May, daily 10am–6pm; 1 June-31 July, daily 9am–midnight; 31 August-30 September daily 10am–6pm.

Lahti

Lahti Sports Centre
Comprises ski stadium, ski jumps, ice stadium, swimming pool, running track, sports hall.
Open: May-September, weekdays 11am–6pm, weekends 10am–5pm.

Lappeenranta/Villmanstrand

Linnoitus (Fortress)
The oldest part of the town. Many sights located here including Finland's oldest Orthodox church, Southern Karelia Museum, fortified walls from eighteenth century.

Lohja/Lojo

Kirkniemi Estate.From the eighteenth century, once owned by Mannerheim.

Mariehamn/Maarianhamina

Four-masted barque *Pommern* preserved as a museum ship.
Open: June 9am–5pm; July/August 9am–7pm.

Naantali/Nådendal

Kultaranta
Luonnonmaa Island
☎ (9) 21–755 390
President's summer residence.
Open: Friday 6–8pm.

Nurmes

Bomba
Ritoniemi (2.5km from centre)
Traditional Karelian house.
Whole Karelian village surrounds it.

Outokumpu

Keretti Mine
Oldest mine still operating in
Finland.
Open: summer, weekends
10am–2pm.

Elna Sivukari's Weaving Shop and
  Pottery
Suutarinkatu 2
☎ (9) 73–51 466
Open: June-August, weekdays
9am–5pm, Saturday 9am–4pm;
September-May, on request,
weekdays 9am–5pm, Saturday
9am–12noon.

Pohja

Billnäs and Fiskars Ironworks
20km from Ekenäs
Established 1640s, still in industrial
use.

Rovaniemi

Santa Claus's Workshop Village
on the Arctic Circle, 10km north of
the town on highway E4.
Open: June-August, daily
9am–8pm; September-May, daily
9am–5pm.

Ruotsinpyhtää

Strömfors Ironworks
55km from Porvoo/Borgå
Established 1698.

Savonlinna/Nyslott

Olavinlinna Castle
Built in a strategically important
location on border of Sweden and
Russia in 1475.

Sund

Fortress of Kastelholm
Tosarby
Built fourteenth century to
strengthen position of Swedish
Crown in Baltic.

Tampere/Tammerfors

Särkänniemi Tourist Centre
Aquarium, dolphinarium,
amusement park, planetarium,
observation tower, zoo.
Open in summer, daily
10am–5.30pm.

Turku/Åbo

Turku Castle
Begun in the thirteenth century.
Restored after World War II.
Houses the Historical Museum of
the City of Turku.

National Parks

**Eastern Gulf of Finland
National Park:** 5sq km, covering
the outer group of islands along the
easternmost part of the south
coast. Seabird colonies abound
throughout.

Helvetinjärvi: 21sq km, a rugged
forest area in northern Häme. Best
known sight is Helvetinkolu, a deep
chasm.

Hiidenportti: 40sq km, a rugged wilderness area.

Isojärvi: 19sq km, situated in Kuhmoinen. The park is composed of sections on the north and west banks of Lake Isojärvi.

Kauhaneva-Pohjakangas: 32sq km, a valuable conservation area by international standards. Rich bird life, pine trees.

Lauhanvuori: 26sq km, famous for crystal-clear springs and streams, several ski and hiking trails.

Lemmenjoki: 2,800sq km, the largest national park in Finland, roadless wilderness, coniferous forests, birch forests, Lemmenjoki River valley, gold panning areas.

Liesjärvi: 6.3sq km, sparsely-populated forest, southern Finland.

Linnansaari: 21sq km, a group of islands in Lake Saimaa. Glens, forests, coves, bare rocks.

Oulanka: 206sq km, wild region bordering on River Oulankajoki, flowering meadows, ravines.

Pallas-Ounastunturi: 500sq km, Lapland mountain plateau, typical mixture of forest and peatland.

Patvinsuo: 100sq km, an expanse of Peatland in the Lieska and Ilomantsi area. Many large animals and birds of prey.

Petkeljärvi: 6.3sq km, a beautiful part of Karelia, pine forests.

Pyhä-Häkki: 12sq km, a sample of southern Finland's primeval forest.

Pyhätunturi: 42sq km, great Finnish fells, deep ravines, bare rocks.

Riistunturi: 76sq km, an untouched wilderness area of forest, bogs, hills.

Rokua: 4.2sq km, coastal sand dunes, ponds, peatlands and kettle holes.

Salamajärvi: 55sq km, situated in the municipalities of Perho, Kivijärvi and Kinnula in the Suomenselkä plateau. Lake areas.

Seitseminen: 31sq km, forest and bog area typical of southern Finland.

South-western Archipelago National Park: 30sq km, a mosaic of rocky islands, richly varied flora and fauna.

Urho Kekkonen National Park: 2,530sq km, stretches from the Raututunturit–Saariselkä area to the east to the forests of the Nuorttijoki River. Wide variety of flora and fauna.

Natural Beauty Spots

The Coast and Archipelago

Giant's Cauldrons, Hiidenkirnut at Korttia, 26km from Porvoo. Worn out of granite, dating from Ice Age about 10,000 years ago. The largest is 4.2m wide (14ft) and 10.3m deep (34ft)

Hailuoto Sands, Hailuoto is an island about 40km from Oulu. Important spot for birds.

Hankoniemi, 130km west of Helsinki — 40km-long peninsula, covered with sandy beaches.

Sandbanks at Kalajoki, 180km from Vaasa on road to Oulu. 3km-long dunes. Just off coast is idyllic fisherman's isle, *Maakalla*, with a twice daily boat connection.

Yyteri Sands, Pori — about 20km from Pori. Bird-spotting.

Turunmaa Archipelago, south-western archipelago is made up of 10,000 islands.

Finnish Lakeland

Pulkkilanharju Ridge, about 35km to north of Lahti on Asikkala–Sysmä road. Great natural beauty.

Imatrankoski Rapids, Imatra. Finland's best harnessed rapids.

Vetroniemi and Keisarinharju Ridges, about 20km to east of Tampere. Beautiful views of western lakeland.

Koli Hills, 70km from Joensuu. Northern Karelia's highest fell. Breathtaking views.

Kelvenne Island, 60km north of Lahti off E4 road — known for great beauty.

Punkaharju Ridge, 30km east of Savonlinna — probably Finland's best known beauty spot.

Northern Finland

Lemmenjoki River valley, 46km from Inari towards Kittilä. Most impressive site in Lemmenjoki nature park.

Saana Fell and Malla nature park, Kilpisjärvi. *Saana Fell* is the best lookout point over the fell landscape. *Malla nature park* and *Malla fell* are beautiful — rich flora, gorges.

River Oulankajoki canyon and *Ristikallio Cliffs* on the River Aventojoki in Oulanka national park about 50km from Kuusama towards Salla Rapids.

Giant's Cauldrons; Hiidenkirnut at Hirvas. 25km from Rovaniemi.

Kevo Canyon, 30km from Utsjoki to south in direction of Inari, 40km long, biggest natural attraction in N. Lapland.

Geographical Terms

Finnish — English
vaara, vuori, tunturi — hill, mountain
huippu — peak
kallio — rock face
selkä, harju — hill ridge
mäki — low hill
laakso — valley
joki — river
koski — waterfall
salmi — arm of sea
vesi — water, lake
ranta — beach, flat coast
saari — island
metsä — wood, forest
suo — moorland
kaupunki — town
kirkko — church
torni — tower
linna — castle
puutarha, puisto — garden, park
katu — street
(maan) tie — road
(kauppa) tori — (market) square

silta — bridge
rautatie — railway
lossi, lautta — ferry

Winter Sports

The following are just a few of the
areas with facilities for cross-
country and downhill skiing:

Jyväskylä
Kemijärvi
Kilpisjärvi
Kolari Yllästunturi
Koli Hills
Kuopio
Kuusamo
Lahti
Muonio
Pallastunturi area
Rovaniemi
Saariselkä – Kaunispää
Salla
Sodankylä
Sotkamo

Annual Events

January
Jyväskylä — Winter Festival
Kuopio — January Fair and
Carnival

February
Helsinki — International Boat Show
Lahti, Vääsky — Skating Marathon
Hämeenlinna — Finlandia cross-
country ski-race

February/March
Inari — Reindeer Driving Competi-
tion
Rovaniemi — Winter Market

April
Helsinki — Easter Festival
Kolari — International Winter
Games

30 April-1 May
May Night throughout the country

May
Valkeakoski — Folk Festival

22/23 June
Midsummer Eve

June
Jyväskylä — Arts Festival
Åland Islands — Mail Rowing Race
Kuopio — Dance and Music
Festival
Oulu — Northern Finland Fair
Helsinki — Helsinki Day

July
Vaasa — Folk Festival
Lappeenranta, Imatra — Finnish
Dance Festival
Savonlinna — Opera Festival

August
Turku — Music Festival
Tampere — Summer Theatre
Helsinki — Helsinki Festival

6 December
Independence Day throughout the
country

Travelling to Finland

By Air
Finland can be easily reached from
all major cities around the world;
Helsinki is the perfect gateway

between east and west. Regular
non-stop flights are scheduled by
Finnair from twenty-three cities in
Europe (DC–9) as well as from
Montreal, New York, Seattle and
Los Angeles (DC–10). Finnair also
run about six flights a week from
London to Tampere via Helsinki.

By Sea
See also page 182.
Finnjet - Silja Line maintains
regular passenger services
between Travemünde in Germany
and Helsinki with the GTS Finnjet
all year round. *Polferries* run a
regular service from Gdansk to
Helsinki. There are daily
departures by the *Silja Line* from
Stockholm to Helsinki, Stockholm
to Turku and from Stockholm to
Mariehamn. *Silja Line* also
arranges attractively-priced mini-
cruises and hotel packages
between Stockholm and Helsinki
and Stockholm and Turku and vice
versa. The package gives you a
full-day in either Stockholm or
Helsinki and includes a berth in a
cabin and meals both ways. Hotel
packages include a berth in a cabin
both ways, accommodation in a
double room plus breakfast at the
hotel of your choice.

Viking Line run a regular
service from Stockholm to Helsinki,
Stockholm to Turku via Mariehamn
and from Kappellskär to Naantali
via Mariehamn. *Viking Line* also
has a cruising programme all year
round between Sweden and
Finland.

Birka Line runs services from
Stockholm to Mariehamn; *Anedin
Line* runs services from Stockholm
to Mariehamn; *Eckerö Line* from

Grisslehamn to Eckerö; *Vaasa
Ferries* from Umeå to Vaasa and
from Sundsvall to Vaasa; *Jakob
Line* run routes from Skellefteå to
Kokkola and from Skellefteå to
Pietarsaari.

See Useful Addresses for
details of the above shipping lines.

Youth and Student Travel
Students can take advantage of
low cost student flights to and from
Finland arranged by the Finnish
Student Travel Service (FSTS) and
other members of the Student Air
Travel Association (SATA). In
general, those eligible to travel on
these flights are:
1. Full-time students at a university, college or other establishment
of higher education.
2. Scholars (minimum age 12
years, maximum age 22 years) in
full-time attendance for a minimum
of a full school year at a recognised
educational establishment.

Eligibility is guaranteed for
holders of ISIC of FIYTO-card
holders only.Youth/student
discounts are also granted on
regular domestic and international
air routes.

Railway, bus and shipping
companies also give reductions to
students and young people under
26 (FIYTO-card holders) on certain
routes and during certain periods.
Information on transportation,
accommodation, tourist services,
cultural and miscellaneous
reductions in the FIYTO brochure
Discounts for Youth Travel.

For detailed information,
contact Travela-FSTS, Mannerheimintie 5C, 00100 Helsinki or
your local Student Travel Bureau.

Travelling Within Finland

By Air
See page 183. For detailed information regarding domestic flights and special reductions, contact Finnair — see Useful Addresses.

By Coach
For services, contact OY Matkahuotto A6, Head Office, Lauttasaarentie 8, 00200 Helsinki ☎ (9) 0–692 20 88.

By Rail
See page 183. For information regarding train times, routes, special discounts, tickets, connections to the USSR and reservations, contact the Finnish State Railways — see Useful Addresses.

By Sea
See page 184. For information regarding Lakeland boat services, contact the Finnish Tourist Board — see Useful Addresses.

Car Hire
A valid driving licence is usually all that is required. Advance deposits are payable at the time of hire. The minimum age of the hirer varies from 19 to 23.

Advice to Car Drivers

As well as the regulations outlined on page 185, the following should also be noted:
1. Foreign vehicles must display an international distinguishing sign.
2. A person living permanently in Finland cannot use a motor vehicle registered outside Finland unless this person is accompanied by the owner of the vehicle.
3. The holder of a small motorcycle (less than 125cc) must be 16 years old or over and the holder of a large motorcycle (over 125cc), car or van must be 18 years or over. A driving licence is not required for a moped (less than 50cc, maximum speed 40km/h (25mph)) However, the driver must be 15 years old or over and the moped must be covered by third party insurance.

Alcohol
Driving with a blood alcohol content of 0.5 parts/1000 is a punishable offence. Penalties are extremely severe if the driver's blood alcohol content is 1.5 parts/1000 or more.

Compulsory Regulations
1. Driver and front seat passengers must wear a seat belt.
2. Moped riders, motorcyclists and passengers must wear a crash helmet.
3. All vehicles must use headlights outside built-up areas. Use of fog lights is permitted only in fog, heavy rain or snow.

Elk and Reindeer Warning
Elk (moose), deer and reindeer abound in Finland and often cross the roads. Warning signs showing approximate lengths of the danger zones are posted in these areas. An elk can weigh anything up to 500–600 kg. Collisions involving these animals are usually serious. Elks are most active at dusk but may be encountered at other times, too. If you are involved in a

reindeer or elk collision, report this without delay to the local police.

Garages are usually open from 7am to 4pm on weekdays. Bigger garages may have breakdown lorries and towing facilities.

If necessary, you can have your windscreen replaced not only in garages but also at some service stations.

Filling stations are usually open from 7am to 9pm, but not quite so long on Sundays. Many stations offer a 24-hour sale of fuel at the height of the season and many of them have cafés.

In the Event of an Accident

Both parties are obliged to give all the necessary information about themselves and the vehicle. Police must be notified in the event of serious injury.

If involved in an accident, one should report it without delay to the Finnish Motor Insurer's Bureau *Liikenneva-kuutusyhdistys*, Bulevardi 28, 00120 Helsinki, ☎ (9) 0–19 251, which deals with traffic accidents involving foreign motor vehicles in Finland.

Parking

Stopping and parking on the left side of the road is prohibited with the exception of one-way road-ways. Stopping and parking is prohibited on pavements; pedes-trian crossings and bicycle paths and also less than 5m (16ft) before a pedestrian crossing or an intersecting bicycle path; at crossroads or less than 5m (16ft) before the nearest side of an intersecting roadway.

Outside built-up areas, parking is prohibited on the carriageway of priority roads. Parking is prohibited on both sides of the road at points designated for passing.

Speed Limits

In built-up areas: Speed limits are indicated by a sign where a speed limit begins and by an additional panel bearing the word 'Aluerajoi-tus' (zone), 'Regional begränsning' (Area speed limit), 'Alue' or 'Zon' (Zone).

Outside built-up areas: Signs may bear the words 'Perusnopeus' (General speed limit) or 'Bashas-tighet' (basic speed limit). Maxi-mum allowable speed for buses is 80km/h, except in Lapland and or motorways where it is 100km/h. Maximum speed for lorries, vans and special vehicles including caravans and cars with trailers is 80km/h. For other speed limits, see page 185.

Accommodation

Hotels and Motels

See also page 186. It is becoming increasingly common for hotels to offer accommodation at reduced rates, especially for groups and during weekends, or for holders of city cards. Offers may apply to accommodation alone or include other services.

Most hotels and motels are new and of a high standard with all modern conveniences, such as a bath and/or shower, WC, telephone and radio in every room. There is almost invariably a sauna and often a swimming pool also. Rooms in country hotels frequently have a balcony. Restaurants in hotels and motels serve meals until late at night and are open to the public as well as guests. There is no limit to the length of stay in a motel. Finnish hotels and motels are open all the year except for the summer hotels, open from 1 June-31 August. These are university students' living quarters used as hotels in summer time and are mostly quite new with the same type of conveniences and services as in an ordinary hotel, but the prices are lower.

Many hotels include breakfast in their room rates. Breakfast is often a *smörgåsbord* with eggs, cold meat, cheese, bread, butter, marmalade, coffee, tea etc.

Service charge is included in the room rate. The service charge for meals and drinks is 14 per cent on weekdays and 15 per cent on Friday evenings, Saturdays, Sundays, holidays and the eve of holidays.

Contact the Finnish Tourist Board for information about the various hotel discount systems.

Farmhouse Holidays

There are about 150 farmhouses which take guests on a full board, half board or bed-and-breakfast basis. They are in genuine rural settings and, almost without exception, close to water. The guest rooms are always clean even if almost without modern conveniences but there is usually a bathroom in the house and a sauna is always at the guest's disposal.

Accommodation is in the main building, separate barns or outhouses. Some farms also have individual cottages for guests; or apartment with kitchen including fridge and electric stove for those who wish to cater for themselves. The guest is almost a member of the family and joins them for their meals. He can have a sauna bath twice a week, walk in the forest, row, fish or take part in the work on the farm, hay-making or looking after the animals.

Classification: Farmhouses are classified into four grades shown by the stars allocated, the best having four stars. The following facilities are provided, but there may be additional items supplied.
**** Electricity, central heating, hot and cold water, WC, separate shower, sauna, beach.
*** Electricity, wood stoves for heating or electric heaters, hot and cold water, WC, shower, sauna.
** Gas light and heating (or oil heating), hot and cold water, WC, sauna.
* Gas or oil lamps, portable heater, chemical closet, cold water or no running water, sauna, no shower.

Prices: Full board prices include accommodation, breakfast, at least two hot meals per day, one of which can be replaced by a packed meal. Half board prices include accommodation, breakfast and dinner. Bed-and-breakfast prices include accommodation and breakfast. Children 50–75 per cent reduction. Bed linen and sauna twice a week is usually also included in the price.

Holiday Cottages

There are about 5,000 private holiday cottages ranging from the humblest fishing hut on the coast or in the archipelago to the luxury log cottages in the lake regions. All the holiday cottages are furnished and cooking utensils, cutlery and crockery are included, as well as bed clothes, fuel for heating, cooking and lighting and in many cases a sauna and boat. The clients need only bring bed linen and towels. Most inland cottages are near a farm, where the tourist can buy food.

Peak season extends from about mid-June to mid-August and from the beginning of January to the end of April.

Classification: Holiday cottages are classified into five grades shown by the stars allocated, the best having five stars.

***** Cottage with at least living-room, two bedrooms, kitchen, sauna, electricity and every modern convenience.

**** Cottage with at least living-room, one bedroom, kitchen, sauna, electricity, no WC or hot water, bed alcove, kitchenette, sauna (own or shared). In general electricity, privy, well.

*** Cottage with at least living-room, bed alcove, kitchenette, sauna (own or shared). In general electricity, privy, well.

** Cottage with at least living-room, possibly bed alcove, sauna (own or shared). Open fireplace, gas stove, privy, well.

* Cottage with living-room/kitchen, sauna (own or shared). Gas cooker, privy, well.

Prices: Rates in a holiday cottage depend on situation, size and equipment. There are usually reductions out of season.

Camping

See also page 188. There are about 360 camping sites in Finland evenly distributed over the whole country. Over 230 camping sites belong to the Finnish Travel Association's national network. They are easily identified by the blue and white sign with a picture of a tent inside a large C. Each site has an official permit from the Ministry of the Interior to operate and they are all officially inspected.

Camping season. The camping season begins in May or June and ends in August or September. Camping is possible in southern Finland for 3 months and in northern Finland for about 2 months, from the point of view of the best weather. However, the camping sites are open much longer and there are some which stay open the whole year round.

Camping cottages. There are many camping sites where a party of campers can stay over-night in inexpensive cottages, or in holiday cottages if the stay is a longer one. In the camping cottages there are usually places for two–six people to sleep, a hotplate or stove, a table and chairs and heating facilities. In a holiday cottage there are in addition cutlery, china and a fridge, and sometimes a sauna. It is wise to take one's own bedclothes for a camping cottage although the kiosk on some sites sells disposable sheets. During the high season there is a demand for holiday cottages so it is advisable to book these in advance.

Caravans. In summer there are about 200 sites where a caravan can be linked to the electricity supply (220 V). In winter there are about 100 such places forming part of winter sports centres, holiday villages, hostels and hotels.

Classification of camping sites. Finnish camping sites are classified into three grades shown by the stars allocated, the best having three stars. *On a one-star site* (*) there are e.g. washing facilities with main drainage, a covered cooking area or place for lighting a fire, WC's and places for washing-up. *A two-star site* (**) has to be guarded at night, equipped with waste pipes, WC's, kitchens, washing facilities with main drainage, showers, children's playgrounds, beaches for swimming etc. *A three-star site* (***) in addition to the services mentioned above, must be guarded night and day; there must be washing facilities equipped with hot water, places for washing and ironing clothes; hot showers and hot water for washing-up, areas for play and ball games etc.

Prices. It costs 22–55mk (1987) depending on the site classification, for an overnight stay at a camping site for a family i.e. two adults, children, car, tent or trailer. The charge includes the basic facilities: e.g. cooking, washing, washing up etc.

For further information, contact the Camping Department of the Finnish Travel Association (see Useful Addresses).

Youth Hostels

Finland is covered by an extensive network of about 160 youth hostels. They vary considerably in both standard and type, some being in small farmhouses, some in manor houses, others in course centres, camping sites, student hostels and so on. Accommodation ranges from family rooms for two to four persons to dormitories for five to ten persons. Almost all hostels have family rooms.

Season: Most hostels are open in summer only; about fifty are open all year round.

Classification: The hostels are grouped into four categories, depending on their facilities. Those in the top category, the four-star hostels, also provide facilities for courses and conferences. The first, one-star category hostels meet the international basic requirements. Some hostels are self-catering, and in almost all of them guests can use the kitchen. Most of the hostels provide light refreshments, some even meals.

Prices: The overnight charges vary between 22mk and 60mk (1987), depending on the category and the number of beds in the room. Sheets are available for an additional charge. Public health regulations prevent the use of sleeping bags.

Visitors are advised to have a valid Youth Hostel membership card from his/her own national youth hostel association. Non-members must pay an additional 'one-night guest card' fee of 10mk (1987) per person per night. There

is no age limit for users of youth
hostels in Finland.

Youth hostels are easy to find
because the signposts leading to
them bear the international 'House
and Fir Tree' emblem of the IYHF
(International Youth Hostel
Federation). Youth hostels
belonging to the Finnish network
are indicated with a triangular
symbol, showing that they meet
internationally approved standards.

Each year the Finnish Youth
Hostel Association publishes a
catalogue of Finnish youth hostels
and their facilities 'Retkeilymajat -
vandrarhem'. It contains valuable
information about the youth
hostels, tips about staying in youth
hostels both in Finland and abroad.
The list is obtainable from youth
hostels and bookshops in Finland
or direct from the Finnish Youth
Hostel Association. (See Useful
Addresses).

Holiday Villages

Finland has over 200 holiday
villages, of which about forty
belong to the Association of
Finnish Holiday Villages.

The villages differ as to layout.
In some the cottages are in a row
fairly close together, in others they
are scattered over the area and
can be as much as 300ft apart.
Many holiday villages are linked
with camping sites.

The cottage usually consists of
a combined sitting and bedroom, a
kitchen with a gas or electric
cooker, fridge, crockery, cutlery
and kitchen utensils. Bed linen and
towels are not always included.
There are often running water and
a WC in the cottage and a sauna is

available in the village. In Lapland
for climatic reasons there is usually
no running water but the log cabins
are otherwise pleasant and
comfortable.

Holiday villages are usually
near to a village where there are
shops and kiosks. If holiday
villages are isolated, they are
sometimes visited a couple of
times a week by a mobile shop,
which in the archipelago is on a
boat.

Peak season. In summer from
mid-June to mid-August. At other
times villages give off-season
reductions. The cottages are
usually rented by the week, from
Saturday to Saturday, but they can
also be rented by the day.
Bookings for the peak season
should be made the previous
winter as most cottages are
booked up by spring. The best
holiday villages are open all the
year and are excellent places for a
winter holiday and skiing.

Prices. In the best villages
these range from 1,000–2,500mk
(1987) per week per cottage, in
some villages luxury bungalows up
to 4,200mk (1987) per week.
Those in the top price bracket have
several rooms, all modern
conveniences and TV in the village.
The best villages also include a
restaurant and a hotel on the site.
From the point of view of the
services or facilities they offer, the
five categories of holiday villages
and accommodation can be
described as follows:

*	simple holiday village/cottage
**	ordinary holiday village/cottage

*** good holiday
village/cottage
**** high standard holiday
village/cottage
***** luxury holiday
village/cottage

Contact the Association of Finnish Holiday Villages for further information. (See Useful Addresses).

Tips for Travellers

Churches

English-language services in Helsinki are held at the Temppeliaukio church ('the church in the rock'), Lutherinkatu 3, at 2pm in the winter and 3pm in the summer, on Sundays and at Lähetyskirkko, Tähtitorninkatu 18, at 10am. In other major cities services are held in English about once a month. For further information contact the International Evangelical Church, ☎ (9)0–406 091/446 776. Other churches in Helsinki: Adventist, Anglican, Baptist, Methodist, Orthodox, Pentecostal, Roman Catholic and Salvation Army. There are also a Mormon church, a Jewish synagogue and a mosque in Helsinki. There are Roman Catholic churches in Jyväskylä, Tampere and Turku, and Orthodox churches in Helsinki and in other parts of the country. Service times vary in difference parishes.

Further information: Information Centre of the Evangelical Lutheran Church of Finland, Luotsikatu 1a, 00160 Helsinki ☎ (9)0–18 021.

City Cards

The *Helsinki Card* can be bought at about thirty-five places in Helsinki including the Hotel Booking Centre (see Useful Addresses), the City Tourist Office, travel agencies and hotels. Valid for up to 3 days (3 days costs 90mk adults, 45mk children 1987 prices) the *Helsinki Card* is useful for unlimited travel on city buses, trams and metro, sightseeing, free entry to about fifty museums and other places of interest; it also includes hotel packages.

The Turku Card may be bought at the Turku City Tourist Office, at the harbour terminals in Turku and Naantali and in hotels. Valid for up to 3 days (60mk adults, 30mk children for 3 days 1987 prices) the *Turku Card* entitles you to free travel on buses, free entry to places of interest in Turku and in Naantali, free extras in a number of restaurants, discounts in certain shops and on a number of sightseeing tours.

Credit Cards

American Express, Diner's Club, Eurocard, Access, Master Card (Master Charge) and Visa are accepted in hotels, restaurants, larger shops, and department stores.

Further information in Helsinki ☎ (9)0–125 11 (American Express), (9)0–694 7122 (Diner's Club) and (9)0–692 2439 for the others.

Customs Regulations

In addition to the regulations outlined on page 177, the following should be observed:

In addition to their ordinary travel requisites travellers may bring in goods to the value of 1,000mk intended as gifts or to be used or consumed by the traveller himself or his family. This amount may not include more than 15kg (33lb) of foodstuffs, of which 5kg (11lb) at most may be edible fats; it is, however, forbidden to import more than 2.5kg (5lb) of butter.
The importation of alcoholic beverages which contain ethyl alcohol more than 52 per cent by weight (= 60 per cent by volume) and kits for making alcoholic drinks is prohibited.

Live animals may be imported only with a permit from the Veterinary Department of the Ministry of Agriculture and Forestry. The mandatory quarantine period in Finland is 4 months. Dogs and cats can, however, be imported from Norway and Sweden provided they are accompanied by a certificate issued by a competent veterinary surgeon in the country of exportation and by a declaration given by the owner of the animal.

Live plants and vegetables: Live plants, floricultural products, potatoes, vegetables, garden stuff and root plants and the like may, in general, be imported only with a phytosanitary certificate issued by the plant protection authorities in the country of cultivation and endorsed by the corresponding Finnish authorities. Without a certificate a traveller may bring fruit, berries, less than 3kg of flower bulbs, rhizomes and vegetables, bunches of flowers and pot-plants from European countries carried by the traveller or in

baggage (but not for sale or planting in open ground).

Products, including souvenirs, made of endangered animals and plants may not be imported into Finland without necessary permits (CITES, Convention on International Trade in Endangered Species of wild fauna and flora).

Pharmaceutical products: The importation of pharmaceutical products, narcotics, certain poisons, and radioactive substances is prohibited without a proper permit. A traveller may, however, bring in small amounts of medicines for their own use.

Firearms: A licence must be obtained for firearms and ammunition imported by a traveller for his own use. This is issued by the police at the place of importation. Usually the permit can be obtained from the airport or harbour police. This certificate serves as a licence to carry firearms for 2 months.

Meat and meat products may be imported only with a permit from the Veterinary Department of the Ministry of Agriculture and Forestry. Without a permit a traveller may import less than 8kg of (e.g. tinned) meat or meat products if these have been rendered free of infectious diseases by heating or other thermal treatment.

Dairy and egg products: Milk, cream and soured milk products, as well as raw cheese and egg products can be imported only with a permit granted by the Veterinary Department of the Ministry of Agriculture and Forestry. However, the following

can be imported without a licence:
a) pasteurised, heat-treated and
sterilised consumer milk products
such as milk, cream and soured
milk products in retail packages, to
a maximum of 8 litres.
b) pasteurised or sterilised egg
products in retail packages, to a
maximum of 4kg.

**Restrictions on the export
of works of art etc.** The
following articles may not be taken
out of Finland without a special
export licence issued by the
National Board of Antiquities and
Historical Monuments (Museovi-
rasto), a regional museum or some
other museum authorised to issue
such a licence:
1. Works of art more than 50 years
old as well as products of the art
and art handicraft industries,
2. Any other objects more than 50
years old possessing cultural or
historical value; and
3. Objects relating to Finnish
national history and distinguished
persons, as well as scientifically
important collections, e.g. of coins,
medals and postage stamps,
regardless of their age.

Exchange Offices
Foreign Exchange Offices: All
banks: open Monday–Friday
9.30am–4pm (office hours may
vary regionally). Helsinki Railway
Station: open 11.30am–6pm daily.
Tampere City Tourist Office open
June-August, Saturday
9am–12noon. South Harbour
Customs Pavilion, Helsinki daily
9am–12am, 3pm–6pm and during
the arrival and departure of ships.
Katajanokka Harbour in Helsinki,
Turku and Naantali harbours during

the arrival and departure of ships.
In Helsinki-Vantaa Airport, open
daily 6.30am–11pm, Turku Airport
Monday–Friday 9am–2pm. Utsjoki-
Nuorgam customs Monday–Friday
9.30am–12.15 and 12.45–3pm.
Also from mid-June to end of
August at Karesuvanto customs
and in Kilpisjärvi Tourist Hotel daily
9am–3.30pm.

Health Care
See page 179. Medicines are sold
at pharmacies (*apteekki*). Note that
chemists (*kemikalikauppa*) only sell
cosmetics. Some pharmacies are
on duty round the clock. All
hospitals have doctors on duty
round the clock. Municipal, central
and regional hospitals charge
40mk (1987) for a visit to an out-
patient clinic and 50mk (1987) a
day in a ward in local hospitals and
in central hospitals. This includes
treatment, doctor's fee and
medicine. Private hospitals are
considerably more expensive.
Information about health care
available round the clock,
☎ (9)0–735 001. There are dentists
on duty in Helsinki round the clock,
☎ (9)0–736 166) as well as an
emergency doctor service (☎ 008
or 000). Emergency hospital
treatment for foreigners with
doctors on duty around the clock:
Helsinki University Central
Hospital, ☎ (9)0–4711. Corresponding telephone numbers in
other towns are available at hotels.

Passports
See also page 176. Although a visa
is not required for a stay of less
than 3 months, it is required after
that period and by foreigners

proposing to take up employment in Finland. Within Scandinavia there are no passport controls between the individual countries which have formed a Nordic Passport and Customs Union. Travellers who plan a trip across the border to the USSR, must have a Russian visa. It is advisable to get it in the traveller's country of origin because it takes at least 8 weekdays to obtain a visa in Helsinki.

Postal Services
See page 177. Poste Restante: In Helsinki at the Main Post Office, Mannerheimintie 11, 00100 Helsinki. Open 8am–10pm weekdays, 11am–10pm Sundays. In other towns in connection with the Main Post Office. Yellow mail boxes (on walls) for collections daily. Stamps available at Post Offices, book and paper shops, stations, hotels.

Service Charges and Tipping
The service charge is included in the room rate. The service charge for meals and drinks is 14 per cent on weekdays and 15 per cent on Friday evenings, Saturdays, Sundays, days before holidays and holidays. The service charge is often omitted from restaurant menus so it is added to the bill by the waiter/waitress. A few extra coins are often left.

The obligatory cloakroom fee to hotel or restaurant doormen is usually clearly indicated. It is usually 3–4mk (1987)

Further information: Hotel and Restaurant Council, Merim-iehenkatu 29, 00150 Helsinki

☎ (9)0–632 488, and Finnish Hotel, Restaurant and Cafeteria Association, Merimiehenkatu 29, 00150 Helsinki ☎ (9)0–176 455.

Tax-free Shopping
Anyone permanently resident outside Scandinavia can shop 'tax free' in Finland, thus saving about 11 per cent on purchases over 150mk. The Finland tax-free shopping stores will provide the customer a cheque covering the tax; this can be cashed on leaving the country, even if the goods were bought on a credit card.

The cheque, together with the goods purchased, should be presented at the point of departure, when it will be paid in cash. Tax-free purchases must be taken out of Finland and may not be used before leaving the country.

Repayment at the following airport transit halls: Helsinki, Turku, Tampere, Mariehamn, Vaasa, Rovaniemi, on board ferries and ships belong to: Finnjet-Silja Line, Silja Line, Viking Line, Vaasa Ferries, Polferries. Also at the main overland border crossings to Sweden, Norway and the USSR. On board cruise vessels, repay-ment is taken care of before leaving port.

Further information: Oy Finland Tax-free Shopping FTS Ab, Et. Makasiinikatu 4, 00130 Helsinki, Finland ☎ (9)0–178 2465.

Taxis
Taxis can be obtained by tele-phone (see telephone directory under 'Taksiasemat'), from taxi ranks or signalled from the street. All taxis have an illuminated yellow

sign 'taksi'. When the sign is lit up the taxi is free. Fares differ slightly in the countryside from those in the towns. The basic fare (September 1986) in Finland was 8.80mk except in Helsinki (9.80mk). The fare rises gradually on a kilometre basis, as indicated by the meter. There is an extra night (6pm–6am) and Sunday charge (2pm Saturday-6am Monday) of 4mk (1986). The waiting charge was 86.75mk an hour in Helsinki and 78.40–83.30mk elsewhere. Price examples: The taxi fare in Helsinki for a 10km journey was approximately 45mk for 1–2 persons. (All 1986 prices)

Telephones ('Puhelin")
See page 178. Phone directories contain white and yellow pages. White pages have an English summary including international dialling information. Reduced rate international calls from 10pm–10am weekdays and all day Sunday.

How to Use the Finnish Telephone
1. Lift receiver and await dial tone
2. Put in 1mk or 5mk coin
3. Dial number
4. Phone will ring or you will hear busy tone

Some Useful Telephone Numbers
International code from Finland to the UK: **99044**
International code from Finland to USA/Canada: **9901**
(Followed by dialling code for the exchange (minus the initial **0**) then the number.)

International code for Finland from the UK: **010358**
International code for Finland from USA/Canada: **011358**
(Followed by the dialling code for the exchange (minus the initial **9**) and then the number.)
Information: **09**
Local directory assistance: **012**
Long-distance operator and long-distance directory assistance: **020**
International operator: **92020**
News in English: **040**
Police, Fire, Ambulance **000**

Local Tourist Information Offices

Ekenäs/Tammisaari
Skillnadsgatan 16
10600 Ekenäs
☎ (9)11–14 600/149

Espoo/Esbo
Tapiontori
Tapiola
02100 Espoo
☎ (9)0–467 652/467 692

Hailuoto
90480 Hailuto
☎ (9)81–601 113

Hamina/Fredrikshamn
Fredrikinkatu 4
49400 Hamina
☎ (9)52–44 320

Hanko/Hangö
PB 10
Bulevardi 15
10901 Hanko
☎ (9)11–82 239/81 800

Heinola
Torikatu 8
18100 Heinola
☎ (9)10–58 444

Helsinki
Pohjoisesplanadi 19
00100 Helsinki
☎ (9)0–169 37 57/174 088

Himanka
Himangan Matkailu OY
68100 Himanka
☎ (9) 68–55 300

Hyvinkää/Hyvinge
Hämeenkatu 30
05800 Hyvinkää
☎ (9)14–2511/251 275

Hämeenlinna/Tavastehus
Häme Tourist Office
Raatihuoneenkatu 15
13100 Hämeenlinna
☎ (9)17–202 388

Iisalmi/Idensalmi
Kauppakatu 14
74100 Iisalmi
☎ (9)77–24 611/223/22 346

Imatra
Keskusasema
PB 22
55121 Imatra
☎ (9)54–24 666

Inari
Piiskuntie 5
Bus Station
99801 Ivalo
☎ (9)697–12–521

Jakobstad/Pietarsaari
Storgatan 11
68600 Jakobstad
☎ (9)67–31 796

Joensuu
North Karelian Tourist Office
Koskikatu 1
80100 Joensuu
☎ (9)73–201 362/201 630

Jyväskylä
Vapaudenkatu 38
40100 Jyväskylä
☎ (9)41–294 083

Järvenpää
Hallintokatu 2
PB 41
04401 Järvenpää
☎ (9)0–29 079

Kajaani/Kajana
City-talo
Kirkkokatu 21
87100 Kajaani
☎ (9)86–25 079

Kalajoki
Bus Station
PB 26
85101 Kalajoki
☎ (9)83–60 505

Kemi
Valtakatu 26
Town Hall
94100 Kemi
☎ (9)80–299 361

Kemijärvi
Koillistunturit ry
Luusuantie 15
98100 Kemijärvi
☎ (9)962–13 777

Kokkola/Karleby
Keski-Pohjanmaan Tourist Office
Pitkänsillankatu 39
67100 Kokkola
☎ (9)68–11902

Kotka
Kirkkokatu 8
48100 Kotka
☎ (9)52–11 736

Kouvola
Varuskuntakatu 11
45100 Kouvola
☎ (9)51–296 557/296 558

Kuopio
Haapaniemenkatu 17
70100 Kuopio
☎ (9) 71–182 584/182 585

Lahti
Torikatu 3B
PB 175
15111 Lahti
☎ (9)18–182 580

Lappeenranta/Villmanstrand
Bus Station
53101 Lappeenranta
☎ (9)53–18 580

Lieksa
Pielisentie 7
81700 Lieska
☎ (9)75–20 500/20 499

Lohja/Lojo
Laurinkatu 46
08100 Lohja
☎ (9)12–201 217

Loviisa/Lovisa
Brandensteinsgatan 13
07900 Loviisa
☎ (9)15–52 212

Mariehamn and Åland Islands/
Åland Tourist Information Office
Storagatan 18
22100 Mariehamn
☎ (9)28–16 575

or
Norra Esplanadgatan 1
22100 Mariehamn
☎ (9)28–12 140

Mikkeli/St Michel
Hallituskatu 3a
50100 Mikkeli
☎ (9)55–13 938/11 951

Naantali/Nådendal
Tullikatu 12
21100 Naantali
☎ (9) 21–755 388

Nurmes
Loma-Nurmes Tourist Office
Kirkkokatu 12
75500 Nurmes
☎ (9)76–21 401/21 770

Oulu/Uleåborg
City Hall
Kirkkokatu 2A
90100 Oulu
☎ (9)81–15 121/15 330

Outokumpu
Sepänkatu 6
83500 Outokumpu
☎ (9)73–5910/51 655

Pargas/Parainen
Strandgatan 16
21600 Pargas
☎ (9) 21–744 880/741 777

Pori/Björneborg
Antinkatu 5
28100 Pori
☎ (9)39–15 780

Porvoo/Borgå
Rauhankatu 20
06100 Porvoo
☎ (9)15–170 145/172 721

Raahe/Brahestad
Brahenkatu 12
92100 Raahe
☎ (9)82–38 475

Rauma/Raumo
Eteläkatu 7
26100 Rauma
☎ (9)38–224 555

Riihimäki
Valtakatu 12
11130 Riihimäki
☎ (9)14–641 225

Rovaniemi
Aallonkatu 2C
96200 Rovaniemi
☎ (9)60–16 270

Savonlinna/Nyslott
Olavinkatu 35
57130 Savonlinna
☎ (9)57–13 492/13 493/13 458

Seinäjoki
Kauppakatu 17
60100 Seinäjoki
☎ (9)64–141344

Sodankylä
Jäämerentie 9
99600 Sodankylä
☎ (9)693–13 474

Tampere/Tammerfors
Verkatehtaankatu 2
33100 Tampere
☎ (9) 31–126 652/126 775

Tornio/Torneå
Lukiokatu 10
95400 Tornio
☎ (9)80–40 048

Turku/Åbo
Käsityöläiskatu 3
20100 Turku
☎ (9)21–336 366

Uusikaupunki/Nystad
Levysepänkatu 4A
23500 Uusikaupunki
☎ (9)22–1551/21 225

Vaasa/Vasa
Raastuvankatu 30
65101 Vaasa
☎ (9)61–113 853

Valkeakoski
Valtakatu 20
37600 Valkeakoski
☎ (9)37–46 997

Vantaa/Vanda
Asematie 4
01300 Vantaa
☎ (9)0–839 31 34

Useful Addresses

Accommodation

American Youth Hostels Inc
1332 'I' Street NW
Washington DC 20005
☎ (202) 783 61 61

Association of Finnish Holiday
 Villages
Luostarinkatu 20
21100 Naantali
☎ (9) 21–752 093

Finnish Travel Association
(Camping Department)
Mikonkatu 25
00100 Helsinki
☎ (9) 0–170 868

Finnish Youth Hostel Association
Yrjönkatu 38B
00100 Helsinki
☎ (9) 0–694 0377

Hotel Booking Centre
Railway Station
Asema-aukio 3
00100 Helsinki
☎ (9) 0–171 133

YHA (England and Wales)
14 Southampton Street
London WC2E 7HE
☎ (01) 836 8541

Advice and Information

American Embassy
Itainen Puistotie 14A
00100 Helsinki
☎ (9) 0–171 931

British Embassy
Uudenmaankatu 16–20
00100 Helsinki 12
☎ (9)0–647 922

Canadian Embassy
Pohjoisesplanadi 14A
00100 Helsinki 10
☎ (9) 0–171 141

Central Bureau for Educational
Visits and Exchanges
Seymour Mews House,
Seymour Mews
London W1H 9PE

Finnish Embassy
38 Chesham Place
London SW1X 8HW
☎ (01) 235 9531

Finnish Embassy
3216 New Mexico Avenue NW
Washington DC 20016
☎ (202) 363 2430

Finnish Embassy
222 Somerset Street West
Suite 401 Ottowa
Ontario K2P 2G3
☎ (613) 263 2389

Finnish Tourist Board
66–68 Haymarket
London SW1Y 4RF
☎ (01) 839 4048

Finnish Tourist Board
655 Third Avenue
New York
NY 10017
☎ (212) 949 2333

Finnish Tourist Board
Northern Finland Offices
Hallituskatu 20/222
96100 Rovaniemi
☎ (9) 60–17 201

Finnish Tourist Board (Head Office)
Asemapäällikönkatu 12B
PB 53
00521 Helsinki
☎ (9) 0–144 511

Helsinki Tourist Association
Lönnrotinkatu 7
00120 Helsinki
☎ (9) 0–645 225

Helsinki Tourist Information Office
Pohjoisesplanadi 19
00100 Helsinki 10
☎ (9) 0–174 088/1–693 757

Municipal Tourist Information and
Congress Office
Aleksis Kivenkatu 143
Tampere
☎ (9) 31–266 52/267 75

Municipal Tourist Information Office
Käsityöläiskatu 4
Turku
☎ (9) 21–336 366

Automobile Organisations

Finnish Automobile and Touring
Club (Auto Litto)
Kansakuolukatu 10
00100 Helsinki
☎ (9) 0–650 022

Sport

Finnish Aeronautical Association
Malmi Airport
00700 Helsinki
☎ (9) 0–378 055

Finnish Archery Association
Mr Esko Salminen
Radiokatu 12
00240 Helsinki
☎ (9) 0–158 2446

Finnish Canoe Association
Radiokatu 12
00240 Helsinki
☎ (9) 0–158 2363

Finnish Equestrian Federation
Radiokatu 12
00240 Helsinki
☎ 0–158 2315

Finnish Golf Union
Radiokatu 12
00240 Helsinki
☎ (9) 0–1581

Finnish Water-ski Association
Mr Raimo Laaksonen
Kalevankatu 3A11
00100 Helsinki
☎ (9) 0–602 933

Hunter's Central Organisation
(Metsästäjäin Keskusjärjestö)
01100 Östersundom
☎ (9) 0–877 76 77

Travel

Anedin Line
Vasagatan 10
S–11120 Stockholm
Sweden
☎ (08) 24 7985 or
Mariehamn ☎ (9) 28–13087

Birka Line (Head Office)
Storagatan 11
22100 Mariehamn
☎ (9) 28–14 450

British Airways
Keskuskatu 5
Helsinki
☎ (9) 0–650 677

DFDS Seaways
Scandinavia House
Parkeston Quay
Harwich
Essex CO12 4QG
☎ (0255) 552000

DFDS Seaways
Tyne Commission Quay
North Shields NE29 6EE
☎ (091) 2575655

DFDS (UK) Limited
9 Wellington Place
Belfast BT1 6GA
☎ (02322) 22467

Eckerö Line
Storagatan 8
22100 Mariehamn
☎ (9) 28–11 011

Finnair
14 Clifford Street
London W1X 1RD
☎ (01) 408 1222

Finnair
565 Fifth Avenue
New York NY 10017
☎ (212) 889 7070

Finnair
625 Pres. Kennedy Avenue
Suite 511
Montreal
Quebec H3A 1K3
☎ (514) 282 1173

Finnair (Head Office)
Mannerheimintie 102
00250 Helsinki
☎ (9) 0–410 411

Finnjet-Silja Line (Head Office)
00161 Helsinki
☎ (9) 0–659 722

Finnish State Railways
(Rautatiehallitus)
Vilhonkatu 13
00101 Helsinki
☎ (9) 0–7071

Jakob Lines
Isokatu 11
68600 Pietarsaari
☎ (9) 67–13011

Polferries
Station Travel Centre (Agents)
00101 Helsinki
☎ (9) 0–177 761

SAS (Scandinavian Airlines)
Pohjoisesplanadi 23
00100 Helsinki
☎ (9) 0–133 443/175 611

Silja Line Inc
505 Fifth Avenue
New York
NY 10017
☎ (212) 986 2711

Silja Line (Head Office)
Käsityöläiskatu 4
PB 210
20101 Turku
☎ (9) 21–652 211

The United States Student Travel
  Service Inc.
William Sloane House
2nd Floor
356 West 34th Street
New York
NY 10001

Vaasa Ferries
Harbour Terminal
65101 Vaasa
☎ (9) 61–116 181

Viking Line
Mannerheimintie 14
00100 Helsinki
☎ (9) 0–176 048

Vehicle Hire

Avis
Fredrikinkatu 36
00100 Helsinki
☎ (9) 0–694 4400

Hertz
Itälahdenkatu 20
00210 Helsinki
☎ (9) 0–675 477

INDEX

Finland is a bilingual country, with a large Swedish-speaking minority living mostly in the coastal areas to the west and the south. This means that many towns and villages in Finland have two names. The name which is placed first is either Finnish or Swedish, depending on the language spoken by the majority of the population of the town or village in question.

Finnish and Swedish dictionaries place the letters **å**, **ä** and **ö** (in that order) at the end of the alphabet after **Z**. But for the purposes of this index they have been treated as **aa**, **ae** and **oe** respectively. The Norwegian characters **å**, **æ** and **oe** have similarly been treated as **aa**, **ae** and **oe**.

Index to Places

Index to Subjects